100 Key Concepts in Environmental Psychology

This accessible book defines 100 key concepts, ideas and processes in Environmental Psychology to provide an introductory reference work that brings together research and theory in a bite-size format.

With contributions from leading figures within Environmental Psychology, each concept is clearly defined and explained within the context of issues around the environment, sustainability, climate change, nature and architecture. This book considers the involvement of psychological, physiological and social processes to understand the mechanisms that explain and contribute to the evolution of behavior and attitudes that relate to our relationship with the environment. Concepts covered include biodiversity, eco-anxiety, place identity, sustainable behavior, climate justice and environmental attitudes.

By integrating ideas from different disciplinary orientations in the field of Environmental Psychology, this book allows for a better understanding of the processes related to the individual-environment relationship, as well as the applications that they allow for in various fields of intervention. This is essential reading for students and researchers in Environmental Psychology, Sustainability Studies, Architecture and Built Environment Studies and related fields.

Dorothée Marchand is a researcher in social and environmental psychology at CSTB (Scientific and Technical Centre for Building, France). She works on well-being, resilience, quality of life and urban quality.

Enric Pol is a professor of Social and Environmental Psychology at the University of Barcelona (Spain). Director of the Research Group in Social, Environmental and Organizational Psychology (PsicoSAO), he is the founder of the Masters in Environmental Intervention and Management, Person and Society.

Karine Weiss is a professor of Social and Environmental Psychology at the University of Nîmes (France). She is responsible for the Masters in Social and Environmental Psychology. She works on risk prevention and adaptation to climate change.

100 Key Concepts in Environmental Psychology

Edited by
Dorothée Marchand, Enric Pol,
Karine Weiss

LONDON AND NEW YORK

Designed cover image: © Getty Images

First published in English 2023
by Routledge
4 Park Square, Milton Park, Abingdon, Oxon OX14 4RN

and by Routledge
605 Third Avenue, New York, NY 10158

Routledge is an imprint of the Taylor & Francis Group, an informa business

British Library Cataloguing-in-Publication Data
A catalogue record for this book is available from the British Library

Library of Congress Cataloging-in-Publication Data
Names: Marchand, Dorothée, editor. | Pol, Enric, editor. | Weiss, Karine, 1971– editor.
Title: 100 key concepts in environmental psychology / edited by Dorothée
Marchand, Enric Pol, Karine Weiss.
Other titles: Psychologie environnementale. English. |
One hundred key concepts in environmental psychology
Description: Abingdon, Oxon ; New York, NY : Routledge, 2023. |
Originally published in French as: Psychologie environnementale : 100 notions clés. |
Includes bibliographical references.
Identifiers: LCCN 2022058404 (print) | LCCN 2022058405 (ebook) |
ISBN 9781032466972 (hardback) | ISBN 9781032466965 (paperback) |
ISBN 9781003382904 (ebook)
Subjects: LCSH: Environmental psychology.
Classification: LCC BF353 .P776 2023 (print) | LCC BF353 (ebook) |
DDC 155.9—dc23/eng/20230310
LC record available at https://lccn.loc.gov/2022058404
LC ebook record available at https://lccn.loc.gov/2022058405

ISBN: 9781032466972 (hbk)
ISBN: 9781032466965 (pbk)
ISBN: 9781003382904 (ebk)

DOI: 10.4324/9781003382904

Typeset in Bembo
by codeMantra

Contents

Contributors

Emeline BAILLY is Researcher in urban planning at the CSTB (Scientific and Technical Centre for Building, France), and she questions the evolution of urban quality and the relationship between the spatial, sensitive and ecological dimensions of cities.

Susana BATEL is Researcher in social and environmental psychology at the Centre for Social Research and Intervention (Cis-Iscte), University Institute of Lisbon (Portugal).

Raquel BERTOLDO is Associate Professor in social psychology at Aix-Marseille University (France). Her main research interest includes science-society relations with a focus on environmental issues, natural and industrial risks.

Marino BONAIUTO is Professor of Social Psychology at the Sapienza University of Rome (Italy). President-Elect (2022–2026) Division #4 Environmental Psychology, International Association of Applied Psychology (IAAP).

Barbara BONNEFOY is Assistant Professor in social and environmental psychology at the University of Paris-Nanterre (France).

Mirilia BONNES is a Retired Professor of the first Italian chair of environmental psychology and Founder of the Inter-University Research Centre on Environmental Psychology (CIRPA, Italy) at the Sapienza University of Rome.

Marie BOSSARD is Doctor in social psychology at the University of Nîmes and Institut Mines-Telecom (France). Her work focuses on exceptional health situations and perceived risks.

Thijs BOUMAN is Assistant Professor in Environmental Psychology at the University of Groningen (Netherlands). He is particularly interested in personal and collective values, and when and how these (de)motivate sustainable action.

Sabine CAILLAUD is Associate Professor in social psychology at the University of Lyon 2 (France) and member of the GRePS Laboratory (UR 4163). Her work focuses on the construction, transformation and adaptation of social thought in different social and cultural contexts.

David CANTER is Professor Emeritus of psychology at the University of Liverpool (Great Britain) and author of numerous works on the interactions between people and their environment. He is one of the founders of the IAPS and created the *Journal of Environmental Psychology*.

Giuseppe CARRUS is Professor of Social Psychology at Roma Tre University (Italy). His research topics include ecological attitudes and behavior, perception of climate change, environment and well-being.

Angela CASTRECHINI is Professor of Social and Environmental Psychology at the University of Barcelona and member of Social, Environmental and Organizational Psychology (PsicoSAO). Her work focuses especially on social and environmental psychological aspects of communication processes, over others

Kevin CHARRAS is Director of the Living Lab Ageing and Vulnerabilities at the University Hospital of Rennes (France). His research concerns the adaptation of the urban, architectural and landscape environment as well as the implementation of psychosocial interventions for people with age-related cognitive disorders.

Valeria CHIOZZA is a doctoral student in social psychology at the Sapienza University of Rome (Italy). Her research focuses on the development and transmission of pro-environmental behaviors.

Susan CLAYTON is Whitmore-Williams Professor of Psychology at the College of Wooster in Ohio. Her research examines people's relationship with the natural environment, and the effects of climate change on mental health and well-being.

Kevin CLEMENTI is a doctoral student in psychology at the University of Strasbourg (France) and member of the SAGE laboratory (UMR 7363). His research focuses on the socio-cognitive representations of space and on the relationship between individuals and geographical objects.

Silvia COLLADO is Associate Professor at the University of Zaragoza (Spain). She studies the restorative effects of natural and constructed environments, environmental preferences and the factors that determine environmental behavior.

José A. CORRALIZA is Professor of Environmental Psychology at the Autónoma University of Madrid (Spain). His work focuses on the human experience of natural and built environments, emotions and the environment and environmental attitudes.

Victor CORRAL-VERDUGO is Professor in the Department of Psychology at the University of Sonora in Hermosillo, Mexico (Mexique). He has published several papers, books and chapters on topics addressing sustainable behavior and its predictors, methods for the study of conservation behavior and models of pro-environmental competency. His current research interest focuses mainly on positive environments.

Kalee DeFRANCE is Post-Doctoral Fellow at the Centre for the Study of Emotional Intelligence, Yale University (USA).

Christophe DEMARQUE is Associate Professor in social psychology at Aix-Marseille University (France) and member of the Social Psychology Laboratory (UPR 849). His research is based on a psycho-social approach to the relationship with time and its influence on the perception of ecological issues.

Sandrine DEPEAU is Researcher in environmental psychology at ESO (Unité Mixte de Recherche, Espaces et Sociétés, 6590-CNRS; France). Her fields of study are mobility, child-family-environment relationships, the ecological model of development and mixed methods.

Patrick DEVINE-WRIGHT is Professor in Human Geography at the University of Exeter (UK). He is an environmental social scientist who draws from disciplines such as Human Geography and Environmental Psychology.

Pierre DIAS is Researcher in social and environmental psychology and member of the DEST laboratory, Gustave Eiffel University (France). His research focuses on social inequalities and identity issues in the regulation of the daily thoughts and practices of individuals in relation to their environment.

Andrés DI MASSO is Professor of Applied Social Psychology at the University of Barcelona (Spain) and Coordinator of the GRICS, Research Group on Interaction and Social Change (AGAUR 2021SGR00233). He explores the relationship between place, power and subjectivity.

Cyria EMELIANOFF is Professor of Urban Planning at Le Mans University (Le Mans, France) and member of ESO (Unité Mixte de Recherche, Espaces et Sociétés, 6590-CNRS).

Gary W. EVANS is Professor of Human Ecology at Cornell University (USA). His research focuses on poverty and the environment of children, the development of environmental attitudes and behaviors in children.

Marie FELIOT-RIPPEAULT is Doctor in Social and Environmental Psychology and Teacher at the University of the West Indies, Martinique (France). Her research focuses on the perception of climate change and, more specifically, on understanding pro-environmental behaviors, and social representations of environmental risks in island spaces.

Marie-Line FÉLONNEAU is Professor of social and environmental psychology at the University of Bordeaux (France) and member of the laboratory of Psychology Lab Psy (EA 4139).

Ghozlane FLEURY-BAHI is Professor of Social and Environmental Psychology at Nantes University (France) and member of the Psychology Laboratory of the French Loire Region (Laboratoire de Psychologie des Pays de la Loire; EA 4638).

Ferdinando FORNARA is Professor of Social and Environmental Psychology at the University of Cagliari (Italy). His research focuses on the perceived quality of place, place-related concepts and the social-psychological antecedents of environmental behavior.

Cristina GARCIA FONTAN is Spanish Architect and holds a PhD in Urbanism, and is Associate Professor of Urbanism and Landscape at the School of Architecture, University of Coruña (Spain), where she coordinates a Landscape Degree. She also coordinates the People Environment Research Group and has a long career in research and projects in landscape and environmental recovery.

Ricardo GARCÍA MIRA is Professor of Social Psychology at the University of Coruña (Spain) and coordinator of the European Research Consortium "ENTRANCES" on the social aspects of the transition to clean energy.

Robert GIFFORD is Professor of Psychology and Environmental Studies at the University of Victoria (British Columbia, Canada).

Fabien GIRANDOLA is Professor of Social Psychology at Aix-Marseille University (France) and member of the Social Psychology Laboratory (UR 849).

Béatrice GISCLARD is Designer and Senior Lecturer in design at the University of Nîmes (France) and member of the Projekt laboratory. Her research concerns citizen involvement and participation in risk management policies and the contribution of social design to these subjects.

Hartmut GÜNTHER is Emeritus Professor of Social Psychology at the University of Brasilia (Brazil).

Harry HEFT is Professor Emeritus of Psychology at Denison University (Ohio, USA). His research interests include ecological psychology, environmental perception, children's environments, behavior settings, way-finding, and the history of psychology.

Bernardo HERNÁNDEZ is Professor of Social Psychology at the University of La Laguna (Tenerife, Spain). His research focuses on place attachment, place identity and pro-environmental motivation, and their relationship with sustainable behavior and environmental law violations.

Bernardo JIMÉNEZ-DOMÍNGUEZ is a Retired Professor of Social Psychology at the University of Guadalajara (Mexico).

Denise JODELET is Emeritus Director of Studies at the School of Advanced Studies in Social Sciences (EHESS, Paris) and specialist in the study of social representations in various fields, including the environment.

Florian G. KAISER is Professor of Social Psychology and Personality Psychology at the Institute of Psychology, Otto-von-Guericke University Magdeburg (Germany). His research interests include attitudes, attitude-behavior coherence, The Campbell paradigm, large-scale attitude and behavior change.

Rachel KAPLAN is Professor Emeritus at the University of Michigan (USA). She co-authored many publications with Stephen Kaplan. Together, they have been among the first to work on nature as a restorative environment.

Céline KERMISCH is Lecturer at the Polytechnic School of Brussels (Free University of Brussels – ULB, Belgium).

Lenelis KRUSE is Retired Professor at the University of Hagen and Honorary Professor at the University of Heidelberg (Germany).

Dimitri LAPIERRE is Associate Researcher at CERISC (French National School of Fire Brigade Officers), in charge of crisis management at RisCrises (France).

Clément LAVERDET is Psychosociologist and Doctor in psychology and Post-Doctoral Fellow at Gustave Eiffel University (France). His research focuses on crisis communication, ecological practices and interactions between road users.

Maria Luisa LIMA is Professor of Social Psychology at the University Institute of Lisbon (Iscte) and Researcher at the Centre for Research and Social Interventions (Cis-Iscte, Portugal).

Siegwart LINDENBERG is Professor of Cognitive Sociology at the University of Groningen and the University of Tilburg (Netherlands).

Rosa Margarita LÓPEZ AGUILAR is Professor of Social Psychology in the Department of Applied Psychology at the University of Guadalajara (Mexico).

Ana M. MÁRTIN is Professor of Social Psychology at the University of La Laguna (Tenerife, Spain). Her research focuses on attributions, personal and social norms, legitimacy and motivation, in relation to environmental law violations.

Eva MOFFAT is Associate Professor in Human Resources Management (CEROS, EA 4429) at the University of Paris Nanterre (France). She works on the work environment, environmental satisfaction, digital organization, telework and sport, mobility.

Oscar NAVARRO is Professor of Social and Environmental Psychology at the University of Nîmes (France) and member of the Chrome laboratory (UPR 7352).

André NDOBO is Professor of Social Psychology at Nantes University (France) and member of the Pays de la Loire Psychology Laboratory (EA 4638).

Sofia PAYOTTE is student in Master 2 of Social Psychology, GRePS Laboratory (UR 4163), University of Lyon 2 (France).

Isabel PELLICER-CARDONA is Professor at the University of Barcelona and the Autonomous University of Barcelona (Spain) and Academic Coordinator of the Inter-University Master in Environmental Intervention and Management: Person and Society.

Goda PERLAVICIUTE is Associate Professor of Environmental Psychology at the University of Groningen (Netherlands).

Thierry RAMADIER is CNRS Research Director in environmental psychology and member of the SAGE laboratory (Societies, Actors, Government in Europe, UMR 7363 of the CNRS), Strasbourg (France).

Patrick RATEAU is Professor of social psychology at Paul Valéry-Montpellier 3 University (France) and member of the EPSYLON laboratory (EA 4556).

Isabelle RICHARD is Researcher in social and environmental psychology and President of the "Environnons" research office (France).

Claudio D. ROSA is a PhD student at the State University of Santa Cruz (Brazil). He has conducted research related to pro-environmental attitudes and behaviors, including efforts directed to assess the impact of nature-based environmental education on these constructs.

Julie ROUSSEL is Head of the Adaptation to Climate Change Unit at the City of Paris and Researcher in the Urban Pedestrian Mobility research group of the Labex Urban Futures (Gustave Eiffel University, France).

Elena SAUTKINA is Professor at the HSE University (Moscow, Russia). Her research focuses on the psychology of global environmental change and sustainability, and the evaluation of interventions.

Alexandra SCHLEYER-LINDENMANN is Associate Professor in psychology at Aix-Marseille University (France) and member of the ESPACE laboratory (UMR 7300-CNRS).

Paul Wesley SCHULTZ is Professor of Psychology at California State University (San Marcos, USA).

Perla SERFATY-GARZON is Senior Lecturer at the University of Strasbourg and Visiting Professor at the Universities of Montreal and McGill, Lund University, Kansas University in Lawrence (Canada). She develops the theory of home, migration and hospitality, identity and appropriation of place through life stages. Her research interests include urban open spaces sociability and heritage preservation.

Henk STAATS is associated with the Department of Social, Economic, and Organizational Psychology at Leiden University (Netherlands). His research interests include environmental preferences, psychological restoration and the analysis and change of pro-environmental behavior.

Daniel STOKOLS is Professor Emeritus in the Departments of Psychological Sciences, Urban Planning and Public Policy, Social Ecology and the Public Health Program at the University of California (Irvine, USA). His work focuses on environmental psychology, environmental stress, social ecology and community health promotion.

William C. SULLIVAN is Professor of Landscape Architecture at the University of Illinois, Urbana-Champaign (USA). He works to understand the ways in which landscapes that we design impact the health and well-being of people. He measures the impact of landscapes on people's hormones, heart rates, brain waves, psychological states and ability to pay attention.

Jean-Paul THIBAUD is Director of Research at the CNRS, UMR AAU-CRESSON (Centre for Research on Sound Space and the Urban Environment, France).

Roger S. ULRICH is Professor Emeritus of Architecture, Texas A&M University and Retired Guest Professor at the Center for Healthcare Architecture, Chalmers University of Technology (Sweden). His work has focused on health-related effects of exposure to nature, and evidence-based health design.

Sergi VALERA is Professor of Social and Environmental Psychology at the University of Barcelona (Spain), Research Group in Social, Environmental and Organizational Psychology (PsicoSAO).

Tomeu VIDAL is Professor of Social and Environmental Psychology at the University of Barcelona (Spain). Member of the GRICS, Research Group on Social Interaction and Change (AGAUR 2017SGR-1500). His research focuses on people and places bonds, and climate change, and environmental behavior.

Inga WITTENBERG is Post-Doctoral Fellow at the Center of sustainability transformation in areas of intensive agriculture, University of Vechta (Germany).

Chris YOUNÈS is Philosopher and Professor Emeritus at the National School of Architecture of Paris – La Villette (France), Laboratory GERPHAU (Philosophy Urban Architecture).

Why write a lexicon of environmental psychology?

The words and concepts of environmental psychology are plentiful and can sometimes seem confusing, given the plurality of researchers and practitioners who have been exploring them for decades. A look back allows us to see that the disconnection with nature and the degraded living conditions first led to a focus on habitat improvement (city, neighborhood and housing), and eventually to the psychology of architecture. Then, we note that the evolution of this interest in the natural environment and the need to preserve nature and natural resources has become a major issue in terms of well-being as well as adaptation to climate change. But, in this situation of climatic emergency, one seeks to preserve essentially human life as we know it, because it is not "life", in all its forms and diversities, that is threatened.

To meet this challenge, there is a strong focus on attitudes and behaviors. While pro-environmental, ecological or sustainable behaviors tend to be interpreted as altruistic, some are hedonistic and reflect more deeply selfish tendencies of the human species. Whether we approach them from the perspective of improving living conditions (despite the effects of social injustice) or changing habits and behaviors to ensure more sustainable behavior, it is important to always consider the involvement of psychological, physiological and social processes to understand the mechanisms that explain and contribute to the evolution of behavior. This raises further questions and raises new doubts. Do we need to generate "general laws of behavior", where sustainable behavior would necessarily be linked to and conditioned by the resources and characteristics of each ecosystem? The immediate environment, whether it is a natural ecosystem or a built environment, is specific to each place because of the contextual variables that characterize it. As early contributions have already shown, the culture of each place (where habits and behaviors are born) has an intrinsic relationship with environmental characteristics and available resources.

Within this line of thought of environmental psychology, there is a great diversity of research bodies and scientific organizations with different orientations, but which it is necessary to know in order to understand the different contributions, sometimes congruent, sometimes contradictory.

The oldest organization, born in the 1960s in the United States – still active and with a recognized worldwide influence – is the Environmental Design Research Association (EDRA). The other reference organization, also international, but of European origin, is the IAPS (International Association for People-Environment Studies). It was born at the beginning of the 1980s from the merger of two European conferences: the IAPC (International Architectural Psychology Conference), which began in 1969 in Scotland, and the ICEP (International Conference on Environmental Psychology), which began in Guilford (England) in 1972. More recently, within the IAAP (International Association of Applied Psychology), in 2013, the section of environmental psychology has been strengthened to independently take charge of the organization of conferences with an international vocation, under the acronym ICEP.

These organizations reflect the most global approaches, with a universal vocation, and their websites are an essential source of resources and accumulated and systematized knowledge. However, we should not underestimate the national or regional organizations, which often develop knowledge that is more closely linked to the particularities and sensitivities of each territorial space, of each ecosystem: ARPEnv (Association pour la Recherche en Psychologie Environnementale) in the French-speaking world, PSICAMB (Asociación de Psicología Ambiental) in the Spanish-Portuguese world, whose influence is developing in Latin America, REPALA (Network of Latin American Environmental Psychology) or the environmental psychology section of the German Psychological Association, to name a few, whether recent or older. Although less well known, other organizations exist in Italy, Great Britain, Sweden, Brazil and many other countries. We can also mention the Australian PAPER (People and the Physical Environment Research) and the Asian AMER (Association of Malaysian Environmental Behavior Researchers), as well as the Japanese Association MERA (Man-Environment Research Association), or the Chinese Association EBRA (Environment-Behavior Research Association).

The websites of these associations (or of events they have organized), which are part of more local territorial scales, are important resources for identifying research and intervention proposals that offer views in harmony with local ecosystems and cultures, an anchoring that contributes to their sustainability.

In this book, thanks to the collaboration with authors and researchers who bring environmental psychology to life in these organizations and throughout the world, we have endeavored to bring together the main words, expressions and key concepts that explain or allow for a better understanding of the processes related to the individual-environment relationship, as well as the applications that they allow for in various fields of intervention. Thus, in addition to bringing together the different disciplinary orientations integrated by environmental psychology, we propose, in the form of a dictionary, the definition of concepts, ideas and processes that we have considered essential and transversal to all approaches, aiming at an integrated approach, from both an epistemological and a methodological point of view. We wanted to invite not only both historical authors and researchers of these concepts and ideas, but also more contemporary researchers who have developed them. This double approach sometimes invites apparent contradictions, behind which we must consider the dynamic, evolving and heuristic dimension of these concepts: contradiction is, indeed, the expression of the conceptual richness of the discipline and the vitality of knowledge.

The selection criteria for the definitions used in this first edition were, therefore, based on the topicality of the terms and expressions (although sometimes their timelessness), their transversality and their plurality. Also, in this dynamic perspective, this work constitutes a first stone to the edifice which could, thereafter, be completed by other concepts.

We would like to thank all the authors for their enthusiastic contributions, their availability and their efforts to produce this work, which was written in a pandemic crisis situation.

Special thanks to Ricardo Garcia Mira, Sandrine Depeau, Lenelis Kruse and Arza Churchmann for their wise counsel.

Dorothée Marchand, Enric Pol and Karine Weiss, as editorial team.

Acceptability – Susana Batel

Acceptability has been used to refer to the extent to which a given idea or infrastructure, normally proposed as having general socio-environmental benefits but involving local costs – like a waste incinerator or wind farm – is (not) accepted by the public/local communities directly affected by it, and the socio-psychological and environmental factors associated with that. Until the 1990s, (lack of) acceptability was mainly studied as the NIMBY (Not in my backyard) effect, that is, the assumption that individuals oppose such facilities out of self-interest, ignorance and irrationality, and that therefore opposition should be overcome (Pol et al., 2006). From the 2000s on, the NIMBY perspective started to be increasingly questioned, and lack of acceptability demonstrated to be mainly related with three factors (Batel, 2020): (1) the socio-environmental and health **risks** and impacts associated with the deployment of those infrastructures – noise, biodiversity loss – and the related unfair distribution of responsibilities and rights (cf. **environmental inequality**); (2) oftentimes, these facilities are deployed through an unjust process, that is, without informing, consulting and engaging affected communities throughout their whole lifecycle, that is, from project to decommission; and (3) there is often a lack of recognition of marginalized groups and of more emotional and symbolic dimensions of people's relations with the places where they live – such as cultural identities and **place attachment** – and of how they are affected by such facilities. The presence of these (in)justices can have several psychosocial impacts, for people's well-being and engagement with their socio-ecological communities (Batel & Devine-Wright, 2020). This critical strand of research on acceptability proposes then that we should move from seeing acceptability as the normative goal, to examining it for socio-ecological justice and equity, while considering the socio-historical, cultural, ideological, spatial and psychosocial embeddedness, at different scales (local to global), of acceptability.

Affordances – Harry Heft

The concept of an affordance was developed by the **perceptual** psychologist James Gibson, based on earlier proposals in Gestalt psychology. An affordance is a functionally meaningful property of the environment perceived

DOI: 10.4324/9781003382904-1

in relation to one's possible actions. The concept takes for granted that activity is the essential property of living things: that organisms directly engage their habitat in the course of everyday activities rather than adopting the stance of a spectator. From an ecological psychology perspective, it is assumed that individuals most immediately experience the environment with respect to its affordances. For example, a surface of support at approximately an individual's knee height is perceived as having the affordance of being sit-on-able. As this example shows, an affordance is neither subjectively imposed on the environment by intellectual processes, nor is it a property inherent in environmental features considered apart from any individual. Affordances are relational properties that conceptually cut across the standard subjective-objective dichotomy. As such, they avoid many perennial problems plaguing theories of knowing that assume an unbridgeable gap between the environment ('out there') and the knower ('inside').

Affordances have great conceptual utility for research in environmental psychology and for design. They provide a way to avoid the paradoxical claim often advanced in the field that the environment is a mental construction: a position that keeps the environment 'out of reach' of individual experience and renders social coordination among individuals a near impossibility. Researchers thus far have profitably applied the concept to analyses of environments for children that promote their development. These efforts demonstrate the relational nature of such an approach by revealing that properties of the environment that are functionally significant for the actions of very young children are not necessarily the same as those for older children owing to differences in body scaling and motor skills, and in turn different from those that are functionally significant for adults as well as for individuals with challenges in mobility. Similarly, with affordances as a guiding concept, designers can plan settings and structures that fit the functional possibilities of different user populations. Moreover, affordances have been profitably applied to problems in ergonomics and the design of tools.

Aggression – Elena Sautkina

Aggression is a purposeful, destructive and offensive behavior that transgresses social **norms** and community laws, damages animate and inanimate objects and physically or mentally harms individuals.

Aggression can be caused by several factors and their combinations: individual (biology, emotions, reaction to stress, personality, lived experiences), socio-demographic (gender, socio-economic status), social (norms, roles, group behavior, stereotypes) or relating to the physical environment (air pollution, noise, crowding, heat).

The physical environmental **stressors**, in the absence of one's perceived or actual control over them (i.e., being able to mentally cope or physically avoid the stressors), become potential triggers of aggression.

Contact with nature and greenery, as well as design providing an adequate **personal space**, acoustics and temperature (including possibility to adjust settings) can decrease mental fatigue and stress, and lead to a reduction in aggression.

Ambiance – Jean-Paul Thibaud

The notion of *ambiance* has been developed and tested in numerous empirical investigations over the last 30 years, essentially within French-speaking research in the humanities and social sciences, and in particular in the field of architecture and urban studies. *Ambiance* can be defined as a space-time experienced in sensitive terms. With ambiance, it is less a question of **perceiving** a **landscape** or measuring an environment, than of feeling situations and experiencing the sensitive contexture of social life. An *ambiance* is of a fundamentally pluri-sensorial nature, summoning simultaneously all the modalities of the perception (vision, hearing, olfaction, touch, taste, movement).

An *ambiance* is always situated and embedded in a material framework. If any *ambiance* is anchored in a concrete space-time, it is not reduced in any case to a physical environment, nor moreover to a subjective and individual state. The notion of *ambiance* proposes an alternative to the classic opposition between a feeling subject and a felt object. It also enables the support of the idea of a shared, embodied, enacted and situated *sensible*. It emphasizes the pathic and affective dimension of any sensitive experience and puts forward its corporal and pre-reflexive content. In no case reducible to the register of the **representation**, *ambiance* shows a power of immersion, infusion and contagion which shapes our body schema and our capacities to feel. It is less a matter of a particular aesthetic appreciation than it leads to restore a thought of the aesthesis and to question the aesthetic discipline itself. *Ambiance* involves the affective tonalities of the situations and can be related to the notion of *Stimmung* in the Germanic world, and of that of *attunement* in the English-speaking world (in English, *ambiance* is sometime translated as atmosphere, or affective atmosphere).

The notion of *ambiance* relies on a transversal approach at the crossroads of the sensitive, the social, the built and the physical. This sensitive approach to inhabited spaces has led to the development of original interdisciplinary methodologies, whether they involve in situ investigation tools (commented walks, recurrent observation, sound reactivation, urban transects), simulation and modeling tools (modeling of ambient physical phenomena, morphodynamic models, virtual reality), or transversal analysis tools (sound effects, sensitive formants, ambient objects).

The research carried out in the field of *ambiance* covers a very wide range of works, from the physical characterization of ambient phenomena to a socio-aesthetics of situated experience, from a sensitive ecology of urban public spaces to a sensitive conception of architectural spaces, from the study of very

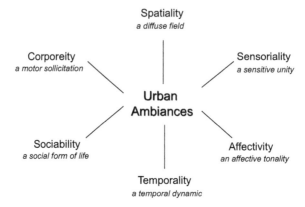

Figure 1 A six-dimensional model, Jean-Paul Thibaud 'Ambiances urbaines, écologie sensible' (*In* Euzen Eymard & Gail, 2013, p. 132).

ordinary urban situations to that of more remarkable places or architectures, from a perspective in terms of urban ethnography to experimentation in virtual reality.

If *ambiance* occupies a particular place in the works on the sensitive world, it is because it engages a strong version of the sensitive. The *ambiance* is not a sensitive domain among others, but rather that by which the world becomes sensitive. It is not an object of perception – as could be, for example, a spectacle or a landscape – but the very condition of perception. In other words, we do not perceive an *ambiance* strictly speaking, we perceive according to it. The *ambiance* is what makes the perception possible, what from which we perceive, what makes the sensible exist. Let us add that the domain of *ambiance* is not an isolated domain, autonomous, independent of the social practices. On the contrary, any setting of an *ambiance* supposes inhabitant performances which activate and actualize the resources of the environment. The *ambiance* is thus the place *par excellence* of the formation of our perceptive habits, of activation of our sensory-motor schemes and of engagement of our socio-aesthetic relation to the world.

(Socio-spatial) Anchoring – Pierre Dias

In its broadest sense, anchoring is a cognitive process that classifies and interprets new information in relation to a pre-existing frame of reference (Moscovici, 1976). This is a psychological phenomenon that leads to a focusing effect (anchoring effect). Individuals rely on the first information that they have already received on a subject to deal with new information received on this same subject.

Through this process, new information enters the already existing social thought (the person's knowledge system) which gives it meaning and existence to become familiar. The new elements to be processed are thus evaluated, hierarchized and instrumentalized according to the categories of thought in memory of the individual. In other words, the processing of information which is complex because it is unknown and a source of doubt leads to a simplification of the reality which is based on the first information received in this field. It is the 'anchor' of thought (Goldszlagier, 2015), which means a frame of reference from which reasoning can develop and influence behavior while minimizing '**uncertainty**'.

The reading grid represented by the anchoring is, thus, based on a substrate of presuppositions which is built in the relationship between the individual and his socio-physical environment. Indeed, addressing the anchoring of cognitions coincides with addressing the anchoring of individuals in their environment, that is, the socio-physical particularities which generate these cognitions. Information is constructed and shaped according to an individual's social identity and his or her **values** and **norms**. In fact, all anchoring takes place in a given socio-spatial environment. Therefore, it is important to consider the socio-spatial dimension of anchoring and to approach it, as proposed by Doise (1992), in a psychosociological way, by considering the thought and its processes as a symbolic position which intervenes in social relations and relations with physical space.

To conclude, everyone will deal with new information (complex) through the anchoring of their social thought (simplification of reality), itself constructed according to the lived environment (insertion in a socio-spatial environment). Anchoring is then both a product and a producer of social relations between individuals, by offering frameworks for understanding and behavior in relation to others. This implies that social thought is inseparable from its environment. It is constructed according to the socio-spatial situation experienced and comes in its expression to mark positions which reinforce socio-spatial borders.

Annoyance – Dorothée Marchand

Annoyance is a sensation that arises from the interpretation of unpleasant information (perception of a nuisance) to which the individual is exposed (a bad smell, an unpleasant sound) and which disturbs his situational comfort. It is directly linked to perceived control. Faced with a nuisance, two scenarios are possible:

- If a person can face to this disturbing information (such as moving away from the smelly or noisy source), he/she can keep control over his/her environment or the situation (psychological process of control) and maintain or restore the initial comfort situation [Link].
- If it is not possible to avoid this discomfort (impossibility to move away from the source of the discomfort, to lower the sound or to ignore it), the durability of the discomfort and the inability to reduce it prevent her

from having control over her environment and from maintaining or re-storing comfort. The situation is no longer just annoying, it has become stressful [Link Stress].

The origin of environmental nuisance does rely not only on its source but also in its interpretation, its perception and in the evaluation of the source of discomfort identified for an individual (Bonnefoy, 2007). It is part of a wider field of representations concerning satisfaction with the living environment.

Architectural Psychology – David Canter

Architectural psychology (known, unsurprisingly, in German as Architek-turpsychologie) is an area of social research and practice that considers the implications for human experience, thoughts and actions of interactions with the built and natural environment. Its initial heyday was in the late 1960s and early 1970s with a seminal conference in Scotland in 1969 (Canter, 1970) and another in Australia in 1974 (Canter, 1974a) and a book of original research the same year (Canter & Lee, 1974). The term fell into disuse but is making something of a comeback in the 2020s, with a number of design and research groups using the term to describe their activities. There was a Psychology and Architecture conference at the University of Texas in 2016 and a conference using the term is planned in Germany for 2021.

The area of study emerged as the Second World War came to an end. At that time, there was a growing democratization of politics combined with awareness of changes in society. This meant that people in authority could no longer decide for the population at large. The growth of the social sciences also reflected a move towards a more systematic understanding of individual and social behavior of relevance to many areas of decision making. Those in power could no longer be relied on to understand how people lived. In archi-tecture this was mirrored by a move towards a more scientific basis for design decision making, reflected in the U.K. in the 1951 Festival of Britain which foregrounded the contribution of science and engineering to modern society, including many aspects of building design.

Across Europe there were government-funded projects, starting in the 1950s to provide guidelines for the massive building program after the de-struction of the Second World War. In the U.K., they were initially studies for housing (Morris, 1961), then offices, shops and railway premises, then schools and hospitals. These studies, typically conducted by civil servants and sociologists, tended to focus on appropriate levels of spatial provision for dif-ferent activities. Other early studies were carried out mainly by physicists and engineers. They examined aspects of thermal comfort, noise annoyance (e.g., Griffiths & Langdon, 1968, who were actually experimental psychologists), and the implications of lighting levels, especially daylight penetration into homes and offices. Much of this work related directly to the impact of the physical environment on productivity (Oborne & Gruneberg, 1983).

The scientific trend in architecture gave rise to research units, such as that funded by the plate glass manufacturer, Pilkingtons, who set up the Pilkington Research Unit, initially studying daylight penetration, then Office Design (Manning, 1965) and subsequently schools. This then developed into the multidisciplinary Building Performance Research Unit (Markus et al., 1972). These studies resulted in a movement of conferences in architectural psychology (IAPC, International Architectural Psychology Conference), without any formal organization, which would become, in the early 1980s, the current IAPS (International Association for People-Environment Studies) association. The acronym of the Australian association PAPER (People and the Physical Environment Research), born at the same time, is more elegant.

The origins in the U.S. in the late 1950s and early 1960s were requests from architects to psychiatrists and psychologists for guidance on the design of buildings which housed people that the designers considered to be very different from themselves, notably psychiatric patients and children. An early account by the psychiatrist Osmond (1957) introduced the, then rather novel, idea that the function of a psychiatric ward should be the basis for design. This was the start of a stream of research that laid the foundations for architectural psychology in the U.S. This gave rise to the Environmental Design Research Association (EDRA), which is still active today.

These developments were encouraged by three early publications from the U.S. which had paved the way for the consideration of the spatial aspects of human activities and experience with architectural implications: Lynch's (1960) *The Image of the City*, Sommer's (1969) *Personal Space: The Behavioral Basis of Design* and Rapoport's (1969) *House Form and Culture*. The area of study broadened out to cover aspects of **landscape** experience and the meaning of building forms. Consequently, although the term 'architectural psychology' was widely used, many of those involved were not psychologists and the areas of study went far beyond those aspects of the environment over which architects have control. This has included somewhat limited studies of the psychology of architects and architectural decision making.

Not long after the designation of the existence of architectural psychology through conferences in the U.S. and the U.K. the label **Environmental Psychology** was introduced in the U.S. with the establishment in New York of an Environmental Psychology Doctoral Program. Although much of the early research under this umbrella dealt directly with aspects of buildings, the promotional power of U.S. researchers led to the terms nudging the label architectural psychology out of common use. With the advent of the 'environmental movement' and the growing awareness of a climate crisis, many social scientists became involved in what might be called 'green environmental psychology'. In many cases, this is an aspect of social psychology dealing with **attitudes** to **climate change** and related actions such as recycling and being more 'environmentally friendly'. With that broadening of the meaning of environmental psychology, architectural psychology became identified as a particular area of the wider field. This does add some confusion because there are important epistemological differences between green environmental psychology and architectural psychology.

From its earliest days, there were theoretical explorations of the ways in which people interact with their surroundings. This is often confusingly couched in questions about the impact of buildings on human actions and experiences. These questions are based on the assumption of what is known as 'architectural determinism'. This is the belief that buildings directly shape what people think, feel and do. A commonly cited quotation from Winston Churchill in his discussion of the rebuilding of the Houses of Parliament after being damaged during the Second World War captures the complexity of even an elementary view of the influence of architecture: "We shape our buildings, and after that they shape us". The interactive nature illustrated by Churchill points to the limits of buildings determining human actions. Many studies show that, except at the extremes of environmental conditions, people are remarkably flexible in their response to the physical environment. Therefore, more complex theories have emerged that explore what people bring to their use and experience of buildings as much as what influence buildings have on them.

A central theory to emerge as part of the move away from a strongly determinist perspective draws on the concept of **'Place'** (Canter, 1977). This is proposed as an aspect of experience in which physical, social, emotional and behavioral facets are all combined. The central premise is that all actions and experiences are spatial and all spaces carry implications for actions and experiences. In its most extreme form, this is embedded in a phenomenological perspective that accepts 'being-in-place' as a wholistic aspect of living (recently reviewed by one of the leading thinkers of this approach; Seamon, 2018). This has its origins in the musings of the French 'philosopher' Bachelard (1958). However, intriguingly, many geographers seem to have got bored with map-making and this phenomenological viewpoint now typically dominates areas of social/human geography (e.g., Malpas, 1999).

One particular strand of theory building has been the exploration of the meaning of places. This has taken on the form of elaborating how and what meanings buildings stimulate. This connected with an emerging interest in the semiotics and was given impetus by Jencks' elaboration of 'post-modern architecture' (Jencks, 1977). As long as the dominant style in architecture followed the (rather ambiguous) slogan ascribed to le Corbusier of 'form follows function', the idea that buildings carried meaning was something of an anathema. Once that idea was undermined, there was room for consideration of what the significance of physical forms might be. Early work brought together by architects Broadbent (1980), Rapoport (1982) provided a variety of perspectives in how buildings generate meanings. The meaning of places is still an active area of scholarship (Castello, 2010).

Research into architectural psychology takes on many different forms (Groat & Wang, 2002). In general, it eschews laboratory studies because they provide such a distinct context that all that can be studied there is the laboratory experience itself. The research design that is regarded as the golden standard in experimental research of the double-blind controlled trial makes little sense when studying people's experience of buildings. They always have a related reason for being there, a role in the building, which cannot be readily simulated for the purpose of research. The practical and ethical challenges of randomly assigning people to different physical environment also limit the use of this research design.

However, the ease of showing people pictures of places and asking them to react to those images has, nonetheless, provided a trend in publications which has been enhanced with the facility provided by digital media, notably videos and virtual reality representations. Surveys and various forms of interviews, which relate directly to architectural experiences, have tended to be the favored form of research. Within the phenomenological tradition, these interviews have usually been open-ended explorations of direct experience, often bordering on autobiography or descriptive journalism.

The influence of architectural psychology is difficult to pinpoint, in part because of the amorphous nature of architecture and the many different stakeholders who influence architectural decision making. However, the ways in which architectural education and the fashion for grand architecture has changed over the past half-century must, to some extent, have been influenced by the debates in architectural psychology. These have included the recognition that people bring their own perspective and aspirations to the use of any buildings and that the idea of 'function' in architecture carries a complex mixture of psychological implications. The involvement of potential users in the design of buildings, with all the benefits that it brings, can also be seen as influenced by concepts and research drawn from architectural psychology.

Attention Restoration Theory – William C. Sullivan & Rachel Kaplan

We have all experienced times when we feel too mentally drained to tackle what we must get done. Despite such mental fatigue, however, we might still have the capacity to go for a run or settle down with a good book. What then is it that gets drained or tired when we experience mental fatigue? The answer is attention, a vital yet under-appreciated human resource. Attention Restoration Theory (Kaplan & Kaplan, 1989; Kaplan, 1995), or ART, concerns the interplay between two kinds of attention, their powerful impact on our effectiveness and what we can do about it.

Two modes of attention

ART grows from a long-standing recognition that we have two modes of attending to thoughts, information and details (James, 1890). More recently, these modes have been characterized as 'top down' and 'bottom up'

(Katsuki & Constantinidis, 2014). Top-down attention, possibly the most important and useful resource humans possess, is what many people refer to as concentrating or paying attention. It is a requirement for planning, problem solving, negotiating, setting goals, monitoring and regulating our behavior, and for engaging in effective social relations.

Top-down attention is voluntary, effortful and goal directed. Neural activity associated with top-down attention makes the object of attention (e.g., a task, problem to be solved) more salient than other stimuli. This is where the effort comes in. To make stimuli more salient, these neural processes highlight the items of interest while simultaneously dampening down or reducing the salience of irrelevant stimuli.

There is a cost to this effort: top-down attention fatigues with use. The longer or more intensively we use it, the more fatigued the neural processes become that underlie top-down attention. After a period of employing focused attention, your ability to keep distractions at bay fatigues and it becomes increasingly harder to direct your attention to the task at hand (Kaplan, 1995).

Though the costs of mental fatigue can be considerable, they are often unrecognized (Sullivan & Kaplan, 2016). With reduced ability to focus attention, people are more likely to be distractible, miss important details and have trouble remembering. We are more likely to be irritable, have trouble with self-management, struggle to resist temptations and miss social cues. Mentally fatigued individuals are less effective in pursuing goals and interacting with others (Kaplan, 1995). In short, we are not at our best when our attention is depleted.

Whereas top-down attention is goal driven and internally guided, bottom-up attention is guided purely by external stimuli and thus is not goal driven. Think of the many situations (e.g., flashing lights outside your window, hearing your name mentioned in a nearby conversation) when despite good intentions it is difficult to sustain focused attention.

There are a host of stimuli that engage bottom-up attention. We often categorize these stimuli as fascinating – that is, in the presence of these stimuli, it is easy to dwell on them. These stimuli include things such as a waterfall, fire, lightening, a wild dog crossing your path, a newborn child, a conflict or competition playing out before your eyes, a good story, a landscape lush with vegetation. Table 1 provides a summary of some of the critical features of top-down and bottom-up attention.

Table 1 Distinctions between the control, effort, costs and benefits of top-down and bottom-up attention

	Top Down	Bottom UP
Under our control?	Yes; internally driven	No; eternally driven
Does it take effort?	Yes; voluntary and effortful	No; effortless
Cost/Benefit	Mental fatigue	Replenishes top-down attention

Attention restoration theory

ART posits that engaging bottom-up attention promotes recovery from mental fatigue. Kaplan and Kaplan (1989) argue that natural settings and stimuli such as green spaces offer 'soft fascination' – they hold one's attention "while leaving sufficient headspace for reflection". Such settings effortlessly engage our bottom-up attention, thus allowing the neural mechanisms that support top-down attention an opportunity to rest and restore. ART proposes four characteristics of restorative settings – environments that draw on bottom-up attention. Restorative settings (1) allow the sense of being away physically or mentally from the demands of everyday routine; (2) offer soft fascination that effortlessly engages bottom-up attention; (3) provide a sense of extent or being connected to a larger spatial, conceptual or temporal world; and (4) seem to be compatible with our purposes and facilitate achievement of our goals in the moment.

Although landscapes that contain natural elements such as vegetation are not the only settings that can relieve mental fatigue, there is a growing body of evidence demonstrating that across various populations a variety of green settings promote recovery from mental fatigue.

Studies conducted using a range of natural stimuli have demonstrated the power of green settings to improve a person's capacity to engage their top-down attention. These findings come from settings in which nature is the dominant element, such as large and small forest landscapes, rural areas, wilderness settings and prairies. They have also come from settings in which nature is present but not at all dominant: urban parks, schools and university campuses, and poor and middle-class neighborhoods. Studies examining ART have drawn on a wide variety of demographic characteristics. The results demonstrate that the positive impacts of green spaces on attention are available to children as young as 7 years old, high school and college students, cancer patients, healthcare providers, AIDS caregivers, public housing residents, children diagnosed with Attention Deficit Disorder, employees of large organizations, and prairie restoration volunteers.

This evidence comes from studies employing a range of methodologies: from randomized controlled trials, quasi-experiments, within and between study trials, and correlational studies. This evidence has drawn on a range of measures employed to assess working memory, sustained and selective attention, visual scan and processing speed, and most recently, from studies using functional Magnetic Resonance Imaging (fMRI).

There is a plethora of opportunities to employ the insights of ART and reduce mental fatigue. An individual might recognize the conditions in his own life that promote mental fatigue and make changes in support of his attention. He can take a break in a natural setting – even urban nature reduces mental fatigue. He can work to create more nearby nature in his community so that, in the long run, he and others will benefit from the restorative aspects of nearby nature.

Behavior and practice – Raquel Bertoldo

The fact of presenting together the terms behavior and practices is useful for analyzing together and comparing how social dynamics which are directly observed might be differently approached depending on the theoretical perspectives solicited. For instance, waste sorting could either be analyzed as 'behavior', when it is directly observed in the field (Schultz, 1998), or declared in a questionnaire in terms of frequency (always vs. never) and context (household vs. work environment) by using a scale. Waste sorting can also be analyzed as a daily 'practice' when the researcher is interested in the cultural context of this action, its history, associated meanings, **social representations**, and shared expectations of this act. Thus, depending on the theoretical approach adopted (Patterson & Williams, 2005), the research questions and methodologies can be adapted even if the actual fieldwork contacted by the researcher – or the 'reality' of the facts! – is the same.

Behavior

Behavior refers to a way of behaving ('Le Robert' dictionary). The term 'behavior' is used in psychology as a reference to the visible actions of living organisms. Behavior has occupied an important place in psychological theories since the work of Robert Skinner on the influence of context or stimuli at the source of observable behavior. The careful study of the conditions (physical or social) at the basis of observed behavior is the main objective of behavioral science, or behaviorism, which corresponds to a tradition of psychology inspired by the studies of R. Skinner. Behaviorism is interested in the S-R relationship, where S corresponds to stimulus and R to response. Thus, behaviorism only included as part of their analysis those observable aspects of the environment or behavior.

From the moment when the organism between the interpretation of stimuli and its responses (S-O-R) began to interest psychologists, these analyses started considering the cognition – this is the moment where the cognitivist revolution took place. The study of cognition has opened important fields of research in psychology related to emotions, memory, intelligence, **social representations**, or more broadly to symbolism.

In environmental psychology, references to behavior are only to a small extent based on Skinner's vision of 'observable' behavior. For at least 30 years, researchers have worked to explain as closely as possible the predictors of pro-environmental behavior, or PEB (Bamberg & Möser, 2007). Different models have been proposed to theoretically conceptualize PEB. Among these, the most widely used are the Theory of Planned Behavior (TPB) (Fishbein & Ajzen, 1975) and the Value-Belief-Norm (VBN; value–norm–belief) model (Stern et al., 1999). Here, behavior is most often measured and estimated on the basis of self-reports (e.g., how many times on average have you used public transport during the last week? 1- never; 5- always).

Practice

According to the definition of the Le Robert dictionary, practice corresponds to a 'voluntary activity in a concrete goal' as opposed to 'theory' but also a 'concrete way of carrying out an activity' as opposed to a rule or a principle. While these definitions illustrate different meanings that the term 'practice' might have for professional psychologists confronted with their 'praxis', this entry will focus on the use of 'practice' and more precisely social practice as a theoretical field of interest in environmental psychology.

The theory of social practices corresponds to an approach developed by sociology to understand and describe social practices beyond not only active agents (humans) but also so-called passive agents (technologies or products). 'Objective' material constraints are thus added to the analysis of representations with the aim of better understanding the concrete result of societal changes. This approach has been particularly useful in the analysis of ecological behavior, the expression of which depends on infrastructure availability or the access to certain technologies, as, for instance, in the field of household electricity consumption (Bertoldo et al., 2015). When applied to the consumption of electricity, for example, the theory of social practices conceives of "households as hybrids of objects and people, which are implied in the (routine) performance of a series of interconnected practices reproduced in the domestic arena with the help of energy as a key resource" (Naus et al., 2014, p. 438). Thus, in this approach, the practices are the culturally contextualized result of "meanings, competences, materials, and connections between these different elements" (Batel et al., 2016).

Behavior Setting – Sandrine Depeau & Karine Weiss

The behavior setting is a conceptual device provided with a wide array of methodological tools, deployed in ecological conditions (i.e., field survey) to better understand individuals' relationships to spaces in a given context. Initially investigated from observations carried out on populations of children, living in two American cities of different sizes, by Barker and Wright (1949), then Barker (1968), it is understood as a basic unit for the behavioral analysis of a set of places on a given scale (neighborhood, city, institution).

It is defined as a set of specific and permanent patterns of behavior in a given space and time that individuals share for the essential functions of the frame, in other words the frame program. It is a self-regulating system that makes behavioral patterns out, in a defined space and time environment. Indeed, individuals are not the primary units for understanding behavior; this one is always embedded in a particular environment. This is why the behavior setting corresponds to a relevant supra-individual unit: a behavior always appears in a specific place, and at a specific time. In other words, each time we visit the same place and at the same moment, we can observe the same behavioral pattern.

Particular attention is drawn to the degree of interdependence between the living (i.e., people and their behaviors) and nonliving (i.e., the physical characteristics of the site, its spatial and temporal boundaries, and the objects it contains) elements that constitute the site: "psychological phenomena and the environments in which they occur are interdependent; they are interdependent in the same way that a part of a system and an integral system are interdependent" (Barker, 1978, p. 41). It is these interdependencies that determine the influence of the behavior setting on the behavior of a large number of individuals, or the 'extra-individual behavioral pattern'. Therefore, a unit defined as a behavior setting corresponds to the following attributes: (1) a recurrent type of behavior, (2) in a particular physical and social structure, (3) at a particular time, and (4) with a **congruent** relationship between the behavior and the physical and social structure.

It is these collective behavioral standards by which a behavior setting can be identified and described: the individuals may change, but the behavioral pattern remains similar. Units defined as behavior settings have a life of their own. For example, a library in a neighborhood or in a university is a behavior setting. It is spatially (building walls) and temporally (opening hours) defined by a set of behavioral patterns that meet the requirements of the site's program (e.g., how to search for, borrow and return a book; how to do things on site, such as reading in silence, limiting copying, etc.; and the variety of occupants of the site – from user to staff to manager). The independence of the behavior setting is a feature that is sometimes misunderstood, as it implies that the site exists independently of the individuals within it, but not independently of the behavioral pattern, which is itself related to the presence of people in the site.

In addition to these basic characteristics, behavior setting can also be explored in terms of their social and organizational characteristics in order to understand the internal forces that explain the maintenance of a site, its disappearance or its transformation, as well as to explain the nuances of involvement between social groups (Gump & Adelber, 1978). Thus, behavior setting can be described in terms of their 'degree of penetration', which allows to characterize types of site occupancy, ranging from 'degree 0 (no occupancy) to degree 6' (marking the role of the site leader).

On the other hand, when viewed on a more global or macro scale, behavior setting can be considered at 'super-ordinate levels' (Barker & Schoggen, 1973), thus allowing to capture the behaviors and activities of specific social groups, such as children, who constitute fairly common study populations in the application of the behavior setting model (Barker & Wright, 1955; Barker & Gump, 1964). Therefore, a set of behavioral sites for a specific set of functions related to a given social group defines the genotype. For example, a set of bookstores or a set of nursing homes. Described in aggregate form, the set of these genotypes for a given group leads to the definition of what the authors call 'habitats'.

The investigation of behavior setting can be undertaken at different scaling levels (city, neighborhood, institution) depending on the original objectives. It often requires an interdisciplinary approach that is able to firstly inventory the distribution, the functional quality and the modes of organization of the spaces studied at the chosen scale (from a variety of documentation) from a social, cultural, political and spatial point of view. From there, the study of behavior setting can use various collection techniques, ranging from travel and activity diaries (for the first phase, for the recording of the time budget and to measure the time spent per individual in the spaces; frequency of frequentation, number of possible sites for a given genotype) to in situ observations (to determine the levels of occupation or the involvement of individuals in the sites, for example). All the characteristics of a behavioral site that allow it to be defined and described are operationalized in the form of an observation grid (cf. Wicker, 1979; Weiss, 2003). Indeed, in the perspective of an ecological approach of behaviors, the authors advocate the non-invasive method of observation, in order to interfere as little as possible with the behaviors we wish to study.

Barker's ecological approach, which focuses on the behavioral description of spaces, originally aimed at a mainly sociocultural description of the use of places. In this way, it makes it possible to understand the place of certain social groups (children, women) in their urban uses, just as it contributes to identifying, through the transformation or disappearance of behavior setting, the mutation of territories and the forms of social segregation in the city. In a more local way, it can be part of a more interventional study in urban design or interior design (day care centers, schools, hospitals).

Since Barker's first studies, the notion of behavior setting has been much commented on, criticized and revisited (Wicker, 1979; Shoggen, 1983; Heft, 2001, *etc.*). Without making an inventory, let us just mention a few lines where this notion is revisited in its application. Thus, the predominance of structure (seen as a limit by some authors), by weakening the consideration of the functions of the site, or at least the motivations and affects associated with the site for a given social group, leads some to question the possibility of sites without (behavioral) structures, based on informal behaviors or behaviors diverted from existing behavioral sites (Perkins et al., 1988); in other words, to detect the uses of spaces, in the hollow of the norms revealed by the behavior settings.

But more diverse methodological approaches for studying behavior setting tend to complement the concept of previously weakened dimensions. For example, the physical and spatial dimensions identified as absent or little considered in Barker's contemporary studies are at the heart of a spatial definition of behavior setting implemented by Moore (1988). This author shows that the prevalence of exploratory and cooperative behaviors of young children in day care centers is greater in spatially well-defined behavioral sites. The spatial definition of behavioral sites remains a crucial point that is reflected in the question of the **legibility** of behavior settings

(Gibson & Werner, 1994). The reinforcement of the model in its subjective dimension (cognitive complement) was also operated by Wicker (1992). More recently, some researches mobilize behavior setting as an inventory to study the resourcing character of spaces, focusing on the perception of the interdependence of spaces and their constraining effects (von Lindern, 2017), when others privilege practical or functional dimensions that find some consistency through the notion of **affordance** associated with behavioral sites in the study by Kyttä et al. (2018).

In spite of the numerous limits that can be found in the ecological model of behavioral sites, which was a pioneer at the time of its emergence (more than 70 years ago), it remains a model that is still often (even if partially) mobilized from a conceptual point of view, for its capacity to maintain an interdependence between the individual and the environment to define their relationships, as well as to apprehend time and space in a global approach. And in this perspective, current methods using sensor technologies (notably datalogger GPS) can meet some of the objectives of the ecological model of behavior settings, notably of the inventory of frequented spaces at the urban scale.

Biodiversity – Marie Feliot-Rippeault

Neologism of the contraction of 'biological diversity' refers to the variety and diversity of the living world from all origins (according to three interdependent levels of organization: **ecosystems**, species and genes) as well as all the relationships and interactions that exist there to maintain a living organism (Art. 2 of the Convention on Biological Diversity, 1992). The human, as a species, is, therefore, part of it.

Recent reports have highlighted dramatic declines in biodiversity and attempts to stem this global loss have proven to be failures (Pörtner et al., 2021). For this reason, research in social and environmental psychology has studied the perception, **social representation** and individual **behaviors** towards biodiversity, in order to design awareness tools to promote PEBs and develop ways to motivate the commitment to biodiversity (Andersson & McPhearson, 2018; White et al., 2020).

The results of field studies highlight the potential counter-productiveness of a discourse only on species (Melcion & Bidaud, 2018). For greater awareness, it is necessary to address biodiversity at the global level, by making the link between Nature and Man and what it can offer him (comfort, survival, etc.). Moreover, to evoke memories of positive and pleasant experiences in nature instead of highlighting the problems to be solved are favorable conditions for adherence to citizen actions for biodiversity.

The scientific literature also highlights all the psychological benefits of nature on our mental health (Pasca & Aragonés, 2021). Indeed, the **connection with natural elements** acts on our affects and our behaviors, and especially on the reduction of urban stress. In that respect, biodiversity provides the main basis for ecosystem services that are important to human life and his well-being.

Climate Change – Raquel Bertoldo

In purely geophysical terms, climate change corresponds to changes over time of averages and variability in terms of temperatures, precipitation, and winds, as well as the impacts of these changes on the atmosphere, the oceans, water, snow, glaciers, land surface, **ecosystems** and living organisms (Pörtner et al., 2021). The Intergovernmental Panel on Climate Change (IPCC) highlights the causal role of human activities in the changes observed since the industrial age. The well-known image of the 'hockey stick' (Figure 2) clearly illustrates the unprecedented increase in average temperatures observed since the industrial age.

It is precisely because human activities have triggered the recent climate changes that psychology has taken a position on this matter. More specifically, the American Psychology Association (APA) published in 2009 a report on how psychological science could support the reduction of greenhouse gas (GHG) emissions, the cause of climate change, as well as to the adaptation to the effects of these changes (Swim et al., 2009). Among the contributions of psychology in the field of climate change, we will focus here more particularly on the understanding of climate change and the associated **risks**.

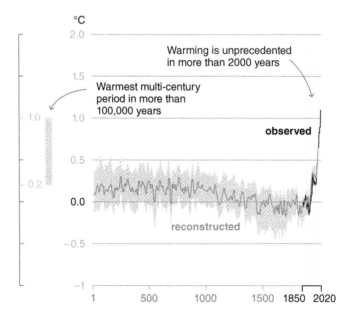

Figure 2 Changes in global surface temperature as reconstructed (between 1 and 2000) and observed (between 1850 and 2020) (Cheshire, 2021).

The public's understanding of climate change has considerably improved since it began to be publicly debated in the 1980s. At that time and until the early 1990s, the public frequently confused climate change with more locally observed environmental issues, in particular those associated with chloro-fluorocarbons (CFCs), pollution and the hole in the ozone layer (Capstick et al., 2015). Then, from the mid-1990s on, concerns about climate change have significantly increased both in the United States and in Europe. The ideas shared on climate change have started to better identify the specificity of the climate change issue compared to other environmental issues. Quali-tative studies show that at that time, the English and North American public associated climate change with melting ice, weather and heat (Leiserowitz, 2005; Lorenzoni et al., 2006). Surveys also show that public concern for the climate issue peaked during the 2000s and that since then there has been a rise in climate skepticism (Poortinga et al., 2011; Smith & Leiserowitz, 2012).

This trend has been confirmed and strengthened since (Bertoldo et al., 2019). One of the explanations put forward for this rise in 'climate skepticism' is that the climate change issue has become a major point of divergence in the political agenda of conservative parties of the Anglo-Saxon world (Dunlap & McCright, 2008). If this question affects the European continent less directly (Engels et al., 2013), it nevertheless impacts international decisions taken re-garding CO_2 emissions through concerns that climate policies might impact the free trade market (McCright et al., 2016).

Along with studies of how the public conceives of and understands climate change, other studies have looked at how the media frames the issue. Boykoff and Boykoff (2007) show, for instance, to what extent current journalistic practices linked to the concern for impartiality have inadvertently given a disproportionate place to 'skeptical' experts, who are nevertheless very much in the minority within the scientific community (Antilla, 2005).

Finally, the perception of the scientific consensus around the anthropo-genic origin of climate change has become, in recent years, a variable of interest for estimating a society's resistance to climate-skeptical arguments (Van der Linden et al., 2015). Different research has shown that the degree to which one perceives anthropogenic climate change as based on a scientific consensus can be described as a fundamental idea, a 'belief' which has been associated with higher levels of concern for the climate situation and for the climate emergency, as well as support for climate change mitigation policies (Lewandowsky et al., 2012; Van der Linden et al., 2015).

Climate Justice – Ana M. Mártin & Bernardo Hernández

Climate Justice is a field of research and a social movement that deals with the responsibilities of climate impact, focusing on the historical, economic, political and social conditions underlying **climate change**. It addresses solutions that support those communities most affected, traditionally disadvantaged due to race/ethnicity, socioeconomic status and/or geographical location. Climate Justice asserts the existence of an unequal distribution of both the benefits and harms of carbon emissions-related activities, and that communities that contribute the least to these activities tend to suffer an uneven distribution of the burdens of climate change. Climate change is a global hazard that reflects and exacerbates existing social inequalities, in terms of who suffer most from its consequences, who are responsible for causing the problem, who are expected to act, and who have the resources necessary to cope with its growing impact. Research has documented this **inequality**, both between and within nations, regarding who are more vulnerable to climate disasters due to race, ethnicity, class and gender. From a Climate Justice perspective, tackling climate change requires addressing social inequalities. The term Climate Justice is used differently by European and U.S. activists. The former focus on the international dimensions of inequality and the flow of resources between states that might require a climate treaty, whereas the latter raise the issue of environmental justice regarding communities suffering from climate impact around the world. Furthermore, although legal scholars use the term Climate Justice for any judicial matter raised by climate change, interdisciplinary and international work shows that the concept goes beyond the legal domain, including principles of distributive, corrective and procedural justice. The unequal distribution of harms and benefits relates to distributive justice; the extent to which some perpetrators have to make restitution due to their responsibility for past damages involves corrective justice; and that the most impacted actors can participate in climate-related decision making refers to procedural justice. The Climate Justice movement seeks to ensure that the evidence on minorities' unequal exposure to climate disasters is incorporated into social policy at the national and international levels.

Comfort and Discomfort – Dorothée Marchand

Comfort has become a standard of contemporary life; a source of multiple norms in the design of living spaces and housing and is considered a factor of **quality of life** (QoL). Research on comfort is most often associated with specific and appropriable environments, such as housing (Pineau, 1980; Sèze, 1994), the school environment (Bernardi & Kowaltowski, 2006) or workplaces (Fischer, 1992, 1997), in which interest has long been performance-based and focused on functional comfort, close to the concerns of ergonomics (Vischer & Fischer, 2005). Ajdukovic et al. (2014) show that comfort at work is more related to the employee's evaluation of his or her work environment and the affective relationship that he or she has with it.

The concepts of comfort, home and home **attachment** have historically been constructed together (Moore, 2000). Both indoor and outdoor spaces have been the focus of research on specific dimensions that contribute to physical comfort. Thus, from the 1970s onwards, numerous studies explored thermal comfort (McIntyre, 1973; Attia et al., 1980; Paciuk, 1990) but without considering its integrated dimension (Marchand, 2007). Nowadays, it is considered that the quality of the living environment corresponds to the sensitivity of the population, which perceives its environment in a global manner (Fleury-Bahi et al., 2017). For Sèze (1994), the living environment constitutes a residential, urban and architectural reality, experienced subjectively and psychologically. This refers to a greater sensitivity to environmental aspects, such as facilities, urban services, green spaces, atmosphere, neighborhood and home. In the field of housing, the post-modern relationship with the environment is reflected in new expectations: in addition to the economic accessibility for all to housing with a minimum of modern comfort, there are new sensitivities regarding the environmental, architectural and spatial qualities of the living environment. Fischer (1997) has also shown that the feeling of being at home is linked to the limitation and control of interactions.

A distinction is thus made between 'sensory comfort', which is linked to the qualities of the environment that address the human senses: light, air, sight, the tactile quality of materials, and 'existential comfort', which concerns the environmental qualities of the living environment that have repercussions on the psychological level, in particular on identity and personal fulfillment (Sèze, 1994). While comfort meets basic needs, a differentiation of requirements is manifested according to specific needs linked to lifestyle, professional activity, social affiliation and previous experiences of comfort (Pineau, 1980). Furthermore, demands and, consequently, satisfaction with comfort are subject to the continuous evolution of needs, which, once satisfied, generate new needs for a given social group. Indeed, the improvement of the living environment increases the degree of subjective affiliation of the individual to a given social class, which then leads to the appearance of higher aspirations and the change of the individual's **value** system (Levy-Leboyer, 1980). Comfort is no longer defined only in technical terms by the designer, it is also defined as a quality perceived by the user. It is no longer enough for technical objects to meet functional requirements; they must also meet requirements linked to the psycho-sociological characteristics of the users. Thus, four main dimensions can be identified in the notion of comfort: (1) material comfort, linked to the satisfaction of primary and material needs; (2) aesthetic comfort, which is subjective and depends on individual perceptions; (3) social comfort, which corresponds to a balance between the need to be with others and the need for intimacy; and (4) comfort of conformity, which marks the belonging to a given social group (Dumur et al., 2004).

Comfort is a complex concept to define, on the one hand because it is difficult to express what makes a situation comfortable or uncomfortable, and on the other hand because comfort is not a directly measurable one-dimensional concept (Dumur et al., 2004). Comfort is related to expectations, perception, mood and situation. Its definition involves both a negative approach (absence of discomfort, which is characterized, for example, by the absence of pain, anxiety, feeling cold, etc.) and a positive approach (satisfaction, perceived control). Marchand and Weiss (2009) have raised the question of the antonymy of comfort: is discomfort the negative of comfort? We have shown, in the context of rail transport, that the dimensions that construct comfort are not the same as those that describe discomfort. For example, while noise appears to be a factor of discomfort and a source of strong complaints in certain contexts, silence or the absence of noise does not contribute to the feeling of comfort. On the other hand, while silence or noise does not guarantee comfort, it is a prerequisite for it. In other contexts, and depending on environmental and individual variables, silence can be a source of **stress** or a feeling of insecurity. Negative elements (which describe a situation of discomfort) act as disruptors of positive elements (which describe a situation of comfort). Thus, comfort is not the opposite of discomfort: the two notions are not symmetrical, but the absence of discomfort is a necessary precondition for the appearance of the feeling of comfort. If the feeling of comfort is made possible after the elimination of discomforts which are sources of discomfort, the absence of **annoyance** does not necessarily guarantee comfort.

At the city level, Marry et al. (2010) focus on the social, physical and functional dimensions of perceived comfort in urban spaces. Taking into account the acoustic, luminous, aerothermal, air quality, sensory and aesthetic parameters, the social dimension, and the urban design makes it possible to explain the perceived discomfort; but the method does not make it possible to arrive at an explanatory model of urban comfort. The notion of comfort appears to be better adapted to interior spaces in which it allows the description of a degree of satisfaction relative to physical environmental dimensions, and to social meanings, notably with regard to social comparison, **values** and **social norms**.

Commented City Walks – Jean-Paul Thibaud

The method of commented city walks belongs to the field of mobile methodologies (Büscher et al., 2011). It consists of investigating while walking. Many devices implement this methodological orientation, whether they rely on itineraries (Petiteau et al., 2018), travelers' routes (Levy, 2001) or go-alongs (Kusenbach, 2003). The method of commented city walks also consists of verbalizing its experience while on the move and finds its originality in its phenomenological positioning. Indeed, in this method particular attention is paid to the sensitive experience of city dwellers and to their ways of feeling and sensing their daily environment. This method was originally experimented in collective research on the sensory environment of underground public spaces (Chelkoff et al., 1997) and formalized in an article published about 20 years ago (Thibaud, 2001).

The main objective of this method is to access the sensitive experience of passers-by by producing accounts of perception in motion. It is based on three basic assumptions. Firstly, we assert the necessarily situated character of ordinary perception, taking into account the sensitive environment of the places crossed, the perceptive conducts of the passers-by and the courses of action in which they are engaged. Secondly, any perception fundamentally implies a movement, however small and tiny, which makes the very act of perceiving possible. The investigation is based not only on situated perception but also on perception in motion, practically implemented in urban walks. Thirdly, it is possible to give an account of the sensitive experience from what can be reported verbally. The descriptions while walking, thus, occupy a privileged place in this investigation device. Three activities are solicited simultaneously: walking, perceiving and describing.

In order to produce these reports of perception in movement and to put them to the test of the fieldwork, a precise protocol is developed asking passers-by (regular users of the places or not) to walk a route with the investigator, while describing as precisely as possible what is perceived and felt during the walk. Immediately after the walk – which lasts about 20 minutes – a reconstruction is made from memory, at a standstill, which identifies and comments the most salient features of the experience. This protocol is applied about 20 times with different people and in variable conditions (possible variety of routes and circumstances). This recorded corpus of the inhabitant's speech is then analyzed according to various reading grids, aiming to bring out the prominence of certain sensitive phenomena, whether they are sound, light, olfactory, thermal or kinesthetic. In order to test the intersubjective content of the descriptions, particular attention is paid to the perceptions that overlap from one passer-by to another. The sharing of the sensitive experience is tested by the redundancy and the recurrence of the comments produced by each city dweller. It is on the basis of these shared perceptions that the sensitive phenomena characteristic of the places crossed are identified. In order to give an account of this phase of investigation, 'polyglot routes' are then produced, consisting of synthesizing all the descriptions into ideal paths that give a reading of the diversity of the experienced ambiances. This heterogeneous arrangement of the plural inhabitant's words preserves a logic of progression and condenses the sensitive experience of the places as documented in the survey.

A return to the field is then necessary. The analysis of the reports of perception during the first phase of the fieldwork is then used as a guide to an oriented observation of the site. The objective is to specify the conditions of emergence of the sensitive phenomena described by the passers-by. The relationship between observation and description is reversed: it is no longer a question of describing what one perceives but of relating the descriptions to what can be observed on site. A set of techniques is then implemented, whether it is ethnographic observations that give an account of social behaviors in situ, sound recordings and photographs that document certain local ambiances, architectural statement and measurement campaigns that inform the physical contexts of the places.

The field of application of this method is relatively extensive: neighborhoods, commercial spaces, museums, train stations, subways, underground public spaces, large urban projects, etc. However, the need for a pathway engages a constraint of scale of the studied site. Thus, the implementation of this method seems more difficult for territories with a very reduced dimension (for example, the domestic space) or on the contrary too vast (a city in its entirety). Finally, this method can be considered as an open method, in the sense that it has given rise to numerous applications and variations. While the methodological hypotheses set the general framework for this approach, the survey and analysis protocol can be modulated – or even simplified – according to the research objectives and the fieldwork. But in all cases, the accounts of perception in motion constitute the basis of this methodological device.

Commitment (theory of) – Fabien Girandola

Decades of research show that it is possible to influence others' opinions and attitudes, choices and actions, without resorting to persuasion and authority. Commitment is a mean of changing ideas and **behaviors**.

The commitment theory was developed by Kiesler (1971) and focuses on the ideological and behavioral effects of performing a given act. For Kiesler, commitment is the link between the individual and his or her actions. For Joule and Beauvois (1998), it is the objective characteristics of the situation which commits or not the individual in his acts and which, beyond that, favor or not the establishment of a link between the individual and his acts: "the commitment corresponds to the conditions of realization of an act which, in a given situation, allows an attributor to oppose this act to the individual who carried it out" (1998, p. 60). The attributor can be an eyewitness, the actor himself, but also any person who would have had knowledge of what happened. The manipulation of the commitment variable can be done according to the visibility and importance of the act (*e.g.*, public *vs.* anonymous act), the reasons given for performing an act (internal *vs.* external reasons) and the feeling of freedom or free choice. Joule and Beauvois (1998) place commitment at the center of free will compliance. Here, individuals have to comply, that is, to perform for others a behavior that they would not have performed of their own free will, and to comply in a context of commitment or freedom. Free will compliance concerns, in a context of commitment, (a) the acts that the individual can perform after having performed those asked of him/her (i.e., foot-in-the-door; Joule & Beauvois, 2017); (b) the cognitive effects, such as new attitudes and beliefs, consequent to performing acts contrary to attitudes or motivations (i.e., cognitive dissonance and rationalization, Festinger, 1957).

Many behavior change techniques are based on commitment. In the context of the environment, these techniques are used to change the behavior of individuals or communities, for example, in terms of energy savings, the use of alternative modes of transportation, sorting, recycling, composting, etc. (cf. Weiss & Girandola, 2010). Joule and Beauvois (2017) list key commitment-based techniques such as foot-in-the-door (i.e., obtaining a low-cost preparatory act before asking for more).

Binding communication

Recently, the binding communication paradigm has unified two disjointed theoretical fields: commitment and persuasive communication. Binding communication consists of making people perform a preparatory act and then spreading a persuasive message. The preparatory act must be carried out in a context of commitment (free choice, no promise of reward or threat of punishment). Research shows that binding communication promotes attitude change, intention to perform a behavior, and effective behavior change. For example, one experiment resulted in increased glass collection. In the classic communication situation, posters were simply put up in local shops in a district to encourage glass collection. In the binding communication situation, a set of action levers was used in another district, in particular a door-to-door preparatory act (answering a questionnaire) combined with information materials. The results show a difference in glass collection (in kg). The inhabitants of the district that benefited from a binding communication sorted and deposited significantly more glass in the containers than the inhabitants of the district exposed to classic communication (+ 57%).

Congruence – Karine Weiss

Congruence refers to the fact that two elements coincide. In environmental psychology, this idea is found in two complementary aspects: we can speak of congruence between **behaviors** and the socio-physical characteristics of a place, or of congruence between environmental qualities and personal characteristics, notably individual goals and sensitivity.

In the former case, the focus is on the congruence between the context and the activities that the subject wishes to perform in the place. Barker (1968), in his definition of **behavior settings**, insists on this congruence between the physical elements of the settings, the living elements, that is, the people, and the behavioral program they deploy in the place. In concrete terms, there is congruence when the place allows or even facilitates the activities that individuals wish to carry out there. If not, a system of regulation is put in place: either by modifying behaviors, which may involve learning congruent behaviors, or by modifying the characteristics of the environment. From a transactional perspective, this is a setting regulation, since individuals as well as objects and characteristics of places belong to the same system.

In the second case, the notion of congruence, or psychological adjustment between an individual and his or her environment, is associated with a state of well-being when the qualities of the context are consistent with his or her goals and sensitivity for certain environmental qualities. It therefore encompasses not only behaviors but also the more affective aspects of the relationship to place. As with the behavior settings approach, the improvement of congruence is characterized both by changes in the environment undertaken by the subject, and by changes in the individual, that is, his or her way of acting, goals or level of aspiration. Moreover, the individual's environmental experiences tend, through a retroactive mechanism, to improve and optimize his or her relationship with the environment (Stokols, 1978). The transaction between the two terms supposes that the individual is involved in both active and reactive phases with respect to the environmental attributes, and that it manifests itself at the cognitive, affective and behavioral levels.

Connection with Nature – Oscar Navarro

Connection with nature has been defined as a self-perceived relationship between the self and the natural environment (Schultz et al., 2004). Some authors consider the valuation of the natural world as an extension of a cognitive representation of self, thus favoring the study of environmental concerns over environmental values as determinants of significant ecological change (Schultz et al., 2004). Another concept considers that in the construction of a self-concept, nature and the self are not independent but linked, as the self-concept comes from a cognitive connection between nature and the self, facilitated by memories of oneself in nature (Thomashow, 1995; Schroeder, 2007; Olivos et al., 2013; Olivos & Clayton, 2017). A recent meta-analysis revealed a strong correlation between measures of connectedness with nature and environmental identity and environmental self-identity (Balundė et al., 2019). These works focus on the cognitive dimension of the connection with nature and in particular its role in the construction of self-identity. Mayer and Frantz (2004) defined the connectedness to nature as an affective individual experience of connection with nature. It reflects a feeling of kinship and an affective individual experience of connection with nature (Mayer & Frantz, 2004). This concept is derived from studies on environmental concerns and has been proposed as being universal regarding the relationship between one's self-image and nature, based on a biophilic disposition (Schultz et al., 2004; Mayer et al., 2009; Olivos-Jara et al., 2020). In the same way, Kals and Ittner (2003), Kals et al. (1999) describe an emotional affinity with nature. They suggest that it is based on biophilia, a concept proposed by Wilson (1984) to express the feeling of an emotional link with the natural world, which means an inborn tendency to focus on life processes.

Connection with nature has been observed to mediate increased positive emotional states as a consequence of experiences in the natural environment

(Mayer et al., 2009). Connection to nature was higher among those who took part in the nature walks, related to the evocation of positive emotions, memories of social experiences in nature and pro-environmental reflections (Mena et al., 2020). Another study examines the relationship between connectedness to nature, spirituality, well-being and sustainable behavior. The results show that connectedness to nature fosters spirituality and personal well-being; sustainable behavior is explained by connectedness to nature and spirituality (Navarro et al., 2020). Correlational studies concur in finding positive correlations between Connection with Nature and different scales of well-being (Howell et al., 2011; Cervinka et al., 2012; Wolsko & Lindberg, 2013) and the psychological health dimension (Cervinka et al., 2012), in different populations, an effect sometimes mediated by other variables such as higher engagement with natural beauty (Zhang et al., 2014). A meta-analysis (Capaldi et al., 2014) incorporating research that operationalized nature connectedness in a variety of ways showed a small but consistent relationship with happiness, operationalized as life satisfaction, positive affect and vitality. Emotional connectedness to nature is a significant predictor of nature-protective behavior (Marczak & Sorokowski, 2018). Some studies have shown how the construction of social identities are closely related to connection with nature and ecological behavior (Arnocky et al., 2007; Hoot & Friedman, 2011; Olivos & Aragonés, 2014). A study revealed that children who perceive themselves as more connected to nature tend to perform more sustainable behaviors; also, the more pro-ecological, frugal, altruistic and equitable the children are, the greater their perceived happiness will be (Barrera-Hernández et al., 2020). Finally, a meta-analysis demonstrated a positive and significant association between connection to nature and PEBs (Whitburn, Linklater & Abrahamse, 2019).

Conservation (the Psychology of Conservation) – Susan Clayton

Conservation psychology (the psychology of conservation) has been defined as the use of psychological techniques and research to understand and promote a healthy relationship between humans and the natural environment. A healthy relationship between humans and nature is one in which nature supports human **well-being**, and humans support the well-being of nature. Because one of the defining characteristics of nature is that it lies outside of human control, it would be a mistake to imply that there is a perfect relationship between human and **environmental health**. However, a degraded and unhealthy environment will ultimately affect the well-being of everyone on the planet, by reducing the availability of the **ecosystem** services we depend on for survival as well as for physical and mental health. The rise of conservation psychology reflects not only an increasing concern for environmental health, but also an emphasis on its interdependence with human health.

In contrast to some areas of scientific research, the subfield of conservation psychology contains an explicit value basis; an emphasis on reducing harmful human impacts on the environment. It also draws at least some attention to practical applications of research. Conservation psychology seeks to direct rigorous research toward the goal of sustainability, and to rely on the results of that research to make recommendations about specific techniques. It is about theory and research aimed at understanding the interdependence between human and natural well-being, and its goal is to make linkages between basic academic research and practical environmental issues.

Despite the applied focus, the goal is not only to promote a healthy and sustainable relationship with nature but also to understand the interdependence between humans and nature – the ways in which people are affected by environmental conditions and vice versa. Some relevant psychological research topics include the impacts of exposure to nature for individual well-being; the ways in which humans interact with nature; perceptions of nature and of environmental **risks**; decision making about environmental policies; conceptions of environmental ethics; and the ways in which people's self-concepts are intertwined with the natural environment.

Broadly speaking, psychologists recognize that individuals are affected by the setting in which they find themselves. Although most psychological research focuses on the social setting, the setting also includes the natural environment and changes in that environment due to things like climate change, overpopulation and the loss of wild **landscapes**. People spend a great deal of time and money interacting with aspects of the natural environment; indeed, a significant proportion of human behavior occurs in a setting that, if not directly in nature, invokes nature through windows, pictures or potted plants. Children's books often include nature and animals. Considering the extent to which people are exposed to nature is one way of thinking about the relationship between humans and nature.

Conservation psychologists are also interested in the motivations that underlie people's interactions with nature: the attitudes and values that encourage people to spend time in nature, and that lead them to care, or not to care, about environmental problems. Care, when fully described, includes cognitive, affective and behavioral components. In order to care about an issue, people must be informed: they should pay attention to the issue and develop some relevant knowledge. Regarding environmental issues, people must recognize the ways in which their behavior can affect the environment and the ways in which those environmental changes, in turn, will affect the things they value. Beyond thought, however, people must feel: they will experience positive emotions associated with nature, and negative ones that are stimulated by the threat of environmental degradation. Finally, people should act in ways that will express both their knowledge and their emotions, and that may tend to minimize or alleviate the environmental threats they are facing.

Conservation psychology should not be considered as a subdiscipline, but as a field or an area of focus. Conservation psychology deliberately enlists contributions from the many subdisciplines within psychology toward understanding and promoting healthy and sustainable relationships with nature. For example, there is a rich history of research within social psychology on predictors of attitude change and on the relationship between attitudes and behavior. Conservation psychologists draw on this research to understand how people might be led to develop more pro-environmental **attitudes** and, more importantly, how, and when such attitudes might lead to more sustainable **behavior**. But conservation psychologists can also draw on developmental psychology, for example, to examine the impact of early experiences of nature; on clinical psychology, for example, to explore the therapeutic role of nature experiences; on consumer psychology, for example, to investigate ways of encouraging more sustainable purchasing decisions; and so on.

The tools it brings to bear are the conceptual and methodological techniques of empirical research in psychology. It offers a new *label* for previous work that existed, as well as a new *focus* to motivate future work and a new *identity* for psychologists interested in this area, encouraging new opportunities for collaboration between conservation professionals and psychologists. Conservation psychology also seeks to provide a community for psychologists across all subdisciplines who want their concern for the future of the planet to be reflected in their professional identity.

Crisis – Dimitri Lapierre & Clément Laverdet

Crisis is part of our daily vocabulary, so many different realities are involved, whether by the multiplicity of events leading to crises (environmental, health, reputational), or by the diversity of issues associated with their management.

The etymological root of the word 'crisis' recalls the notions of complexity and fracture: the ancient Greek 'krisis' means 'to separate, to judge'. It is the moment of judgment, of the fracture between two antagonistic times, a 'before' and an 'after' crisis, which is followed by a new state. A crisis situation is, therefore, a threat to the usual functioning of an organization and/or part of human society, the emergence of an 'unsafe' state (Fink, 1986). It is the "extreme difference between the expected functioning and the existing situation that causes the perception of threat" associated with a crisis (Billings et al., 1980, p. 306, in Seeger et al., 1998). However, the crisis situation is different from the successive 'perceptual readjustments' that lead one or more aggregates of individuals to consider the situation as risky, from the point of view of potential managers, publics or victims (Turner, 1976). Indeed, a threat can form without giving rise to a perception of crisis by managers (e.g., preparations for an attack over several months; a ship drifting towards a port over a few minutes; a succession of bad decisions that lead to accidents, sometimes over years). Incompatibilities between expected normal functioning and beliefs about the current and future situation produce a succession of perceptual readjustments, which eventually converge on a 'complete perceptual readjustment', consisting of considering that the situation has returned to normal.

For Coombs (2015), a crisis is the "perception of an unpredictable event that threatens important health, safety, environmental, or economic expectations of stakeholders and that may have an impact on organizational performance and/or negative consequences" (Coombs, 2015, p. 3). This (possible) threatening cognition is different from the effective management of the crisis and its consequences. Also, this definition does not account for the adjustments and strategies of crisis management, which are the points of interest in social and environmental psychology: while the universal goal of crisis response is to reduce or contain damage, each type of actor pursues its own specific crisis management and communication objectives (Seeger, 2006). In order to better understand these issues, we will focus on the three states that mark a crisis and that underpin different strategies (Dautun, 2007):

- Firstly, a crisis is marked by a dynamic state in which rapid changes lead to stressful situations requiring rapid cooperation from the actors. This phase is known as acute and follows the event that triggered the crisis.
- The second phase is an unstable static state, in the sense that the evolution of the acute phase depends on the crisis management that is carried out.
- Finally, the last phase is the so-called stable static state, where the situation can no longer get worse. The main difficulty here is to regain control of events in order to promote resilience.

For this reason, Heiderich (2010) considers a crisis to be a transitional moment that can lead to a definitive break between two states, thus requiring crucial decisions to be taken urgently and with discernment, subject to the judgment of reality and, above all, highlighting dysfunctions (Roux-Dufort, 2007; Crocq et al., 2009).

Crisis management

Crises are often non-linear and sometimes unpredictable events to which one must adapt. In this context, various authors (Lagadec, 1991; Dautun, 2007; Crocq et al., 2009; Heiderich, 2010) propose a set of successive or superimposed stages to understand some of the recurrent issues of crises and their management. The first stage, relating to a 'normal' situation, is not systematically analyzed. However, these authors agree on the following path: warning signs are not taken into account, or are taken into account too late, which leads to a triggering event. The latter plunges decision makers into the crisis, leading to an emergency response phase.

In summary, a five-phase process can be used to describe the chronology of crisis management: (1) Warning signs may occur and not be sufficiently considered, or too late, and/or without sufficiently effective management. They lead to the event triggering the crisis (Lagadec, 1991). This first phase corresponds to an accumulation of fragilities (Heiderich, 2010), allowing a crisis to occur. (2) Following the triggering event, the decision makers are

Figure 3 Different stages of crisis management.

faced with the obligation to act in a degraded situation despite disorganization, a high level of stress, and a dynamic and unstable environment where information is lacking (Crocq et al., 2009). This acute phase highlights a series of failures within the crisis unit, that is, a phase of disruption (Lagadec, 1991), of breakdown, of disorganization of systems (Heiderich, 2010), revealing dysfunctions (Dautun, 2007). This rupture phase is also the one that generates the most impacts during the evolution of the crisis. (3) Despite a psychological state marked by the stress of decision making, the response phase must be initiated: decision makers must manage the crisis and organize rescue and relief operations (Dautun, 2007), with the major objective of stopping the escalation of events (Heiderich, 2010). The assessment of the situation is essential in order to manage its evolution. (4) When the most critical actions of the crisis have been completed, the progression towards a state of equilibrium (Heiderich, 2010) corresponds to the post-crisis phase. This phase should lead to the resolution of the crisis. (5) Once the equilibrium point is reached, the crisis is over; it is the return to normal. In principle, feedback is then carried out in order to take note of the decisions taken, their consequences, failures, etc., and to make recommendations for improvement for a future crisis or crisis management exercise.

Crowding – Gary W. Evans & Kalee DeFrance

Crowding occurs when there is more social interaction than desired and is often accompanied by feelings of being cramped or constrained and perceptions of diminished control. Crowding is typically measured by indices of density such as people per room or square meters. Although crowding is a psychological experience and density is a physical measure (Stokols, 1972), most research operationalizes crowding as density. Measures of interior crowding have more impact than external indicators such as people/hectare or census tract. Crowding is a common environmental stressor that produces elevated biomarkers of **stress**, negative affect, interpersonal strains, particularly social withdrawal, as well as psychological distress (Bilotta, Vaid & Evans, 2019). Ironically, people who live under more crowded conditions are more likely to have diminished social support from their fellow residents. Parents in crowded homes are less responsive to their children's needs (Whipple & Evans, 2022). Stress outcomes from crowding are robust and have been demonstrated in the field and experimentally. Whereas there are reliable cultural and ethnic differences in personal space, there is little support for the widely held belief of cultural differences in tolerance for crowding. Children who live in crowded residences have poorer academic achievement, and experimental laboratory and classroom studies reveal greater aggression when resources are insufficient (Bilotta, Vaid & Evans, 2019; Whipple & Evans, 2022). Design factors, including greater light, more open vistas, higher ceilings and more architectural depth (interlocking rooms), may attenuate the adverse impacts of crowding.

Cultural Theory – Céline Kermisch

Cultural theory has been initiated in the 1960s by the British anthropologist Mary Douglas, who studied primitive societies from a functionalist standpoint (Douglas, 1966, 1979). She observed their tendency to make a selection among beliefs about dangers, ensuring the stabilization of the social order in place. The generalization of this observation constitutes the founding hypothesis of cultural theory, that is, social structures and cultural biases maintain themselves mutually. The notion of cultural bias is understood here very broadly, covering all the cognitive and axiological contents, that is to say all the beliefs and **values**, ways of perceiving the world and more specifically **nature**, as well as the different ways of managing them. The notion of social structure – or social form – refers to the type of interpersonal relationships involved in a group or network.

Mary Douglas defines four types of social structures, depending on two dimensions: the importance of the sense of belonging to the group (the *group* dimension) and its degree of hierarchy (the *grid* dimension). On that basis, she distinguishes between the hierarchical form, the egalitarian form, the individualistic form and the fatalistic form. For hierarchical forms, group cohesion is essential and these groups are highly hierarchized. The roles of individuals are clearly specified, and the related distribution of resources is often inequitable. Egalitarian forms also value group membership, but these groups are not hierarchized. Social constraints are linked to the preservation, by the group, of the external border against intrusions, and to the control exercised, on behalf of the group, over the behavior of individuals. For individualistic and fatalistic forms, the degree of integration into the group is very low – therefore we rather speak of networks. The degree of hierarchy in fatalistic forms is high. In this social form, individuals do not have the possibility to carry out personal transactions, their autonomy is minimal and their social roles are fixed. On the other hand, the degree of hierarchy of individualistic forms is very low. There, individual autonomy is important, conditions are very competitive, and their members exercise control over individuals from other social forms, in particular those from fatalistic forms.

Each type of social structure corresponds to a cultural bias, which integrates the way of perceiving nature conveyed by myths. These myths only make sense within the social structure in which they are deployed and they justify the institutional measures they are associated with.

Hierarchical forms adopt a myth of nature capable of preserving itself as long as humans do not transgress certain limits, in which case nature becomes vulnerable. From an institutional standpoint, regulations consisting of avoiding unusual events are necessary, which gives scientific expertise a key role.

Equality and purity are essential values for egalitarian groups. The exclusive character of the group associated with the importance of not being expelled from it is essential. Their demand for purity leads them to fear external threats – especially environmental ones. Thus, egalitarian groups conceive nature as fragile and vulnerable to human intervention. Therefore, the institutions treat the ecosystem with extreme caution, favoring lifestyles respectful of the fragility of nature and multiplying preventive measures.

On the other hand, the myth of nature specific to fatalistic forms reflects a conception of nature that is unpredictable, and from which we cannot learn anything. Hence, it is impossible to deal with nature. The only conceivable 'strategy' is to improvise in the face of unpredictable events.

Eventually, the individualistic forms – guided by the spirit of the market economy – adhere to the image of a benevolent nature, capable of preserving global equilibrium whichever way people are behaving. In this context, institutions resort to trial and error when facing **uncertainties**. This myth of a generous and abundant nature, compatible with *a laissez-faire* attitude towards nature, ensures the viability of the individualistic form. Yet, it could not prevail in other types of social form because it would be inconsistent with the values they promote.

It appears thus that cultural theory conceives social structures and myths of nature to be closely tied.

Eco-anxiety – Karine Weiss

Eco-anxiety is a concept that has appeared in the media over the last 10 years. It corresponds to a form of **stress** felt in relation to environmental changes, and more particularly in the face of climate change and its consequences. The APA defines it as a 'chronic fear of environmental doom' (Clayton et al., 2017). This state of anxiety is linked more broadly to fears about the future from both an egocentric and an ecocentric perspective. Thus, given this **temporal perspective**, it would essentially concern younger people: those under 35 are, indeed, more sensitive to eco-anxiety than older subjects (Coffey et al., 2021). Because it is still an emerging concept, it reflects a variety of meanings according to the scientific productions: it can refer explicitly not only to anxiety (Clayton, 2020), but also more broadly to a range of negative emotions associated with the perception of climate change (Clayton & Karazsia, 2020), the fear of seeing environmental conditions deteriorate or of experiencing an environmental disaster (Clayton et al., 2017), or even the fear of collapse. Also, some authors include, in their analyses of eco-anxiety, the emotional responses of subjects who have experienced extreme climate events. The framework thus goes far beyond, according to the research, anxiety about the environmental future. Yet, "The key roles of uncertainty, unpredictability and uncontrollability in general anxiety tell of the fundamental characteristics of eco-anxiety. Overwhelm seems also a major factor" as for eco-fatigue (Pihkala, 2020, p. 12). And, in all cases, eco-anxiety describes negative emotions associated with environmental issues. It does not, or very rarely, refer to anxiety disorders, but much more often to moral emotion, "based on an accurate appraisal of the severity of the ecological crisis" (Pihkala, 2020, p. 14). With the concept of **solastalgia**, Albrecht (2007) highlights the impact of negative emotions related to a state of helplessness and distress caused by the disruption of an ecosystem.

Other closely related terms are sometimes used to refer to eco-anxiety, such as '**climate change** anxiety' or 'ecological stress' (Coffey et al., 2021). Stanley et al. (2021) differentiate eco-anxiety from eco-depression and eco-anger. In particular, they show that eco-anxiety is not likely to lead to behaviors related to environmental protection, and that only eco-anger is associated with individual ecological behaviors. In fact, one study shows that 70% of Americans are worried about the climate, and of those, 59% feel helpless about the issue (Yale Program on Climate Change Communication, 2019). As with **eco-fatigue**, eco-anxiety could therefore be associated with **learned helplessness**, reflecting the inability to act to improve the future situation. It is also linked not only to personal characteristics, such as a sensitivity to anxiety, but also, and even more strongly, to the fact of being exposed, through one's profession or personal situation, to climate change indicators: farmers or climate scientists would, thus, be more likely to develop eco-anxiety (Pihkala, 2020).

Ecocentrism – José A. Corraliza & Silvia Collado

Psychology, driven by the seriousness and force of environmental problems, has long been engaged in the study of the impact of human behavior on the genesis and dimensions of the so-called ecological crisis. In 1973, Maloney and Ward called for the need to reconceptualize the object of study by proposing to understand, predict and modify the human **behaviors** that affect the ecological crisis. They conclude that "we must 'go to the people' in an attempt to understand these behaviors. We must determine what the population 'knows' regarding ecology, the environment, and pollution; how they feel about it; what commitments they are willing to make; and what commitments they do make"; Maloney & Ward, 1973, p. 584). In the almost 50 years since this powerful call, environmental psychology has included among its tasks the study of environmental beliefs, feelings, commitments and behaviors. In fact, this task has given rise to a green environmental psychology that articulates its contents around, among others, ecocentrism.

Ecocentrism describes the structure of environmental protection beliefs and **attitudes** that is characterized by three central contents:

- the tendency to value nature for its own sake, considering it to have intrinsic value;
- human beings are part of all living beings on an equal footing (rejection of the exceptionalism of the human species);
- people have a specific responsibility for environmental deterioration.

Ecocentrism is opposed to anthropocentrism, which assumes a utilitarian view of nature and the resources it contains, defends the subordination of nature to human **well-being**, and believes exclusively in the sufficiency of technological resources to deal with the consequences of the ecological crisis. Ecocentrism and anthropocentrism form two different visions of the environmental question, as Thompson and Barton (1994) state in a classic reference. Based on this proposal, it is thought that the two dimensions would be independent and, indeed, there would be anthropocentric people who support the protection of nature and its resources for their value in themselves, and other anthropocentrics, whose environmental attitudes are based on a utilitarian view of nature and the environment. However, empirical research has not indisputably confirmed the independence of these two motivations. Thus, people can hold beliefs and attitudes based on both anthropocentrism and ecocentrism.

Ecocentrism defines a pro-environmental orientation of environmental attitudes and beliefs. This orientation may, in turn, be the consequence of a concern for nature itself or a reflection of a concern for the impact that the degradation of nature may have on human well-being. In this sense, Amérigo (2009) proposes to differentiate within ecocentrism a dimension based on safeguarding nature for its intrinsic value (biospherism) and another in which nature must be protected because it is seen as a resource for human well-being, so that the self and nature are difficult to separate (ego-biospherism). And these two dimensions are complemented by the strictly anthropocentric motivation. In this sense, empirical research on the content of ecocentrism (Amérigo et al., 2005) shows that it is a motivation articulated on two poles of the same continuum: in one the self in nature (ego-biospheric) and in the other nature itself (biospheric).

The use of the term ecocentrism has been generalized to other areas. Thus, it is the basic principle of environmental ethics as "a worldview that recognises the intrinsic value of ecosystems and the biological and physical elements that make them up, as well as the ecological processes that connect them spatially and temporally" (Gray et al., 2018). In this sense, as Taylor et al. (2020)

point out, ecocentric ethical reasoning is essential to promote the development of ecologically responsible people, sustainable and egalitarian societies,
and to protect life on Earth.

Eco-district – Tomeu Vidal

An eco-district is a specific area of a city whose objective is to integrate the
social, environmental and economic dimensions of sustainability. The development of eco-districts is a way to accomplish the common **sustainability**
objectives proposed by international organizations (Aalborg Charter, Leipzig
Charter, UN 17 SDG). An eco-district is a way to develop urban sustainability at district level and to put that city in a higher position in the list of
sustainable cities. It is often referred to as a sustainable neighborhood.

Several classification systems and assessment tools certify the sustainability of
a neighborhood (LEED ND, Breeam Communities, HQE A, Star Communities, *etc.*). These standards analyze different aspects (governance assessment,
transportation and linkage, social and economic **well-being**, energy assessment and **climate change**, natural resources conservation, built environment
and land use) to integrate a natural and human **ecosystem** that connects ecological excellence, social well-being and economic vitality (Flurin, 2017).

Bottero et al. (2019) propose four major dimensions of sustainability in
eco-districts: energy and natural resources, socioeconomic dimension, **mobility** and urban design. The results of their 14 European case analysis show
a major role of energy aspects. They highlight efficiency and technology-
oriented approaches, with the risk of producing non-democratic self-learning
systems that do not concern the people (smart cities). But the most relevant
result is the lack of research into aspects related to the social dimension of
sustainability, such as the inclusion of the marginalized, and the questions
of communication, participation and engagement of the population in the
neighborhood. Despite the risk of creating green gentrification, eco-districts
provide an opportunity to move sustainable experiences to a higher scale
(city, region...) and strengthen learning among the different actors of the urban environment (residents, city planners, political authorities...).

Eco-fatigue (Green-fatigue) – Enric Pol & Dorothée Marchand

Green-fatigue (or eco-fatigue) refers to the fatigue linked to an excess of
information or pressure related to ecological issues that tend to make people
feel overly responsible or even guilty. Riechmann (2015) reports a weariness
and a disdain for environmental messages and the ecology movement. This
trend towards trivialization is linked to the marketing of ecology (green marketing) and sustainability, which encourages practices that are disconnected
from climate issues.

Woods (2010) describes green-fatigue as the feeling of being overwhelmed and believing that personal action will not achieve the desired results. This tendency would be more assertive for individuals who view themselves as having less personal responsibility, low perceived self-efficacy or a sense that they are unable to change things. All of these characteristics are associated with personality and cognitive traits such as external locus of control, inflexibility and lack of confidence in meeting challenges. Woods (2010), Strother and Fazal (2011) relate eco-fatigue to **learned helplessness** which is related to a perceived lack of control over events that are expected to lead to sustainability problems.

A distrust has developed regarding the credibility of commercial companies' sustainability discourse (Moscardo & Pearce, 2019) which is perceived as instrumentalizing ecology for economic purposes. Thus, the multiplication of alarmist messages calling for individual ecological responsibility provokes mental saturation and leads to a response opposite to the one expected: citizens become disengaged, and their environmental awareness and PEBs decrease.

Green-fatigue can have emotional implications and lead to confusion, stress and anxiety that can result in cynicism, apathy, helplessness and inaction (Greenberg, 2008; Turtle, 2008). The notion of eco-fatigue is then close to the concept of **solastalgia** developed by Glenn Albrecht and that the philosopher builds from the emotional and empirical dimension of a negative relationship with the environment.

While Strother and Fazal (2011) describe green-fatigue as an anxious response to excessive and confusing communication about sustainability, Albrecht understands it in terms of a loss that affects the self and an intimate relationship to place. For Pol et al. (2017), the perception of this loss linked to the changes of place to which people are attached generates a feeling of incapacity to decide or act on the phenomenon which is in line with the learned helplessness highlighted above.

This experienced helplessness leads to **eco-anxiety**, which translates the state of anxiety and fears generated by catastrophic scenarios that accompany climate change (Pol, 2020).

Ecological Model in Environmental Psychology – Sandrine Depeau

The ecological model can be defined as a taxonomic formalization of nested life contexts to study, in a systemic way, the psycho-sociological processes involved in the individual-environment relationships. Being part of the ecological approach of psychology, it allows to consider them in a holistic approach and in a plurality of dimensions attached to various levels of spatial and temporal scale: from the micro level (individual, even intra-individual dimension) to the macro level (cultural and political dimension).

The Bronfenbrenner's model (1977b; Bronfenbrenner & Morris, 1998) is the most common one. It was conceptualized in the legacy of Lewin's and Vygotsky's works (Bronfenbrenner, 1977a) to explain certain processes of individual development. It originated in the 1970s, following observations made by the author about the effects of the major upheavals in American society on children's development (Bronfenbrenner, 1974) and following his interest in the quality of the links between the various living spaces of a child and his or her family. Observing the phenomena of alienation and isolation of children in certain contexts, he denounced the important part of social inequalities that were dependent on the transformations of society and experienced in a differentiated manner according to social groups. Isolation would be linked to the unequal interactions of children in their daily lives (especially with their parents), the causes of which are to be found in the structural changes of certain institutions that support the daily lives of families: the professional occupation of parents, the neighborhood and services, the city, etc. Hence, the model proposed (Bronfenbrenner, 1977b) to study the quality of the links between the various living spaces of an individual and its impact on the developmental processes consists of a complex system composed of environmental units (of different spatial scale in interdependence) specified here by taking the example of the role of play in the development of the child:

- *The microsystem* is defined as the immediate site (setting) that supports the immediate active interactions of the individual with the environment, at the proximal level of the processes to be studied. At this scale, the physical characteristics of the site (constraints, stimuli), the roles and activities deployed in this site are the most important notions to consider (for example: the home, the nursery, a play area). However, the observation of interactions within a site only makes sense in relation to other sites, in other words, the mesosystem.
- *The mesosystem* defines the relationships between the two sites of the micro-system; for example, the forms and role of play can only be understood by considering a broader field, linking the home and the school, but also the places of extracurricular activities or the nearby homes. Therefore, it concerns all the links (communications, interdependence) between sites that can explain some of the proximal processes (observed at the micro-systemic level). The number of sites making up this level is limited by the capacity to investigate several sites at the same time. The classic example refers to the neighborhood, which is, for Bronfenbrenner (1993), as much a meso as an exosystem.
- *The exosystem* corresponds to the broader set of social structures and organization, of patterns or indirect experiences (such as parental stress, for example) that govern the life of other systems, and therefore indirectly condition developmental processes. This system includes both the amenities of a neighborhood, the rules of use and accessibility of sites, and the

forms of change in social structures that impact the meso-system (e.g., the social and geographic mobility of parents, working hours, etc.). The individual is not directly affected by this system but is concerned. For example, the school-catching maps, by organizing the daily movements of families and their children, conditions certain resources. (Depeau, 2003). It is also through this system that children will come into contact with the community of peers and experience the values of society and observe collective life. It is also through this system that it is possible to consider social groups, but by observing them differently (Bronfenbrenner, 1977). The rules and structures at this level only make sense, however, if we consider the value systems and the kind of cultures prevailing at the macrosystem.

- *The macrosystem* includes the ideological and institutional system of a culture or a 'subculture'. It provides the basis for a social thought, sometimes unique. For example, the question of children's play in the city also raises the question of their place in society and therefore in the city (*cf.* hygienic policies or the hyper-functional conception of spaces).

The initial model was revised several times by Bronfenbrenner, in order to consider the temporal dimension, on the one hand, and to introduce a more ontological dimension anchored in the individual's biological system, on the other. The temporal dimension, which is crucial in developmental processes, is apprehended at different levels of scale (Bronfenbrenner & Morris, 1998): *micro-time* (time related to the microsystem, biological time, time of an activity related to the process under study), *meso-time* (related to the meso-system, i.e., the measurement of the times or durations of activities associated with it, such as the flexibility of working hours or parents' schedules), and *macro-time* (otherwise called the chrono-system) is the historical time (related to changes in society). On this last point, Bronfenbrenner specifies that "whatever psychological phenomena we study, they always take place in a particular culture and at a particular point in history" (Bronfenbrenner, 1993, p. 33).

The attention paid to the temporal dimension in the understanding of the developmental processes of the individual in his or her living spaces also implies grasping not only the transformations, changes and forms of alterations, but also the stages (Bronfenbrenner & Morris, 1998). These points of change (or stages) are defined as ecological transitions described as *normative* (key event in the life history, such as starting school, college, first job, etc.) or *non-normative* (not predictable, more variable between individuals, such as the mourning of a loved one, divorce, etc.) (Bronfenbrenner, 1986). Transitions are forms of events that occur throughout a person's life. This is why this model, initially theorized in the field of child development, is not limited to this period but applies to other life cycles, as long as development is understood throughout life.

The full application of the ecological model remains a challenge for research. However, despite a more recent evolution towards the biological field

(Bronfenbrenner & Morris, 2006), it is still often cited and applied to inspect the place of children in urban environments (Depeau, 2003, Depeau et al., 2023), or to act in public health, education, urban planning, etc. Moreover, although it was admitted (notably by the author) that all the prerequisites are impossible to consider in the application of the model, some can be noted. Thus, the longitudinal approach remains the most suitable for crossing synchronous and diachronic times and identifying ecological transitions. Similarly, the interest in so-called 'proximal' processes is crucial. Moreover, by fitting into the transactional paradigm of environmental psychology, it remains useful to understand the individual-environment relationship as a molar unit within (as in any system) each entity defines the other and where any change at one level leads to a change at the other level, thus producing a new entity.

In addition, the relational approach, which is used to formalize life contexts, makes it possible to describe intra- and inter-system links. In this respect, it is a relevant approach, because it is operational and more elaborate, in order to understand, for example, the role of social structures in the processes of individual development. Bronfenbrenner specifies that "social class is usually treated as a linear variable rather than conceptualized in systems terms, for example, in terms of the social network in which a person is a participant (...) or the structural requirements of the work in which a person is engaged" (Bronfenbrenner, 1977b, p. 527).

In the end, the fact of considering as central the individual in his relation to the environment, and of understanding the environment in a form of complexity where physical and social forms count as much, induces to adopt a multi-level or multi-scale approach (convening interdisciplinary approach) to understand what conditions certain psychological processes. Hence, if the strict application of the ecological model remains questionable (Tudge et al., 2009; Heft, 2013), it remains important in the field of human and social sciences, and sometimes without being explicitly mentioned.

Lastly, we may wonder if this model is not for environmental psychology what Doise's (1982) multi-level model (intra-individual, interpersonal, positional and ideological) represents for explanation in social psychology.

Ecological Psychology, the German Heritage – Lenelis Kruse

Early beginnings: ecological approaches in a historical perspective

The widely quoted though also criticized statement by Hermann Ebbinghaus (1908) "Psychology has a long past, but only a short history" is, in fact, a proper description for the history of **environmental psychology** in Germany. The early beginnings of environmental psychology in Germany are not only of local interest but its proper recognition could also clarify the origins and developments of 'environmental psychology'[1] – to use the term here as a comprehensive or umbrella term to encompass many different denotations and connotations – from the 1960s on.

If at all reference is made to the historical roots of environmental psychology, its European background is considered and reference is made to several refugees to the U.S. in the 1930s, first of all to Kurt Lewin (1890–1947). Egon Brunswik (1903–1955) is mentioned as another great precursor who uses the term environmental psychology (e.g., Gifford 5th ed., 2014, p. 6). On the other hand, Brunswik (1943) uses only once the term 'molar environmental psychology' to label a research area that has to deal with 'psychological ecology' (the intra-environmental correlations of object–cue relationships) on the one hand and 'ecological psychology' (the organism's adjustments or achievements concerning these correlations) on the other hand.

It becomes obvious that the story of the early European beginnings of environmental psychology is still very little known, although the first conception of a 'psychology of the environment' ('Psychologie der Umwelt') (Hellpach, 1924) had already been described in some detail by Kruse and Graumann (1987) in the *Handbook of Environmental Psychology*, edited by Stokols and Altman. Among these initiation periods, it is worth mentioning at least three authors, who have had a projection and impact: Willy Hellpach, Jacob von Uexküll et Roger Barker.

Willy Hellpach (1877–1955), German psychology professor and physician (1877–1955), developed the first part of what he later integrated as 'Psychology of the Environment' (1924) already since 1911 under the title of 'Geopsychischen Erscheinungen' (geopsychological phenomena), which has been a reference work. It was the beginning of a systematic study of "the impact on the human mind of weather and climate, soil and landscape" that Hellpach published under the title of 'Geopsyche' (1911b). This publication was apparently very rarely noticed by researchers in psychology, but obviously recognized by geographers, as this book was published in 1977 in its 8th edition.[2]

In a volume of the important Abderhalden's *Handbook of Biological Methods*, Hellpach conceptualized his 'Psychology of the Environment' (1924). In addition to the 'natural environment' and the impact of geo-psychological facts on mental life, Hellpach saw the 'social environment' with its 'social psychological facts' originating from other human beings, and eventually the

---

1 'Environmental psychology' in inverted commas is used to signify a general/umbrella term and not a specific concept.

2 In contrast to later conceptualizations Hellpach did not distinguish between a geographical and a behavioral or experienced environment, but instead differentiated two modes of impact of geopsychological effects on the organism, (1) via "impressions" ("Eindruck") by means of immediate sensory impacts and (2) via tonic "influences", e.g., physiological processes that affect the organism and have thereby an impact on mental states ("Seelenleben").

'cultural environment' that has been created by humans with their fellow humans, objectified in books and laws, streets and vehicles, buildings and states as well as institutions, all of which have effects on our mental life. One important objectification of cultural and historical facts is the built environment, and thus Hellpach conceptualized a 'tectopsychology' which he elaborated in his book 'Mensch und Volk der Grossstadt' (1939), which was also influenced by the Zeitgeist of critique of civilization, of growing cities and of the 'nervousness' of urban life at the turn of the 19th to the 20th century.

It is these three 'circles' of geo-psychological, socio-psychological and cultural psychological facts that constitute his 'Psychology of the Environment' (1924).

That Hellpach's contributions to the upcoming environmental psychology in the 1960s is not known is due to the fact that although his books had been translated into several languages it was the beginning of the Second World War that prohibited English translations.

Jacob von Uexküll (1864–1944) introduced the term 'Umwelt' into biology as a construct for the species-specific environment in contrast to an extra-individually conceptualized 'Umgebung'. By means of its sensory organs, an organism perceives a sensory environment ('Merkwelt'), and accordingly, it is by its specific effector organs (hands, paws, beak etc.) that a motor environment ('Wirkwelt') is acted upon. Corresponding to specific sensory and motor organs, the environment consists of objects with respective sense qualities as well as motor qualities, which have a cue function for the organism. This means that structurally different organisms live and function in different 'Umwelten'. Generalized to the human level, 'Umwelt' has now become the term for the subjectively meaningful surroundings of an individual or group. Under the German label 'Umwelt' the definition as 'environment-as-experienced-and-acted-upon' was even taken over in English language dictionaries (cf. Harré & Lamb, 1983).

Martha Muchow was influenced by v. Uexküll from the University of Hamburg but even more by her teacher and mentor William Stern (1871–1938). He was a well-known professor for developmental psychology at Hamburg University who was as a Jew dismissed from his position and emigrated first to the Netherlands and 1934 to the U.S. His student and assistant Martha Muchow, interested in the 'Lebensraum' (life space) of the city child, obtained her theoretical concept on the basis of William Stern's conception of 'personal world' (including 'personal time' and 'personal space') (Stern, 1938) as well as with reference to v. Uexküll's subjective and species-specific environment. In her study that was published after her early death by her brother (cf. Muchow & Muchow, 1935), Martha Muchow looked at the life of an urban child in Barmbeck (a quartier of Hamburg) from three different perspectives, using specific methodologies. The space 'in which the child lives', outlined on city maps, was differentiated from the space 'which the child experiences', assessed through interviews, questionnaires, children's drawings, and eventually the space 'that the child lives' that was identified by using (unobtrusive) observations. It was this last category of lived space (similar to the phenom-enological concept of 'gelebter Raum' or life world) that proved to be most child-specific and much different from adults' lived space in the same area.

Almost every introduction or textbook on environmental psychology will honor **Kurt Lewin (1890–1947)** as important founding father of the field.

Before Lewin was forced to emigrate to the U.S. in 1933, he had already developed his concept of environment as part of his field theory dealing with the interdependence of person and environment. According to his concep-tion, psychological processes are not a function of individual processes, such as needs, interests, intelligence and habits, but they can only be understood as a result of person and situation which Lewin calls 'lifespace', the total situa-tion at a given moment (See Lewin, 1936, 1943, 1951).

Lewin's emphasis on the subjective experience of the lifespace was crit-ically received by some of his students, especially by Barker and his group.

Roger Barker (1903–1990), following Lewin's idea of psychological ecology, argued, "Scientific Psychology knows nothing and can know noth-ing, about the real-life settings in which people live in ghettos and suburbs, in large and small schools, in regions of poverty and affluence" (1969, 31) and suggested in his major work, 'Ecological Psychology' (1968,1):

> Ecological psychology is concerned with both molecular and molar be-havior and with both the psychological environment (the life-space in Kurt Lewin's terms; the world as a particular person perceives and is oth-erwise affected by it) and with the ecological environment (the objective pre-perceptual context of behavior; the real-life settings in which people behave).

Starting from the idea of biological ecology (Haeckel, 1866), Barker and his associates intended to study the richness of daily lives of children, that is, the 'stream of behavior' in their natural habitats. Psychologists should not inter-fere with naturally occurring events and processes but should win their data as 'transducer' from holistic and unobtrusive observations and recordings of behavior, in specific 'Behavior Settings'.

Afterwards, the behavior setting concept was further developed in different directions, for example, integrating cognitive and social psychological aspects. Kruse (1986) defined behavior settings from the very beginning as 'social set-tings', as the environmental context of behavior setting was never described in physical terms or in the language of architecture. It was rather determined by social norms and collective habits that made up the 'coercive' character of behavior settings, accepting or excluding resp. certain behavior patterns.[3]

---

3 Kruse (1986) tried to bridge the gap between different concepts by reconciling the ecological concept of behavior setting with the cognitive concept of "script", and the linguistic concept of "frame" and proposed a research perspective of contextualizing behavior in social situations.

Driving forces and incentives for an institutionalization of modern 'environmental psychology' in Germany

Looking at the development in the late 1960s and early 1970s from a contemporary point of view, the growth of environmental concern is often seen as a major driving force. Reference is made, for example, to 'The Limits to Growth' (Meadows et al., 1972). However, the driving forces are much more diverse (cf. Kruse & Graumann, 1987; Kruse & Funke, 2022). Predominantly but not exclusively with a view from Germany, it will also explain the different denominations for the new (or rather old) field, such as environmental psychology, ecological psychology/'Ökologische Psychologie' and 'ökologische Perspektiven' /ecological perspectives:

1   A major driver originated from within the discipline of psychology, in particular social psychology and, more general, also in sociology and other social sciences. Until the 1950s, we find a neglect of things, of concrete spaces and places, as prerequisite, means and goals of social behavior and social relationships. That was psychology 'without things' (Graumann, 1974) and 'Umweltverarmung'(environmental impoverishment; Kruse, 1974).

2   Connected with these deficits and addressed from the very beginning by scholars developing environmental or ecological conceptions by Hellpach, Brunswik and Barker, in particular, was a critique of the dominating experimental paradigm and suspicion concerning the external validity of laboratory research, that means the reduction of everyday individuals and groups to experimental subjects in standardized artificial laboratory settings, confronted with molecular stimuli instead of subjectively meaningful objects and places.

3   While 'architectural psychology' (**Canter**) had already begun to study the effects of physical features on perceptions, behaviors and well-being of individuals, in Germany the situation became more relevant and serious after the Second World War, with the need for rapid postwar reconstruction and housing. Only years later, the shortcomings of this kind of planning became increasingly apparent. The new towns and quartiers did not meet the respective needs of children and adolescents, of housewives and the aged, etc. A well-known psychoanalyst raised his voice and criticized the 'inhospitality of our cities' (Mitscherlich, 1965). Increasing complaints and loud criticism stimulated architects to turn to psychologists and sociologists.

4   As mentioned before, the presently most pressing and potent driving force for 'environmental psychology' research and application is increasing environmental concern and the need to find solutions for more sustainable lifestyles and modes of QoL. In the early 1970s and 1980s, first research interests and application approaches under the label of environmental protection focused on local problems like noise, crowding, littering, energy use, air pollution, etc. The shift from local to global and back

to local problem solutions started in the early 1990s (e.g., Kruse, 1995). The observant reader will remember Hellpach's geo-psychological phenomena as well as his analyses of urban strains and stresses.

Environmental and ecological psychology: German conceptions

A signal for the beginning institutionalization of 'environmental psychology' in Germany was a first symposium at the biennial conference of the German Psychological Association in 1974 (cf. Kaminski, 1976), also recognizing the 50th anniversary of Hellpach's introduction of a 'Psychology of the Environment' (1924). At this occasion, it was suggested to frame the field of 'environmental psychology' with two different terms: 'ecological psychology' for more fundamental and comprehensive analyses of people-environment interactions, and 'environmental psychology' for more applied approaches studying environmental problems (noise, pollution, energy) and respective problem-solving approaches or technological practice. This differentiating labeling was only rarely reproduced.

Another line of thinking followed the idea that ecological psychology should not be established as a new separate psychological subdiscipline but rather *permeate all fields of psychology with an ecological perspective.* That would mean greater concern for representative research designs, focusing on concrete everyday environments and natural groups, overcoming the neglect of things, of spaces and place, and define 'person-environment-interactions' or even stronger 'interdependencies' as the proper unit of research, using more field studies and nonreactive methodology to realize more holistic approaches.

A first German handbook under the title of 'Ökopsychologie'(ecopsychology) (Kruse et al., 1990) had chosen to present a comprehensive overview about multidisciplinary origins of ecological psychology as well as the great variety of concepts, methods and topics, including fields of application, to direct attention to the wealth and value of psycho-ecological thinking for interdisciplinary cooperation.

In recent years, the field of environmental or ecological psychology has grown considerably, in many countries. The global change, in particular climate change, and the great challenges for society to move towards sustainable development became important. They are a chance and a necessity for environmental and ecological psychology to get involved, become partners in interdisciplinary and transdisciplinary initiatives for understanding, managing and solving these existential problems.

Ecology – Alexandra Schleyer-Lindenmann & Karine Weiss

The term 'ecology', from the Greek 'oikos' (house, habitat) and 'logos' (discourse, science), has two meanings.

On the one hand, in the biological sciences, it refers to the study by ecologists of the interactions (mutual influences) between living beings and their environment. In this sense, ecology was defined by the physician and biologist Ernst Haeckel in the 19th century (Haeckel, 1866) as the science of the relationships between organisms and their environments. Its advent was part of the scientific revolution of the 19th century, which went beyond the description and taxonomy of organisms, a mechanical vision of the world that originated in the Age of Enlightenment, to address the issue of variation and change, in short, evolution, a theory proposed by Darwin (1859). This interest in understanding change encourages the observation of **ecosystems** with all their elements and their mutual influences; to take into account time – short (ontogenetic – over the life of the individual) and long (phylogenetic – over the life of the species), as well as the variability in space that testifies to the adaptation of the organism to its environment.

A distinction is then made hereafter between fundamental ecology, or natural ecology, which focuses on the study of the structure and functioning of ecosystems, and applied ecology, which takes into account the action of human beings on the environment, with the aim of rational management of nature to limit the negative consequences of this action. Another speciality, global ecology, aims to study the interactions between ecosystems at the global level. This approach is particularly relevant to the problems of **climate change** and **biodiversity** on a global scale. Global ecology also emphasizes the action of humans on ecosystems and thus requires an interdisciplinary analysis of necessarily anthropized ecosystems, integrating life and earth sciences as well as human and social sciences. Ecology shares with psychology not only fields of study (for example, ethology), methods (observation in natural situations), but also concepts to be studied (such as territory). Observing and understanding human **behavior** in its 'natural' environment has inspired psychology, partly because of questions about the ecological validity of behavior observed in the laboratory, but also because of the postulate that the individual and its environment form an interdependent system. The study of this 'human being-environment' interaction has been formalized in environmental psychology, notably by the transactional approach (cf., for example, the ecosystemic model, Bronfenbrenner, 1979).

On the other hand, this term also refers to the environmental protection movement, led by ecologists or environmentalists. This movement was born out of an awareness of the negative effects on the environment of the cultural evolution of the human species, particularly since the industrial revolution, which was followed by the 'ecological revolution', marking the impact of ecological thinking on the whole of science.

The scientific and political (or ideological) aspects are closely linked: the ecological movement can be considered to have originated following the publication of the book *Silent Spring* by the biologist Rachel Carson (1962), which denounced the harmful effects of pesticides, particularly on human beings and birds. This book created an awareness that led to the creation of environmental movements, resulting in the banning of DDT (Dichlorodiphenyltrichloroethane) in the U.S. in 1972. This period also saw the publication of the follow-up work to the Club of Rome (Meadows et al., 1972) and the Stockholm Conference, marking the importance of ecological issues in the scientific, economic and political fields. At the same time, Hardin (1968) described the 'tragedy of the commons', which was to become a major contribution to ecology, emphasizing the problem of the overexploitation of resources, which had no technical solution, only a moral, and therefore human, one.

Psychology also took up this issue in the 1970s, with the aim of helping to change human behavior that had negative consequences for the environment: called in turn 'green psychology' (Pol, 1993b), 'natural psychology' (Gifford, 1995), 'conservation psychology' (Clayton & Myers, 2015), this field of environmental psychology questions individual aspects in order to help people evolve towards PEB. An interdisciplinary approach by ecology and psychology is still necessary and should be encouraged in the face of environmental problems such as the reduction of biodiversity, pollution or, more generally, the mitigation of, and adaptation to, climate change.

Ecosystem – Karine Weiss

In ecology, the ecosystem is the basic unit of analysis of nature, consisting of living beings that evolve in a delimited environment with specific biophysical characteristics.

Environmental psychology favors the approach of applied ecology, integrating the human factor and its impacts as central to the study of ecosystems. This anthropocentric perspective took shape in 1971 with the 'Man and the Biosphere' program, which, under the aegis of UNESCO, aimed at improving relations between populations and their environment by coordinating the natural and social sciences. Today, one of the objectives of this program is to "preserve natural and managed ecosystems by promoting innovative approaches to economic development that are socially and culturally appropriate and environmentally sustainable" (Lima Action Plan 2016–2025). Humans, therefore, remain at the heart of the ecosystem, whether through their use of ecosystem services or through their actions to preserve the biosphere. Ecosystem services, defined as "the socio-economic benefits derived by humans from their sustainable use of the ecological functions of ecosystems" (EFESE, 2016), are taking on a central role in the relationship between humans and the ecosystem: they make it possible to become aware of the value of ecosystems and to integrate this value into development strategies, at both the local and the more global level. Thus, these services, associated with the state of ecosystems, are evaluated at the global level by the United Nations (United Nations Millennium Ecosystem Assessment) in order to measure the impact of their evolution on the well-being of human societies, but also with the aim of conserving and using these systems in a sustainable manner. Similarly, the restoration and safeguarding of essential ecosystem services are becoming government priorities. In return, ecosystems are now being monetized, in particular through indicators in terms of wealth produced, the benefits of maintaining them in good condition and the costs of degradation.

Environment – Mirilia Bonnes

The *environment* is the *physical environment* – in spatial (and temporal)/physical terms – of *everyday-life individual experience*, ranging from the more *built-up* – in architectural and engineering sense (as *setting* or *place*) – to the more *'natural'* ones – in a geographical or bio-ecological sense (as *place* or *eco-system*) – and differentiated along its *spatial scale*: small (house or tree), medium (neighborhood or wood) or large-scale (city or park). It is often also defined as a *social-physical environment*, since the daily life physical environment is always also a *social environment*. Following the *ecological revolution* of the last century, expanding from bio-ecology to various other *new ecological sciences* (including social and behavioral sciences) and guided by the UN *Programme on Sustainable Development* – with its dynamic and long-term perspective on *environmental sustainability* – the environment is increasingly conceived as a *socio-ecological system* (982).

Environmental Attitudes – Florian G. Kaiser & Inga Wittenberg

Environmental attitudes and *environmental concern* are often used interchangeably. But only environmental attitude – not environmental concern – is included as an index term in the *Thesaurus of the American Psychological Association* (Tuleya, 2007). In psychology, attitudes are personal valuations of people, ideas and all kinds of objects. This valuation of, for example, a sound, such as the chirping of crickets, can differ among people and over time. For example, while Peter generally loves the chirping of crickets, he hates it when he is trying to sleep. As such, attitudes are unobservable mental entities (e.g., Bassili & Brown, 2005).

Attitudes are thought to become evident in what people say and do, via processes with varying degrees of intricacy. Thus, they become recognizable in verbal, affective or otherwise behavioral expressions (e.g., Rosenberg & Hovland, 1960). For example, disliking the construction of a new power plant might be expressed through signing a petition opposing the construction of the plant or in malicious glee when the construction firm runs into difficulties. Accordingly, people's attitudes tend to be identified based on their verbal and nonverbal acts (e.g., Kaiser & Wilson, 2019).

Environmental protection and nature-related attitudes

Environmental attitude traditionally concerns two objects. The first of these attitudinal objects that people value to a greater or lesser extent is *environmental protection*, or its inverse, environmental degradation (e.g., Dunlap et al., 2000), or more specifically, environmentally protective behaviors, such as recycling paper or commuting by bike. The spectrum of environmentally protective behaviors is broad and encompasses actions in domains such as pollution prevention, reducing energy and resources consumption, and sustainable transportation, mobility and sustenance.

The second object that people value to a greater or lesser extent that falls under the term environmental attitude is the *natural environment* or *nature* (e.g., Thompson & Barton, 1994), or more specifically, certain acts involving the use of nature and certain activities in nature, such as camping, hiking or taking walks in the forest. This distinction into environmental protection-related attitudes and nature-related attitudes pervades the history of the environmental attitudes construct.

Whereas people's valuation of environmental protection is sometimes referred to under the term *preservation*, people's valuation of nature and the use of nature is referred to under the term *utilization* (see, e.g., Bogner & Wiseman, 1999; Milfont & Duckitt, 2004). Studies applying this model typically find that, in contrast to what most would expect, people who value nature and its use value environmental protection *less* and thus do not engage in environmental protection.

In their variant of Bogner and Wiseman's model of environmental attitudes, Kaiser et al. (2013) found the expected strong ($r \geq 0.50$) and positive relation between environmental protection-related environmental attitude and use of nature-related environmental attitude. Thus, their model variant suggests that people with favorable views of environmental protection simultaneously hold favorable views of the natural environment and activities in nature, and vice versa. Kaiser et al.'s proposed variant of Bogner and Wiseman's model falls within the Campbell paradigm (see, e.g., Kaiser et al., 2010). This paradigm contrasts with the conventional view of the relationship between environmental attitudes and behavior in which an attitude – as an unobservable mental entity – *causally* elicits either other mental (cognition or affect) or behavioral responses (see, e.g., Rosenberg & Hovland, 1960).

Attitudes as reasons for behavior

In the Campbell paradigm, attitudes are defined as the recurrence probabilities of a given class of *behavior* (e.g., environmentally protective behaviors). As such, attitudes are mental entities that can be directly observed in behavior

(Henn et al., 2020). This functional link between attitudes and the probability of engaging in attitude-relevant behaviors is mathematically captured with the Rasch model (see Rasch, 1960/1980):

$$\ln\left(\frac{p_{ki}}{1 - p_{ki}}\right) = \theta_k - \delta_i$$

In this equation, the natural logarithm of the ratio of person k's probability of engagement (p_{ki}) relative to the probability of non-engagement ($1 - p_{ki}$) in a specific environmental protection behavior i (i.e., its odds) is the result of the difference between k's environmental attitude (θ_k) and the costs of behavior i (δ_i). In other words, a person's attitude must offset the specific costs of a particular behavior before the behavior has a reasonable chance ($p_{ki} \geq 0.50$) of being implemented. Expectedly, concern for the environment is unlikely to be expressed – even when doing so would be undemanding – when an actor has absolutely no regard for environmental protection.

The functional link between attitudes and behavior arises because the goal implied by the attitude – for example, protecting the environment – functions as the reason behind behavior (Kaiser, 2021). Ordinarily, when people aim at achieving a goal, they are able to choose from among a variety of behavioral means. Irrespective of their commitment level to a goal, though, people strive to achieve their goals in a cost-effective, rational manner (Kaiser et al., 2010). Thus, in striving to reach a specific goal, people favor more convenient over more demanding or otherwise costly goal-directed behaviors. For example, people are more likely to express environmental concern on a survey than to engage in strenuous and unpleasant practices such as commuting by bike in inclement weather.

As a consequence, people's valuation of an attitudinal object (e.g., environmental protection) or commitment to the attitude-implied goal (e.g., protecting the environment) becomes recognizable through the barriers and obstacles, the behavioral costs they overcome (Kaiser & Wilson, 2019). The higher the behavioral costs people overcome, the higher their commitment to the goal underlying these behaviors. Conversely, when the slightest inconvenience is enough to stop people from taking the corresponding behavioral steps, their commitment to protecting the environment can be presumed to be weak.

Grounded in such a *final* (i.e., means-end) view of the attitude-behavior relationship, environmental attitudes prove their durability against the test of time (Kaiser et al., 2014) and, as attitudes generally manifest in an array of behavior, attitude change appears to be an extremely powerful lever for behavioral change (Henn et al., 2020). Even more importantly, various experimental studies have also revealed that environmental protection-related attitude and behavioral costs jointly determine – as mutually compensatory *causal* factors – engagement in manifest environmentally protective behavior (for a list of studies, see Kaiser, 2021). As such, these studies contradict the notion of an attitude-behavior gap, in which people seem to advocate an environmental protection-related attitude without engaging in corresponding environmentally protective behaviors (see, e.g., Gifford, 2014).

Environmental Communication – Angela Castrechini

Environmental communication focuses on how people obtain information and understand environmental issues while exploring how environmental concern is generated, elaborated and used by citizens. Cox (2013) states that environmental communication is "the pragmatic and constitutive vehicle of our understanding of the environment as well as our relationships to the natural words; it is the symbolic medium that we use in constructing environmental problems and in negotiating society's different responses to them" (p. 19). This definition is based on the premise that beliefs, **attitudes** and **behaviors** towards the environment are mediated or influenced by communication. In addition, in this area it is recognized that the media and public spheres constitute the discursive spaces in which environmental issues of social relevance are built and dialogued. Thus, mass media and social media have a fundamental role in the construction and consolidation of **social representations** about the environment, since these are developed, 're-think', 're-cited' and 're-presented' through communication and social interaction in daily activities, while being influenced by the media (Moscovici, 1994).

As a field of study, environmental communication is the development of empirical theories and studies that examine the role, techniques and influence of communication on environmental issues. Cox and Depoe (2015) establish the beginning of this field with the creation of the academic journal *Environmental Communication* in 2007, which coincides temporarily with the creation of the *International Environmental Communication Association* (IECA) in 2011. However, Díaz-Pont et al. (2020) place the beginning of environmental communication in the 1960s and identify three stages in its development: the first related to the industrial impulse and its impact on the environment; the second, in the 1990s characterized by the rise of environmental awareness and the development of government actions that resulted in international agreements and commitments of the business sector; and the third stage, in the 2010s related to the development of social networks, generating the network society and favoring digital and local activism. In each of the stages, they identify key milestones, from the book *Silent Spring* by Rachel Carson (1962) and photographs of the Earth as seen from space, passing through the Rio Summit 92 and the rise of international non-governmental organizations (NGOs) and their web platforms, up to the digital activism of *Fridays For Future*.

In this development, different actors take center stage and different discourses predominate: first, the scientific one, with emphasis on arguments such as the preservation and conservation of natural resources and, second, the political one with the rise of environmental protection policies and legislative measures (Castrechini et al., 2014). In the last stage, direct messages and imperatives from activists and citizens dominate, demanding commitment and the search for solutions to the environmental crisis, specifically the climate crisis. However, in times of crisis, such as the economic crisis of 2008 or the health crisis of 2020, caused by COVID-19, a decrease in messages and a change of emphasis on socially relevant issues are detected, which distance citizens from environmental commitment (Pol et al., 2017).

In some cases, environmental communication is characterized by adapting the results obtained from scientific developments to the general population, doing an informative and, to some extent, educational task. Another relevant aspect is **risk** communication. It implies knowing how to communicate the seriousness and possible impacts of environmental problems on the human being (health effects, resource depletion, etc.) and, at the same time, the urgency that merits responding to these situations.

However, environmental communication as a professional activity involves a series of difficulties reported by scientific research: it is not an easy task to have to communicate topics that due to their multicausality are complex and, in some cases, abstract or not visible to the human eye. Thus, for example, various studies suggest that climate change is usually perceived as a distant phenomenon, capable of affecting people, places and times outside their own (Bonnes et al., 1997; Gifford, 2011). This perception of remoteness translates into cognitive and emotional responses of low intensity, which lead to reducing the priority that people give to this phenomenon, this being lower than that given to other social issues (Nisbet & Myers, 2007).

Additionally, environmental issues are often controversial and conflicting positions converge that reflect different political and/or economic interests or that report contradictory scientific findings. Along the same lines, environmental communication can be full of technicalities, not understandable to the general population. Sometimes, a sobering tone underlies the messages, predominating negative tones with sensationalist or catastrophic formats that can lead to inaction, apathy and even a certain **eco-fatigue** (Pol et al., 2001). Sometimes, the discourses are well founded, but they remain opposite and polarized, generating ambivalence and uncertainty in the citizen, which often seeks or prefers simple causation relationships, which enhances the *fake news*.

On the other hand, it is easier to reach people who are aware of environmental issues (and even so, there are different levels of awareness) while there are great difficulties in reaching people who do not show interest in these issues or who are even skeptical, as is the case of **climate change**. All these difficulties highlight the need to develop contextually situated, geographically and temporally close messages, and specific to different types of audiences.

In this sense, environmental communication is materialized in the design and implementation of plans, programs and communication campaigns

(Norton & Grecu, 2015). It focuses on building messages to change **attitudes** and habits in relation to the environment. Some of the most used information strategies to promote PEB are providing information, setting goals, promoting **commitment**, inciting action and providing feedback. These strategies have been employed with varying degrees of success and are recommended for use combined and tailored to the target (Abrahamse & Matthies, 2018).

With technological developments that promote communication formats increasingly based on screens and mobile devices, mediating communication at all levels, interpersonal, group and social, content is as important (and influential) as the way in which information is presented (Lazard & Atkinson, 2015). In turn, social networks can influence conventional media on scientific issues while they can have a greater influence on individuals' perceptions of different topics due to their public and participatory nature (Williams et al., 2015). An example of this is the relevance that *influencers* have acquired, who, thanks to their attractiveness, similarity to their audience and the use of first-person, non-dogmatic, nor aggressive communication are effective since they encourage followers to try their proposals – such as 'do-it-yourself' o 'live one day waste-free' – evidencing the importance of psychosocial processes such as social identity, minority influence and social learning (Chwialkowska, 2019).

The results of the studies help in the conception, development, and design of messages, allowing to rethink the design of specific messages, as well as the development of broader campaigns with greater emphasis on the variables of the communicator and the message, as well as the audience. Adapting the messages to the already existing perceptions, values and attitudes of different audiences will make the political debate about this complex reality more understandable, relevant and personally important.

Thus, the results of research in the field of environmental communication are translated – or should be translated – into recommendations aimed at public and private organizations, as well as at non-profit organizations that fight in defense of different environmental challenges, to make more efficient use of communication channels. At the same time, they could also translate into recommendations to help users, especially those who have less experience using social media, distinguish the most reliable information online.

Environmental Education – Claudio D. Rosa & Silvia Collado

One of the biggest global challenges is dealing with the serious environmental problems that threaten the present and the future of life on Earth. There is a growing awareness of the detrimental effects that human **behavior** has on the **environment** (Steffen et al., 2015). Human behavior not only compromises environmental quality, it ultimately jeopardizes people's health. As an example, the latest world's pandemic caused by COVID-19 has been linked to deforestation, which highlights the nature-health interconnection (Brancalion et al., 2020).

The current ecological crisis requires not only technical solutions, but also a strong adherence to individual and collective environmentally-friendly behaviors. One frequently used strategy aimed at enhancing PEBs is through participation in environmental education initiatives (Hume & Barry, 2015). In his classic definition, Bogan (1973, p. 1) describes environmental education as "the process that fosters greater understanding of society's environmental problems and also the processes of environmental problem-solving and decision-making". The idea behind this perspective is that people do not behave in a pro-environmental way because they lack knowledge about environmental issues and about the negative impact that their actions have on the environment. Thus, the provision of knowledge would lead to engagement in PEBs. Based on this approach, the focus of environmental education has traditionally been to increase participants' awareness about environmental problems, their consequences, possible solutions and alternatives.

Although increased knowledge may lead to taking action in favor of the environment, this is not always the case, and other behavior determinants, including motivation, connection to nature, environmental attitudes, values and social norms, play a role in people's PEBs (Schultz & Kaiser, 2012). Accordingly, environmental education strategies have been updated to face the complexity of PEBs from a holistic approach. As such, environmental education could be defined as the process that fosters one or several behavior determinants (i.e., knowledge about environmental issues, pro-environmental attitudes) with the ultimate aim of increasing PEB. Researchers should put effort into obtaining a deeper understanding of how, why, for whom and under what circumstances different forms of environmental education enhance PEBs. For example, while environmental education initiatives have traditionally taken place indoors, the provision of environmental education in natural settings is seen as a more effective approach to increase PEB (Kuo et al., 2019). More specificity about the psychological pathways that lead to PEB through participation in environmental education initiatives will help develop specific guidelines for environmental educators and, ultimately, more effective environmental education programs.

Environmental Health – Ghozlane Fleury-Bahi

Environmental health examines the possible links between health and environmental factors, targeting not only direct effects on health by environmental agents, but also their effects on the psychological dimension of health. Hence, the field of environmental health studies the impact of environmental factors on somatic health, together with their effects on psychological health, **well-being** and the **QoL** of potentially exposed populations. According to the World Health Organization (WHO), the environmental factors implicated in the field of environmental health can be physical, chemical, biological, social or psychosocial. The following are considered to be environmental factors with the potential to impact health: (1) physical characteristics of the indoor or outdoor environment, such as noise, temperature, UV rays, radioactivity or electromagnetic fields; (2) factors of exposure to pollutants and chemical or biological agents in the home or workplace (atmospheric pollution, exposures to asbestos, lead or pesticides, air contaminated by biological agents…); together with psychological, social and organizational factors generating stress at work (such as workload or harassment). The field of environmental health also targets the impact of environmental agents that could be considered as **emerging risks** (nanoparticles, endocrine disruptors, magnetic fields…), together with the issue of vectors of pathogenic agents (ticks, tiger mosquitoes…). An environmental health policy consists of acting on these various factors in order to enhance knowledge of their effects, reduce exposure risks, prevent risks and improve the health of populations.

Environmental Inequality – Cyria Emelianoff

(Translation: John Crisp)

Environmental inequalities can be defined as inequalities in access to environmental resources and amenities, in exposure to pollution, **risks** and damage, and in adaptation to environmental change. They express the idea that, regardless of the territorial scale considered, populations or social groups are not equal with respect to environmental decline, change or risk. Good quality environments are scarce and disputed resources. Multiple in kind and extremely fast-changing, environmental inequalities arise from the dynamics of resource capture, of socio-spatial segregation, of environmental deprivation and exclusion, such as those found in designated traveler sites or refugee camps (Emelianoff, 2010).

These inequalities have a long history, notably in the shaping of milieux, particularly urban spaces, but have become particularly acute in this industrial and Anthropocenic era. The day-to-day environment is largely the product of human activities and public regulations, such as industrial policies, policies for infrastructure and sanitation, for the protection or rewilding of natural spaces, for traffic calming, etc. (Diebolt et al., 2005). However, urban design and planning choices, policies on the environment, on sustainable development and on socio-ecological transition, have often been socially regressive, ignoring the problems of justice associated with environmental problems, and have hence come to be perceived by a section of the population as illegitimate.

Beyond obvious disparities in living and working conditions, environmental inequalities refer to environmental injustice, to the different ways in which populations are treated depending on their social status in the broad sense, a process that is anchored in history (Pellow, 2000). The concept emerged in the 1970s in the crucible of the struggles for decolonization and civil rights. Protest movements by dominated, racialized or disadvantaged groups began to reject their experience of territorial dispossession or pollution exposure. The environmentalism of the poor (Martinez-Alier, 2002) and ecopopulism (Szasz, 1994) highlighted the environmental injustices at the heart of the relations between North and South: the grabbing of natural resources since colonization, social conflicts for access to and control of resources, the export of toxic waste to developing countries as industrialized countries adopted environmental regulations. A second interpretation of environmental injustice took shape in the U.S. at the local scale, revealing the overexposure to risks and pollutants among Southern populations in the Global North. The movements that came to the fore in the 1980s showed how racial discrimination drove minorities into 'toxic' environments.

A third aspect of environmental inequality concerns the impact of unequal **vulnerabilities** on the capacity to adapt to environmental changes. Almost all the deaths and injuries caused by so-called natural disasters, in particular climate disasters, occur in developing countries, where societal protections are largely lacking (Roberts & Parks, 2007). Insecure land tenure and informal housing, the urbanization of high-risk areas, the absence of crisis management plans, of access to healthcare and of political representation, all exacerbate the risks. Equally unequal is the capacity of people to leave areas where they can no longer live safely or that can no longer meet aspirations that are deemed essential. The result is a game of musical chairs between migrants moving into cities in the hope of economic and cultural emancipation, and previously urban populations fleeing the excessive constraints resulting from environmental and health crises.

Inequalities between individuals and social groups come into play at every stage of the adaptation process: access to information, preparation, protection, evacuation and political action (Van Valkengoed & Steg, 2019). Intergenerational inequalities are particularly striking. The ecological, health, social and migratory consequences of Global Change are threatening the future. Immersed in a regime of growing ecological instability, the younger generations oscillate between anger and **eco-anxiety**, between civil disobedience, flight and self-protection.

The environmental resources and **threats** are simultaneously material, sociocultural and subjective. They are governed by perceptions, sensibilities and representations, and they can affect people's health, living conditions and life expectancy. The risks and consequences of environmental degradation – and hence the associated inequalities – have often been made invisible or denied on the pretext of the need to protect jobs, with the active collaboration of industries, public authorities, health professionals and trade unions (Duclos, 1987). A second form of denial arises from people's embeddedness in their locality, their **place attachment** and to neighborhood life, which forge a spatial identity, a sense of community. The wish to defend one's day-to-day environment wins out over negative representations (Moser & Weiss, 2003). The situation is akin to that of people who declare themselves satisfied with their life because they have internalized the normality of the deprivations they experience by adapting to their social and cultural environment (Nussbaum, 2012).

To become aware of environmental problems, their impact and the associated inequalities, requires access to information or to knowledge that is, on the one hand, profoundly inegalitarian, and, on the other hand, the more difficult to bear, to even recognise, for those whose everyday constraints are the more acute. Beyond a certain threshold of understanding, inequalities in self-defense and coping mechanisms come into play: for example, political or legal action, practices such as avoidance, monitoring, self-protection, escape, access to healthcare or self-medication. Social groups and individuals, thus, directly transform their environment in order to increase its resources (physical and/or psychological) or to mitigate its threats, either in situ or through migration. However, access to a safer environment is not available to all. There are many who have neither the means nor the power to refuse or to escape the deterioration in their living or working environment.

Environmental inequalities thus depend on the ways in which environments are shaped, on dominance relations (colonial, social, intersectional) and on sociocultural norms that determine what people are or are not prepared to do, to accept, in the light of their social class, their membership of an ethnic group or a minority, their gender, their age and their state of health (situations of disability), but also in the light of subjective factors. The capacity for mobilization and for mobility shapes these inequalities, which are not solely governed by processes of political exclusion. Indeed, where should polluting and dangerous infrastructures be located, where can people find shelter from the effects of Global Change? While environmental inequalities reflect injustice in distribution, in procedures, in recognition and in capabilities (Schlosberg, 2007), they, above all, demonstrate the collapse of a development model that threatens destruction for multiple populations, generations and living species, the most dominated first of all. It is, therefore, urgent to learn how to repair these environments that ravage us (Stengers, 2019; Blanc et al., 2022).

Environmental Justice – Bernardo Hernández & Ana M. Mártin

Environmental justice refers to the unequal distribution of environmental burdens and benefits between different social groups, connecting the environmental problem with social justice. Research on environmental justice is interdisciplinary and suggests that the burdens of risk are found in communities or minority groups, disadvantaged due to racial/ethnic, socioeconomic status and/or geographic location. These investigations demonstrate that groups with lower status in society experience a disproportionate share of environmental risk, exacerbated by social conditions that increase **vulnerability** to environmental damage. The disproportionate imposition of environmental risks to these populations is based on their low financial, political and informational resources, and it is known as environmental injustice or environmental inequality. Environmental racism is the form of environmental injustice that first attracted the attention of civil rights activists, academics and politicians in the U.S. in the 1980s. Environmental racism is the subject of an interdisciplinary body of literature that focuses on the unequal impacts of environmental pollution on different social classes and racial/ethnic groups. The concept of environmental justice was later broadened to include differences in race, economic status, sex, gender, age and capabilities, as causes of the unequal distribution of environmental impacts. Currently, inequalities are also related to recognition, capabilities and participation in the decision-making process, not only over pollution, but also on natural resources. Driven by the process of globalization, environmental justice has become a global movement that connects local environmental conflicts that regularly arise around the world. Furthermore, environmental justice has expanded the concept of environment protection to the places where people 'live, work and play'. Research on environmental justice suggests that, due to their heightened vulnerability, disadvantaged individuals, groups and communities have different understandings and concerns about environmental issues. Other concepts related to environmental justice include energy justice, water justice and climate justice.

Environmental Management – Isabel Pellicer-Cardona

Environmental management is understood as the decision-making process aimed towards minimizing the impact of human activity on the physical, biological and social **environment** and to protect and safeguard natural, social and cultural values. Environmental management is based on the idea of **sustainable development** and the need to find procedures for action that make society's relationship with the environment sustainable, therefore it is linked to the conscious choice of resources, means and actions that are respectful of the surroundings, without undermining the integrity and stability of the natural system, seeking to avoid the degradation of the environment.

The concept of environmental management and what it encompasses has evolved throughout the years. It started as an incipient concern for the environment, but it is directed more towards the physical consequences. However, its actual birth is considered to have been in the early 1970s in the U.S., due to the Environmental Impact Assessments that were carried out there and gained momentum with the approval of The National Environmental Policy Act (NEPA) on 1 January 1970. NEPA called for environmental factors to be taken into account in technical and economic decisions as soon as possible. The importance of taking environmental factors into account quickly spread to other countries and generated reports, meetings and conferences. The effects of this, such as the Brundtland report (cf. **Sustainable development**), the Rio '92 Declaration on Environment and Development and subsequent meetings, gave way to the formalization of environmental management, which gained importance in the 1990s, materializing in the increase of environmental legislation. This legislation involved the regulation of processes and the use of law to force change in personal, societal and organizational **behavior**. This inevitably required the contribution of psychology. In this way, concern for the environment became increasingly important, becoming a key element in the planning of any human activity and in a transdisciplinary field.

As indicated by Pol et al. (2010), environmental management concerns both companies in the world of production, exploitation of natural resources, waste management, etc. and service companies, NGOs, civil associations, public administrations and citizens, and it is linked to social responsibility, which is why it concerns everyone and not only the administration and/or large companies, although it is more common to speak of Environmental Management Systems (EMSs) in the latter.

EMSs are tools that seek to reduce environmental impact and improve efficiency by taking as a measure some objective criteria that arise from the recommendations and regulations of international bodies, public or private organizations and the legislation of each territory. Although each EMS has its own peculiarities, they are based on a cycle of continuous improvement, which monitors, develops and implements the environmental policies of an organization or body, whether public or private.

The most common EMSs are ISO 14001, the most widely used standard for environmental risk management, and the European Eco-Management and Auditing Scheme (EMAS), although there are also informal EMSs carried out by internal programs through which organizations or stakeholders manage their interaction with the environment.

Finally, a dimension that is also linked to environmental management is environmental marketing, although it is sometimes limited to what has been called 'green washing' or image cleaning of organizations.

Environmental Psychology – Enric Pol[4]

Environmental Psychology is the part of psychology that aims at studying and understand the behavioral, psychological and psychosocial processes derived from the relationships, interactions and transactions between people, social groups, organizations and communities, with their socio-physical environments (natural, built and technological) and available resources. It intends to understand and interpret the socio-environmental situation, and from it to generate new forms of action and intervention.

The interpretation-understanding from action-intervention enables and enriches the generation of theoretical knowledge of a psycho-socio-environmental character. Environmental Psychology is often closely related

---

4 I want to express my gratitude to Lenelis Kruse, for his critical reading and suggestions for this text.

to other disciplines that address environmental impacts affecting psychoso-cial and **behavioral** phenomena, while psychosocial and behavioral aspects influence the planning, construction and destruction of artificial and natural environments. Environmental Psychology tries to generate, discover, develop and test general laws of behavior, but behavior is necessarily linked to the peculiarities or differential facts of each **place**, of each **behavior setting**, of each **ecosystem**. Currently, Environmental Psychology has a broad, diver-sified and unclear program (if we look at our 'conferences' and publications). We will try to clarify why.

Many texts place the origin of their subject, the 'environment', in the 1960s, 1970s or even later in the 20th century, depending on their specific focus. But there is evidence that the real origins go back to the beginning of the 20th century. This is reflected in the multiple names the discipline has taken at different times in its history: Geopsyche (Hellpach, 1911b), Umwelt Psychologie (Hellpach, 1924; Muchow & Muchow, 1935; von Uexküll, 1909, 1934) (cf. **Umwelt**), **Ecological Psychology** (Kurt Lewin, Roger Barker et al. in the 1940s–1950s), **Architectural Psychology** (Lee, Canter, Küller and many more during the 1960s–1970s), Psychology of **Space** (Moles & Rohmer, 1972; Korosec-Serfaty, 1978, and others in French-speaking area), Environmental Psychology (Proshansky et al., 1970), Psychology of **Sustain-able Development** (Schmuck & Schultz, 2002), **Psychology of Conser-vation** and later Psychology of **Climate Change** (Clayton et al., 2015), and also names that are not explicitly linked to psychology, such as the case of **Social Ecology**.

We may ask then, what do these issues have to do with each other? Do we really have an 'identity' as '*Environmental*' Psychology? Do we have the right to call ourselves 'Environmental' Psychology?

Three axes of maximum nuclearization can be taken within the current form of the discipline: (a) What does **sustainable behavior** and preven-tion of **Climate Change** mean? (b) What role do urban form and housing play today, as **habitat?** (c) What are the main psychological and psychoso-cial processes involved in the person-environment relationship? We always talk about **perception, appropriation, attachment, identity**, but there are others. We may ask which came first: 'sustainable behavior' or urban form and houses as habitat? As can be seen from the above-mentioned entries, what gave rise to the first formal expressions such as Environmental Psychology (*Umweltpsychologie*, as it was first named in Germany in 1924, by Hellpach) was the social malaise and the precariousness of housing linked to the indus-trial revolution and the rapid growth of cities in the 19th century. This gave rise to critical approaches to housing analysis from Friedrich Engels (1845, 1872), the analysis of social relations in the city (Simmel, 1908), community relations (Tönnies, 1887) or early architectural movements that explicitly at-tempted to introduce 'nature' into the city, even in the form of stone flowers (e.g. Modernism, Art Nouveau, Modern Style, Jugendstil).

Furthermore, in the 19th century, with the advances in (natural) sciences, there was a growing awareness that health problems, epidemics, etc. were related to poor environmental conditions in living environments. This led, among other things, to the emergence of the first approaches to what we now call Environmental Sciences. Thus, Haeckel (1866) had introduced the term **ecology**, and Uexküll (1909 ff), created a kind of 'subjective biology' by differentiating between 'Umwelt' and 'Umgebung' (surrounding) showing that each organism, depending on its sensory and motor organs respectively, lives in its specific environment (Umwelt). Thus, the 'Umwelt', as it is experienced and acts in a species-specific way, is different from an extra-individual environment (Umgebung) (it raises the necessary differentiation of a species-specific ecosystem, and the Umwelt as an environment common to all species, and so many others). And this is 'transferred' to psychology, directly or indirectly, giving rise to concepts such as **behavior settings**, within the ecological psychology of Roger Barker (trained with the German émigré Kurt Lewin) among others, during the 1940s and 1950s.

In the social sciences in general, there is also a growing concern about these questions. Wundt leaves the laboratory when he wants to analyze why the peoples and cultures of the world are so different (this was his participation in the *Völkerpsychologie*), something that will influence and lead his pupil William Hellpach to produce his 1911 book *Geopsyche*. Moreover, within the climate of social and environmental concern of this period, it should also be noted that Simmel's social concern (1908) is explicitly in the background of the formation of the first empowering authors of the Chicago School of Sociology (Park and Burgess).

On the other hand, there was the architectural innovation of the Bauhaus (created in 1919 by Walter Gropius and Mies van der Rohe) – with links to GESTALT – and other movements of modern architecture. These movements, in addition to new aesthetic forms, wanted to find constructive forms that would allow affordable and dignified housing for the industrial workers who were concentrated in the cities. This will create a climate of interest and sensitivity all over Europe, but especially in Germany, which is the basis for the first explicit expressions of Environmental Psychology and other related formulations (see *Ecological Ps*, Lenelis Kruse; *Umwelt*, Hartmut Gunther).

Taking these aspects into account, four stages can be distinguished in Environmental Psychology (Pol, 1993, 2006, 2007): (1) Early beginnings, (2) American transition, (3) Architectural Psychology and (4) Green Environmental Psychology. These four stages have deep links with each other, even if they are sometimes not entirely obvious.

The beginnings range from the turn of the 19th century to the 20th century, including the emigration of researchers from Germany to the U.S. in the 1930s, in the pre-war period. In other works, we have called this process the 'American Transition'. Without this *'transition'*, one cannot understand the background that gives rise to the **architectural psychology**, which spans from the early 1960s to the 1980s.

Then, awareness – technological, social and political – of environmental issues as a reflection or confluence/combination of the natural environment, the built environment (especially urban), food, agriculture and food-producing population, the economy (production and consumption), the social interaction, etc. led to the elaboration of the Brundtland Report of 1987, and to the 'formalization' of Sustainability as an 'integrating' concept (a period we have called Green Environmental Psychology, but it must be borne in mind that being 'green' is not necessarily sustainable). Later (at the beginning of the 21st century), the awareness of the degradation of environmental conditions shifts the focus to global warming and the Psychology of Sustainability (Schmuck & Schultz, 2002) appears first, and then the Psychology of **Climate Change** (Swim et al., 2009; Clayton et al., 2015), which involves prevention and adaptation, resilience and risk management.

This puts processes such as **values, attitudes, behaviors, social representations**, the role of **nature** as a restorative element of personal and social **well-being** or the rethinking of the very concept of **QoL** at the center of the discipline.

The conclusion of all this, as seen in the latest developments in the discipline, is that now, in order to improve the **well-being** of citizens, we cannot design cities, **habitats** or built environments that are not emission-neutral and that are also 'enablers' (not 'determinants') of environmentally desirable **behaviors** (individual and collective), while at the same time allowing for the restoration of **biodiversity**. This is what leads to what are sometimes called *nature-based solutions* (NBS), but which often end up in approaches that are too naïve and non-disciplinary. Moreover, they are often not sustainable! This would require the integration of ecological needs, economic survival and well-being, and socio-psychological well-being. What we need today are new concepts of **QoL**, based on **sustainable development** (including social justice and just cultural developments).

Environmental Quality – Ferdinando Fornara

In the definition of the European Environmental Agency (2004), environmental quality has been conceived as a general term which refers to properties and characteristics of the environment, such as air and water purity or pollution, noise, access to open space, visual effects of buildings, and the potential effects which such characteristics may have on physical and mental health (caused by human activities).

Environmental quality can be assessed in either 'objective' or 'subjective' terms. In fact, for detecting and measuring the environmental quality of a given object or place, we can distinguish between technical evaluations, based on machines or experts' judgments producing 'hard' measures, and users' evaluations, which rely on the 'soft' measures based on the subjective experience of such an object or **place**. Examples of the first kind of evaluation, defined as Environmental Quality Indices (EQIs: Craik & Zube, 1976) and reflecting the 'technical' (Gifford, 2002), 'objective' or 'expert' (Bonnes & Bonaiuto, 1995) environmental assessment, are represented using sensors measuring air quality or the urban green space (in square meters) per inhabitant. Examples of the second kind of evaluation, defined as Perceived Environmental Quality Indexes (PEQIs: Craik & Zube, 1976) and reflecting the 'observer-based' (Gifford, 2002), 'subjective' or 'layperson's' (Bonnes & Bonaiuto, 1995) environmental assessment, can be given by residents' perceived air quality or green spaces quality of a city or a neighborhood. A further kind of layperson's environmental assessment is provided by the Observer-Based Pollution Indexes (OBPIs: Craik & Zube, 1976), which derive from the rating of panels of observers who are specifically trained for that (e.g., for air quality judgements). An example of the latter is represented by the creation of a unit of perceived measure named 'decipol' (Aizlewood et al., 1996), which refers to the detection of pollutants emitted by the office equipment.

An expert's technical assessment and a layperson's observational assessment of environmental quality stem from different **values**, beliefs and goals that are developed by the experts versus the laypersons' communities. Such differences mirror the socio-psychological processes of social construction of environmental issues, where social conflicts and controversies affect environmental descriptions and evaluations (Bonaiuto & Fornara, 2017). For instance, the quality judgment of urban green areas could be discrepant between experts and laypersons, since experts such as biologists or natural scientists tend to assess the quality based on 'naturalistic' features (e.g., the biodiversity rate), whereas laypersons deem important characteristics such as the green area accessibility and usability. Thus, different perspectives could produce different (and sometimes opposite) evaluations of the environmental quality of the same object or place. Despite that, environmental quality ratings, which can play an important role at various levels (e.g., orienting policy interventions or individuals' touristic choices), have usually been based only on technical assessments – due to their 'objectivity' appeal – whereas the investigation of laypersons' evaluations has been substantially neglected. Apparently, an exception – at the institutional and international level – seems to be provided by the 'European Common Indicators' (ECI) Project, supported by the European Commission and the European Environmental Agency, that includes both technical and layperson assessment measures of environmental quality of urban contexts (Ambiente Italia Research Institute, 2003). The set of ten indicators included 'subjective' measures (i.e., citizen satisfaction with the local community), other self-reported measures (i.e., local mobility and passenger transportation, journey by children to and from school, products promoting sustainability) and 'objective' measures (i.e., local contribution to global climatic change, availability of local public open areas and services, quality of local ambient air, sustainable management of the local authority and local business, noise pollution, sustainable land use, ecological footprint). Thus, only one out of the ten indicators cover the 'subjective' side of environmental quality, that is, the place as it is perceived by the people who experience it.

Indeed, a deeper analysis of the two types of environmental quality assessment shows that 'hard' measures are not so objective as they appear, whereas 'soft' measures can reduce the weaknesses of subjectivity. In fact, technical evaluations rely on human 'subjective' choices (by experts or decision makers) concerning which factors to take into account and how to measure them (e.g., which services to consider for the rating of neighborhood quality and which basket of indicators) and sampling times and places (e.g., where to locate the air quality sensors and what is the timing of data collection) as well as the interpretation of results. On the other hand, users' evaluations, which are derived by definition from individual experience-based responses, can be investigated through the development of reproducible measures that reach the standards of validity, reliability, sensibility and usefulness (Craik & Feimer, 1987).

Indicators of perceived environmental quality have been developed for various kinds of environmental objects or places, such as the **landscape** (mainly natural), the urban context, public or private facilities (mainly built places, such as schools, hospitals, elderly residences, etc.). As to the assessment of perceived quality of the landscape, an example of a tool measuring aesthetic and visual quality is the Scenic Beauty Estimation (SBE: Daniel & Boster, 1976), which is based on a prediction model as a function of various physical features of the environment, each contributing to a different extent to the overall SBE. Concerning the perceived quality of urban places, various tools have been developed, particularly for the neighborhood level, such as the Perceived Residential Environmental Quality Indicators (PREQIs), which include different versions in a variety of linguistic contexts, for example, French (Fornara et al., 2018), Swedish (Ferreira et al., 2016), Chinese (Mao et al., 2015) and Persian (Bonaiuto, Fornara, Alves, Ferreira, Mao, Moffat, Piccinin, & Rahimi, 2015). Regarding public or private facilities, an example is provided by the Perceived Hospital Environmental Quality Indicators (PHEQIs: Fornara et al., 2006; Andrade et al., 2012).

Investigations on perceived environmental quality of spaces, either at the urban (or neighborhood) level or at the building level, can take the form of a Post-Occupancy Evaluation (POE), which refers to the users' assessment of areas after they have been occupied by the users themselves, in order to figure out whether and how much such areas are congruent with users' needs and expectancies, and then modify those elements which receive a negative assessment (Zimring & Reizenstein, 1980). More specifically, according to the definition of the US Federal Facilities Council (FFC, 2001) the POE focuses on how much a building's performance suits occupants' health, safety, security, efficiency, psychological comfort, aesthetic quality and satisfaction, after the building has been occupied for some time.

In sum, environmental psychology literature has witnessed the effort of developing proper tools and procedures for detecting laypersons' assessments of environmental quality, in order to integrate (and be compared to) technical measures for improving the design and management of spaces within a 'user-centered design' perspective (Gifford, 2002).

Feedback – Béatrice Gisclard

Knowledge is acquired through practice, experience or result or observation; experience is a polysemous term that refers to both people and objects. Etymologically, *experientia* in Latin meant 'trial, test, attempt' or 'acquired experience, practice'. Feedback applies to the individual, but it can also concern broader levels such as the social group, the organization or the environment, both as a device and a process. From a temporal point of view, it can be understood as a circulation from the present to the past (in a reflective approach) as well as from the present to the future (in a preventive approach). Feedback can be seen as a grammar of interpretation,

> a kind of hard disk in which acquired experience is stored. A chess champion has a stock of several thousand games, played or learnt by heart. He will draw from this library in order to identify analogies with known situations and to identify possible options very quickly.
>
> (M. Goya, quoted by Tripier, 2007)

Shared feedback at the collective level is widely documented in the literature, because it is used in the study of organizations (e.g., civil security, the army, air transport or health) where the group takes precedence over the individual. From an interactionist perspective, the actor gains access through feedback to a systemic understanding of the event of which he could only have a fragmented vision. Used in the context of accidents, feedback does not point to failures but helps to understand their origins in order to improve processes and achieve high levels of reliability (High Reliability Organizations). This stimulation aims at organizational transformation by projecting into a future activity through scenarios, fed by a collectively reinterpreted past. These multiple approaches form the basis of a so-called learning organization. Weick (1995) has highlighted the importance for actors to find meaning (sensemaking) in the interpretation of the event in order to be able to act together: deprived of meaning, individuals are no longer able to interact correctly. According to the author, the environment cannot be objectified but is the result of the interaction between the organization and its context, particularly through communication. In post-disaster situations, feedback is used in the reconstruction phases (Build Back Better) to identify factors that would reduce vulnerabilities. However, many authors point out the limits of this approach, which poses the paradoxical injunction to rapidly rebuild the damage while requiring the capitalization of memory and reflection. On another scale, Kahn (1999) postulates that our collective inertia in the face of the current ecological catastrophe is rooted in what he calls 'environmental amnesia'. It is explained by the fact that generation after generation nature is degraded and that the feedback that each person has with regard to it is less than that of the generation before. This situation prevents us from measuring the extent of the degradation and the change of the reference frame.

Goal-framing Theory – Siegwart Lindenberg

Goal-framing theory (Lindenberg & Steg, 2013a; Steg, Lindenberg & Keizer, 2016; Lindenberg, Six & Keizer, 2020) focuses on the role of social contexts in making salient differing overarching goals (sometimes also called 'mind-sets'), thereby influencing agents' cognitions, actions and decision-making processes. It is, thus, a theory that is particularly important for analyzing social influence processes on the meso and macro level, such as environmental behavior, compliance, social contagion, governance and sustainable cooperation. The theory is widely applied not only in the field of environmental **behavior** (such as green consumer behavior, energy use, recycling, travel behavior, clean production, resource protection; Lindenberg & Steg, 2013a; Steg et al., 2016; do Canto et al., 2022) but also in the fields of organizational governance (Birkinshaw et al., 2014; Weber et al., 2023), social contagion (Lindenberg et al., 2020), adolescent behavior (Dijkstra et al., 2015), self-sufficiency (Serido et al., 2020) and hypocrisy (Lindenberg & Steg, 2013a, 2013b; Lindenberg et al., 2018). Its basis is the phenomenon known as 'shifting salience' or 'changing activation' of goals: only those goals that are salient (activated) at the moment are relevant for behavior (Lindenberg & Steg, 2013a; Steg et al., 2016). Overarching goals capture the entire mind (combining cognitive and motivational processes) and activate entire classes of goals, such as searching for 'what's in for me?' (relating to any kind of goal leading to personal gain) versus searching for 'what is the appropriate thing to do here?' (relating to any kind of goal leading to what is morally right). Mostly all three overarching goals are activated to some degree (so that motivations are mostly mixed), but at any given time, one of them is the most salient (see Figure 4). The theory identifies (1) the most important overarching goals, (2) the dynamics of these goals, and (3) factors

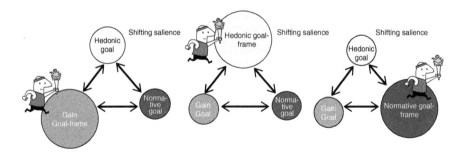

Figure 4 Shifting salience effects: Situational factors can make one overarching goal particularly salient.

that make one or the other of these overarching goals to be particularly salient for an individual or groups at a given time.

The most important overarching goals

The theory highlights the role of three distinct types of overarching goals (Lindenberg & Steg, 2013a; Steg et al., 2016). There are two 'ego-centered' overarching goals: the hedonic and the gain goals. The *hedonic* goal is focused on improving the way one feels within a particular context in the short term. When salient, the subgoals that it activates are variously related to need satisfaction; to the avoidance of negative feelings; to seeking pleasure, comfort, positive experiences and thoughts; and to the avoidance of effort.

The longer-term overarching goal, concerned with improving or maintaining one's resources, is called the *gain* goal. When salient, it is variously related to activated subgoals associated with material resources, material security and status.

Finally, there is an overarching goal oriented towards the collective: the *normative* goal. This goal can be described as the desire to act appropriately in the service of a supra-individual entity, involving commitment to a collective or joint identity – a social 'we' and, possibly, also nature (as the most inclusive 'we'). When salient, it is variously related to activated subgoals such as behaving in a prosocial way (say by helping others), collaborating (say, for a joint enterprise) or saving the environment.

The most salient overarching goal 'frames' a situation, that is, it governs what is activated in our mind, determining what kinds of subgoals are activated, and what we pay attention to, what we ignore; what parts of our knowledge system is activated; what we like and dislike at the moment; what we expect others to do; which goal criteria are important. For example, when the hedonic goal is activated, it leads agents to evaluate situations and actions in terms of their potential to make one feel better. A salient gain goal induces financial motivation and leads agents to evaluate situations and actions in terms of their potential return. When the normative goal is activated, it leads agents to evaluate situations and actions in terms of their potential to serve collective goals and in terms of 'doing the right thing'.

Dynamics of overarching goals

First, the overarching goals are competing, so that their relative strength matters when they are in conflict at a particular moment (such as avoiding effort versus doing what is right).

Second, much of the dynamics of overarching goals derives from the fact that, 'naturally', that is, without special interference, they differ in their power to become the most salient goal and thereby to heavily influence what kinds of subgoals are activated, and what we pay attention to, what we ignore, etc. This difference in strength derives from the evolutionary role of these goals.

The hedonic goal, being linked to the satisfaction of fundamental needs, is naturally the strongest. The gain goal, being linked to resources needed for the satisfaction of fundamental needs, is naturally weaker than the hedonic goal but stronger than the normative goal which very likely evolved in order to gain adaptive advantages from living in larger groups, and is, therefore subservient to the 'ego-centered' overarching goals. In the literature, this natural pecking order is often (partially) described in terms of the power of the 'affective system' of the brain. The ubiquitous phenomenon of rationalization for solving a conflict between overarching goals in favor of the naturally stronger goal also speaks to this pecking order (such as a person pouring turpentine down the sink mumbling 'I already protect the environment in other ways'; or the person refusing to insulate her house, saying 'I cannot afford saving the world all by myself').

Importantly, this natural order of strength can be changed, and it is the focus on this change (by shifting saliences) that makes the goal-framing theory so relevant for analyzing the meso and macro phenomena mentioned above. Circumstances can make people be more committed to moral or biospheric goals than to pleasure, avoidance of effort or caring about money. However, for this change, the weaker overarching goals need extra support, from culture, institutions, or from other people giving the good example. Only with these special supports will the normative goal not be pushed into the background to lose much or all of its influence.

Third, while one overarching goal is the most salient at a given moment, the other two exert their influence from the cognitive background (creating mixed motives on a regular basis). For instance, even a person who is committed to saving the environment will be influenced by how much that costs or how much effort it takes. Yet, the influence of an overarching goal from the cognitive background on behavior is much weaker than from the foreground. For example, when the gain goal is in the background and the normative goal in the foreground, people will pay much less attention to costs than when the gain goal is salient.

Factors that influence the salience

The salience of overarching goals changes due to changes in the external (say, what other people do) and/or internal (say, values) environment of the individual. The salience of the hedonic goal increases with visceral stimulation, such as cues that create or activate threats to or possibilities for the satisfaction of fundamental needs (such as hunger, sex, comfort, social approval, affection), or cues that frustrate expectations or create anxiety, or experiences of unfairness.

Because of the difference in natural strength of the overarching goals, the most pressing question is: what supports can make the normative goal become and remain the salient overarching goal against the strong pull of the gain and hedonic goals? This question is paramount not only for environmental behavior, but also for the contagion of compliance with legitimate rules, and for governing sustainable cooperation.

The *first* important support for the salience of the normative goal comes from compatible hedonic and gain aspects in the background. They take the sting out of the competition between overarching goals. For example, following **norms** or doing the right thing for the environment may give one a good feeling and generate social approval (a hedonic 'warm glow' support) and it may also save money in the longer run (a financial gain support). Such background support is essential for the salience of the normative goal.

Second, values are guiding principles in human life and influence the salience of overarching goals (Lindenberg & Steg, 2013b; Steg et al., 2016). Values often develop in response to threats to one's way of life (such as threats to the natural environment or to one's culture) guided by science (Lindenberg & Steg, 2013a, 2013b). Even though they are personal, they are strongest when shared with others. The most important groups of values are akin to the overarching goals: hedonic, gain-related and normative values (Lindenberg & Steg, 2013a; Steg et al., 2016). It has been shown that the latter contain two important subtypes: social (concerned with human relations) and biospheric (concerned with nature and the environment) (Steg et al., 2016). For environmental-friendly behavior, biospheric values support the salience of the normative goal in two ways: directly and via providing meaning and personal relevance and therefore a hedonic warm glow to environmental-friendly behavior.

Third, formal and informal rules are only covered by the normative goal if they are seen akin to norms (Lindenberg et al., 2020). For this to happen, rules must make sense and relate to beliefs of efficacy, and the less room they leave for rationalization, the more likely they will be followed voluntarily. For example, abstaining from eating meat in favor of the environment is fostered by a strong belief in the link between eating meet and negative consequences for the environment. Political, cultural and social institutions (i.e., established rules) can, thus, have a strong influence on the salience of the normative goal if they are 'legitimate' by making sense and also by providing hedonic and gain supports from the background (Lindenberg & Steg, 2013a). In democracies, values can influence institutions via public discourse (guided by serious science) and elections (Lindenberg & Steg, 2013b).

Fourth, the behavior of other people, especially as it relates to norms, has a strong influence on the salience of the normative goal (Lindenberg & Steg, 2013a). Observing respect for shared norms will increase, and observing disrespect will decrease its salience, which creates collective cycles. Thus, processes of social contagion are very important for the meso and macro level of voluntary compliance, prosocial and pro-environmental behavior (Lindenberg et al., 2020).

Finally, contexts that convey a sense of 'joint production', that is of jointly achieving a common goal, are a strong support for the salience of the normative goal (Birkinshaw et al., 2014).

The dynamics of goal-framing highlight just how interdependent people are with regard to the mainsprings of their behavior, and that it takes virtually all five supports to approach sustainable guidance of behavior by the normative goal.

Home (chez-soi) – Perla Serfaty-Garzon

Home refers to the universe – physical or intangible – strongly invested by a subject, whether the latter is an individual or a group. Endowed with its own social characteristics and atmosphere, this universe is inhabited by this subject in adequacy with himself/itself, in a durable or temporary way.

An intangible home – such as a language or a collective history – is intimately associated by the subject with the mastery of the field of meanings and with the cultural, social and ethical issues of this home, as well as with the identifications and **attachments** that the latter elicits in him. A subject's ability to recognize himself in an intangible home is, thus, an event of his personal consciousness of inhabiting in his own way a shared heritage, affectively or by thought, in a way 'from the inside'.

Home as a physical expanse covers a wide range of places whose meanings and scale can vary greatly, ranging from a house, a neighborhood, a city, a region, a country or the Earth. It is, however, to the concrete house, situated in the world, that the notion of home is most commonly and closely associated, and often understood as a synonym.

The house introduces differentiation within space – *spatium* – by conferring on certain acts, such as the establishment of limits and of an interior, a founding significance of place which elicits an imaginary of huddling, of withdrawal into oneself and into the family, of peace and freedom. However, doors and windows, as well as the variations in approach routes to the house – side and front alley, threshold, etc. – and its near-home environment – garden, yard, private park, etc. – of the house reflect the diverse expressions of the relations between the outside world and the sphere of the intimate. Such expressions take the form of separations, connections, keeping the outside world at a distance or closer to home, and all are at stake in the act and experience of hospitality.

The interior, for its part, does not coincide with a single psychological universe. Deriving from the Latin adverb '*intus*' which means 'inside', and sharing a common etymology with the term 'intestines', its polysemy refers to the homology between the inhabited interior and the interior of the person. The former offers a landscape with multiple tones, going from the *intimus*, that is, 'what is most interior', the intimate of certain rooms, to the more 'public' character of others, that is, the most open to the stranger to the home.

As an example, the living room, despite its recent evolutions, remains the place where the inhabitant allows himself the most to be seen and where he plays with refinement the game of appearances and revelation to the strangers to the home. In the mode of variations on intimacy, the bathroom for its part balances between hygienism and sensuality, bringing to the surface the contradictions of modesty and narcissism. The house thus implies the existence of a given project to inhabit which, moreover, engages space – *spatium* – through its **appropriation**, in the construction of the dweller's self.

The examination of two of the Latin words that convey today the meaning and sense of home allows a deeper understanding of the latter. The abstract noun *mansio*, or 'dwelling', deriving from the verb *manere,* 'to dwell', to stop, to stay in a place, gave the French '*maison*' or house, as well as the English 'mansion' and 'manor'. The French preposition '*chez*', deriving from the Latin *casa*, means 'at the house of', 'in', or 'among'. '*Chez*' forms with the French personal pronoun '*soi*', or 'self', the expression '*chez soi*', usually translated in English as 'at home'. The concept of '*chez soi*' conveys at once the sense of being at home in one's place as well as the inhabitant's awareness of his presence to himself, that is, of his interiority.

Both home and *Chez soi* designate the stay, the habitation or dwelling in a place, of leaving and coming back to it, that is, the experience of duration and its fragmentations, as well as the weaving and potential tearing of emotional ties with this place. The two terms also refer to the family group, all domestic affairs, lineage or dynasty. As such, both represent relationships between people, between them and the spaces of the shared territory, as well as between them and domestic objects.

The moral ties, of belonging, solidarity and affiliation among the inhabitants ensure the overall security and stability of the home and the *chez soi*. But they also reveal the power relations, hierarchies and implicit or manifest inequalities of these places. The latter both constitute spaces of potential violence, conflicts of place and visibility. They bear witness to the alteration, over the stages of each person's life, of the dynamics of solitude and community life, its adjustments, and arrangements, as well as the confrontations between the dwellers' domestic objects. These spatiotemporal dynamics reveal a mode of a subject's inscription in space, a habitual way of inhabiting and of being together, as underlined by the etymological origin of the term 'to inhabit', the Latin *habere* – to have, to hold – which expresses the continuity of a way of being in a place.

Beyond its synonymy with the house, the understanding of the concept of *chez-soi* takes us farther than the concept of home, as it opens, with the personal pronoun '*soi*', or 'self', the fundamental perspective of the subject's consciousness of being instituted in his interiority.

Interiority is presence to oneself, separateness, and the subject's intimate, inner 'at home' place. To assume himself as such, the subject must be separated from the other, and he receives his existence from this separation. Protected in the secrecy of his inner dwelling, the subject thus necessarily transcends himself to welcome the other. It is from inhabiting his own inner sphere that the subject can remain in the world, experience his spatial anchoring, establish places, build a house to access the experience of being at home in the world, as well as the experience of hospitality. Inhabiting physical space is grounded in the interior abode.

This inner dwelling is a place where movements for the establishment and renewal of its borders, the protection of its sovereignty and its autonomy are constant. It is permanently active to avoid the pitfall of withdrawing into itself, self-confinement and drifting towards self-alienation. Withdrawing into oneself alienate one's capacity to welcome the other. In its effort to transcend itself and open itself to the other, however, the inner dwelling must escape the risks of being overwhelmed by the assignments imposed by the other, of being expelled from itself and handed over to the other without recourse. These vacillations, recaptures and restorations of the subject's sovereignty in the secrecy of his interiority and the intimate temporality that unfolds there throughout the subject's life underline the openness and nomadism simultaneously inscribed in each one's original *chez soi* and its dual dynamics. On the one hand, the *chez-soi* hopes to be anchored both in the interior home and in the physical house, located 'in the world'. On the other hand, it aspires to open to the other and experience shared journeys, hospitality and encounters.

The ontological scope of the continuum between the interior dwelling and dwelling in the world opens the perspective of a subject who, to inhabit, must establish his concrete home, *chez soi*, in the hope of making it, through active appropriation, constitutive of himself. The resonance of the appropriation gestures on the inhabitant himself results in a heightened dwelling awareness which, when the test of reality imposes it, will support his capacity to dwell elsewhere and to renew the actions and gestures which make and remake, through time, his dwelling.

Founded on the continuity between one's interior abode and the home in the world, the sense of home, *chez soi*, is thus the awareness of taking on the constant effort to protect one's interiority and one's secret, as much as that of transcending their vacillations to open to the other.

Hospitality – Perla Serfaty-Garzon

Hospitality is the act of meeting and mutual recognition requiring at least two people as well a space in which to take place. We call that place home, whether it refers to a built dwelling, a neighborhood, a city, a country or the Earth.

Hospitality is a major value, carrying a powerful evocative force stemming from the ancient Greek and Roman body of ethical thought, the foundational philosophical, ethical and theological texts of the Hebrew Bible and the New Testament. The figure of Abraham remains a guiding reference and a living part of the monotheistic traditions as he embodies unconditional hospitality through his tent's four openings at the four cardinal points to welcome any traveler arriving from all directions, extending full and fearless hospitality to unknown people, showing complete discretion as to their origins, affiliations, or reasons for their travels, and eagerness to bring material and spiritual comfort to them. Hospitality remains a forceful part of our living humanistic worldview. It is, indeed, understood as an ethical risk taking. Few ever confess that they are not hospitable and routinely assume the quasi-synonymy between hospitality and warm welcome.

Yet, an elaborate set of time, spatial and moral rules of hospitality are followed by both hosting and hosted hosts to ensure its regulation and dynamics, before, during and after their encounter, through a range of material and symbolic markers enforced by the potential hosting host. Such rules help securing homes, thus inevitably recognizing there is a risk, if not a danger, of confrontation and hostility between both hosts. They are supposed to tame and limit open hostility, confine it to a latent state, while, at the same time leaving room for welcome.

From the apparently benign but powerfully symbolic force of the fence marking the end of the public domain from the beginning of the potential hosting hosts' private sphere of his house, and the dramatic, sometimes ceremonial walk and almost theatrical approach to the alley, the porch or the stairs, the guests walk to the complex place that is the threshold. This is the place where the first threat of intrusion can occur, where the hosting hosts' sovereignty might be questioned. Indeed, it is already shaking on its foundation. Alertness and eager screening of the guests happen there, in a silent confrontation which will be resolved only by the decisive steps taken by the hosting hosts to welcome or not their visitors. The hosting hosts must answer immediately the inner question of allowing – or not – the guests 'to be' within his house, and the encounter between both sides to 'take place' in it.

Because the guests are defined by their position of exteriority to the home, the nature of the threshold is the place where the latent hostility contained in hospitality is evaluated, hopefully tamed and resolved into a tentative welcome. That welcome constitutes an implicit contract, an engagement for mutual restraint and respect where the hosting host remains a sovereign in his home, dictating the uses of its territories and time-related practices. It engages the guest to accept to be served by the host without usurping the latter's place as sovereign in their home nor becoming a parasite. To the eyes of the hosting hosts, the threshold is transgressive, as it represents the place where lies the mutual acquiescence to the terms of such a contract.

The vestibule, where the hosting host re-enters into their own home, thus signaling the welcome, becomes then the place of the first appeasement between hosts and guest and opens a wider possibility for mutual recognition.

From near-home territories to the vestibule, the dance between the desire to act hospitably and the potential reversal of the latter into hostility is on the mind of everyone involved. It is a dance made more elaborate by a number and nature of several material elements that highlight the complexity of the issue at hand. A traditional doorknocker, for example, upholds the suspense of who is coming from the outside world until the moment when the host opens the door. The more suspicious doorbell with camera enacts hospitality from a place of distrust. The careful screening of guests through the door intercom system is equivalent to stronger frontiers between the outside world and the private home sphere. In more upscale residential buildings, a finely furnished and spacious entrance impresses social status on the entering visitors, while stopping their gaze from preying beyond the aesthetics of the controlled façade.

The dynamics of hospitality take on a special character with the door to the house. This Janus figure opens to two antagonistic worlds, separating while at once bridging the spatially and temporally self-centered domestic sphere with the shared public domain. The door's shape, size, materials and symbolism come together in an infinite play on sternness, ambiguous transparency, austere closure or casual protection of the home. The door is everything but passivity. It addresses the issue of strangeness and foreignness of potential visitors, heightening the welcoming host's confrontation with alterity, the strength of their identity and, most of all, their inner capacity to dwell safely within themselves.

People are permanently aware that they are securing their homes to keep the outside world out. They want to hold their authority over who may enter their home, to deny to the guest, as both their prisoner and potential master, the power to lord over them or to place them at his/her mercy. Contrary to Abraham, but nevertheless in line with his stature as a guiding unconditional hospitality figure, they maintain their sovereignty over their homes by exercising filtering, and a degree of violence, while, at the same time, transcending their fears and extending conditional hospitality.

Potential guests interrupt their hosting hosts' mental and spatial focus on themselves, as well as the flow of their personal time. Hospitality, thus, requests that hosting and hosted hosts assume a double movement or self-expropriation and interruption of their own self-centeredness. They both must allow time and room for the other, let him/her be in their respective homes, step inside each other's dwellings for each one to 'take place' and be able to express themselves at their own time. This logic of gift and counter-gift in hospitality implies forms of renunciations and reciprocity, as well as the intentional and benevolent interruption of the flow of one's personal time.

It is at the pivotal moment when the hosting host makes the effort to get beyond and above his centeredness on his own self to welcome a guest, that they are most vulnerable to the blurring of boundaries between their self and the self of the guest. Separation, which guarantees the strength of the subject's intimate identity, becomes unstable and must be restored by the hosting host.

The guest, however, faces that same risk as he must assume, at the same time as his host, an effort for mutual recognition. Under these conditions of respect for material and symbolic markers and of shared efforts towards self-limitation, hospitality, indeed, takes place.

Housing – Perla Serfaty-Garzon

The notion of housing designates, in zoology and botany, the spatial area occupied by – and adapted to – an animal or plant species. For geographers, sociologists and ethnologists, this notion covers a system of human settlement within a **territory**, that is, the spatial distribution and modes of localization and dissemination of human habitations. Sometimes replaced by the term 'milieu', it has also designated, in sociological works of the beginning of the 20th century, the general housing conditions of a given population.

Anthropology has underlined the passive nature, despite its necessity, of human dwellings' shelter dimension. It has shown that their spatial distribution, architectural types and devices, interior layout, variations in the use of materials, refer less to a utilitarian conception of the dwelling than to an intention to translate a cultural model of social life. The inhabitant's goal is to constitute for himself and his group a meaningful and relevant unit within the social space of his culture. As such, houses and housing represent, beyond their capacity to provide shelter, comfort and respite, major facets of material culture, expressing the mentality of the inhabitants, their way of life and their relationship to their environment.

Housing and its multiple sociological, demographic and economic ramifications are at the center of people's concerns. As a system of population and territorial devices, it reflects the structure of a social system, carries a heavy ideological weight and constitutes a significant political issue.

Housing is strongly defined by its territorial anchoring. It raises fundamental issues, such as the dwellings' location and its ramifications in terms of social status (the suburb, the popular vs. the affluent neighborhood, etc.), **well-being** (density of medical services, local services, etc.), **comfort** and day-to-day life (schools, sports and cultural facilities, etc.), and social hierarchy. It is built in line with the cultural **norms** of a given era and the heavy socioeconomic determinants weighing on it.

Homes are, for their part, strongly defined by their status as shelters and interior spaces, as well as the personal identity and symbolic issues attached to them. As such, they cannot be considered a merchandise like any other. However, they constitute commodities that are at the center of the specific rents and acquisitions markets. They are also considered as heritage assets intimately linked to the concepts of transmission and family histories' continuity. Charged with both financial and emotional issues, their status is thus made more complex by filiation questions, power relations or rivalry within siblings, and the recognition of each person's place within their family.

People attach great importance to their home and its environment. They regard as acute and pressing the societal problems attached to the issue of housing, such as its affordability, residential social diversity, the marginalization of certain groups in so-called 'sensitive neighborhoods', substandard urban buildings, social exclusion and homelessness. In this regard, recent debates on the poor quality of air and water, or soil pollution in neighborhoods and villages located near sources of pollutants and populated by minorities, advance the concept of environmental racism, which is itself based on the more general ideas of a right to a healthy environment and to **environmental justice**.

The inhabitants express a growing demand for the resolution of these problems by social actors, and towards the State. Although considerably complicated by the many agents acting on several scales, the issue of housing, because it intimately affects residents, sometimes also mobilizes them during collective actions. Their expectations confirm the historical achievements of defining housing as a public problem. They bear witness to the will to see the role and responsibility of public authorities extended to curb market abuse, promote innovative policies and major state housing programs.

Such programs have, for example, implemented policies for social housing and the founding of new towns which, moreover, contribute to the construction of a specific relationship between inhabitants and their homes. But if these policies' technical, architectural, urban planning and financial standards affect the inhabitants' dwelling modes, people also exercise their skills to adapt to and sometimes subvert their dwellings so as not to become, thanks to their place appropriation, strangers to their own living space.

The symbolism of housing accentuates the complexity of its status. This symbolism is expressed in several ways, including, for example, the option in favor of a particular district of residence, urban centrality versus the suburbs, which are an integral part of the social image of the inhabitant. Furthermore, the address of a home situates, confirms and consolidates the dweller's legitimacy of place within communities, such as the neighborhood, as well as friends, family, cultural or professional networks. Homes establish the relationship of their inhabitant to society. *A contrario*, a person recognized as 'homeless' loses, at the same time as his territorial grounding and his address, the legitimacy of his place within the social group, thus constituting homelessness as the dwelling experience's ultimate trial.

Within the larger issue of housing, the complexity and significance of the home extend in the inhabitant's intention, through the relationship he maintains with it, his acts of place appropriation and his modulation of its openness and closure, to transform his living space into a home, thus opening the issues of dwelling, intimacy, interiority and hospitality.

Landscape/Landscape Quality – Maria Luisa Lima

In general, landscape refers to the visible features of an area of land. In environmental psychology, however, it is always analyzed as part of the interaction with individuals and groups (Uzzell, 1991). Although landscape has a physical presence and an ecological side that can be analyzed by other disciplines with no reference to its use or to the transactions with people, our perspective of landscape includes necessarily the perceptions [Link], meanings and uses of the spaces. For this reason, the three approaches to landscape that we will develop here go beyond its objective and material features, to include the subjective experiences, preferences and representations of the space [Link], the (socially) constructed meanings and symbols given to the settings and the **affordances** of the place to develop different types of activities. Finally, we will apply these perspectives to the analyses of landscape changes.

Evaluating the landscape

One approach to landscape from environmental psychology adopts a cognitive approach, focusing on the ways people perceive, assess and develop preferences for a particular type of landscapes. Within this perspective, some authors have identified the dimensions underlying scenic evaluation and aesthetic appreciation. For example, Kaplan and Kaplan (1989) proposed complexity, coherence, mystery and **legibility** as basic constructs for landscape assessment. Another important topic in landscape studies is wayfinding and space orientation, mainly with the use of mental maps (cf. **spatial cognition**). One important contribution of this perspective to landscape studies is the demonstration that people's views of the spaces are structured by predictable dimensions, and that they are different from the ones used by policy makers or landscape architects (Uzzell & Lewand, 1990). However, this perspective often assumes homogeneity within the groups, and ignores the individual and group variability of landscape perception.

Feeling the landscape. A second approach to landscape focuses on the meaning of the landscape to the individuals or groups. It includes an experiential or phenomenological perspective where the landscape is thought of as imbued with individual feelings, interpretations and expectations, often associated with a strong emotional tone. This phenomenological approach focuses on the experience of people in place, including either positive (even sublime – Bethelmy & Corraliza, 2019) experiences of landscapes or negative (Tuan, 1979), even traumatic ones (Proudfoot, 2019). They often include a deep, narrative and qualitative approach. Another perspective focuses on the collective emotional experiences, associated with social meanings given to the landscapes. In this perspective, the importance of emotional **attachment** to the (existing or imagined) landscape for sustaining and reproducing collective identities is noted. Although the link between landscape identity and the narratives about the self is not always consensual (Ramos et al., 2016), **place identities** include a shared (usually positive) view of the landscape, that is often used as a symbol of the group. As natural landscapes are central topics in the representations of nations, people with stronger national identities have more positive feelings about the quality of the landscape (Bonaiuto et al., 1996). As landscape has an important role in creating an identity narrative, it is often a support for nostalgia in communities that live away from home (Brinkman, 2009). Another consequence of this collective perspective is that landscapes become a domain where conflicting social groups debate their different symbolic place representations (Nogué, & Vicente, 2004; Batel et al., 2015; Bettencourt & Castro, 2015). This approach stresses the process of attributing meaning to the landscape, and the potential for conflict that comes with the emotional and social dimensions of landscapes.

Experiencing the landscape. A last domain of research on landscapes analyzes the uses of spaces and its consequences, namely for health and **well-being**. Considering landscapes from a functional perspective and identifying its **affordances** (Gibson, 1979) allows for the analysis of the activities that can be developed in the place, namely recreational activities, thus permitting the design of the spaces considering specific behaviors (Helft, 2014; Menatti & Casado da Rocha, 2016). Another important line of research in this domain analyzes the therapeutic side of landscapes, in particular natural ones (Bell et al., 2018; White et al., 2021), as restorative environments (Staats, 2012). In fact, the exposure to natural landscapes (either in a walk, observing through a window, or looking at a picture or a video) is related to reduced **stress**, improved attention, better recovery from illness, and improved mood and general **well-being** (Velarde et al., 2007; Ward Thompson, 2011).

Changes in landscape. Given the importance of landscapes to the different domains of our lives, it is only natural that changes in landscape are involved in complex decision-making processes. The Council of Europe approved in 2000 and amended in 2016 the *'Council of Europe Landscape Convention'* that clearly recognizes the multidisciplinarity of this domain. In the preamble, it states that the landscape "is a basic component of the European natural and cultural heritage, contributing to human well-being and consolidation of the European identity"; and in article 5a it states that landscapes should be recognized as "an essential component of people's surroundings, an expression of the diversity of their shared cultural and natural heritage, and a foundation of their identity" (CoE, 2016). Changes in landscapes and the definition of landscape quality are not processes that can be environmentally managed without the involvement of both social and natural sciences. In fact, landscape changes have the potential to threaten the identities of the individuals and the communities, as they can put at risk the sense of distinctiveness of the landscape (if the changes ignore landscape identity), the sense of continuity between the past and the present (making it difficult to articulate place memories), the sense of autonomy and self-efficacy for the new uses proposed for the landscape, and the sense of self-esteem if the new image of the landscape is not positive (as in the case where changes include industrialization of natural spaces) (Twigger-Ross & Uzzell, 1996). From our perspective, a successful change in landscape can be achieved with collaborative work that includes not only the architectural and ecological dimensions of the project, but also the psychological ones – the cognitive, emotional and behavioral aspects mentioned above. Positive processes of landscape change imply the co-creation of spaces, the involvement of the communities and the openness to innovation from the different stakeholders and knowledge. Although there are barriers in these processes (associated with the scale of the observations, the time and resources involved, the different languages between disciplines – Raymond et al., 2010; Lima et al., 2012 – and even epistemic dimensions – Castro, 2021), they can be overcome with a **place**-based approach (Clayton et al., 2016). There are now several published successful examples that can be used in future landscape interventions (e.g., Lubis & Langston, 2015; Cowell & Devine-Wright, 2018; Hedblom et al., 2020).

Learned Helplessness and the Environment – Enric Pol

The concept of learned helplessness is a contribution by Martin E.P. Seligman (1975), based on his experiments with animals, which later allowed him to apply it to explain different human pathologies, such as depression and the self-perceived inability to solve problems in one's daily life and future expectations. It can be defined as an *inadequate passivity or demoralization*, which *largely explains depression, that can lead to physical illness and even death* (Peterson et al., 1995). In many of his publications, he *examines the learned helplessness in reference to the contemporary culture of individuality and personal control*. In contrast, his own approach led him to propose what would be the basis of later Positive Psychology (Seligman & Csikszentmihalyi, 2000) based on works that were also very old, such as *Learned Optimism* (Seligman, 1990/2006), in which he proposes personal and community strategies similar to what is often included under the term 'empowerment'.

His approach is focused on research on situations that are directly linked to common themes in Environmental Psychology. Thus, for example, Baum, Aiello & Calesnick (1978) analyze *the relationship between prolonged exposure to architecturally mediated social density and the motivational deficits characteristic of learned helplessness*. They find an explicit relationship, with nuances depending on the situation. But above all, they found that, *as expectations of control diminished, the response of helplessness increased*. This leads them to conclude the key importance of the person's expectations of control.

Peterson and Seligman (1983) analyze the effect of *victimization* on the person, and find that during the episode of victimization, victims learn that responding is futile. It creates an expectation of future powerlessness, and some victims become numb and passive.

But much earlier, Klein et al. (1976) had shown in an experimental situation that when depressed subjects attributed their failure to the difficulty of the problems rather than to their own incompetence, their performance improved markedly. This leads them to conclude that failure itself is not enough to produce impotence deficits in the person, but it does lead to a decrease in the belief in personal competence.

This places the phenomenon of *causal attributions* as a key element in the effects of failure or the perception of incapacity to control in people (Dweck & Goetz, 1978). This situates the dominant **social representations** as one of the elements that will influence the social construction of helplessness. Therefore, also of the communicative processes, the mass media and ICTs (see Environmental Communication).

There are two ways of approaching environmental information: one that seeks the involvement of the person in the resolution of the environmental problems prevailing at any given moment, with an empowering effect; and the other that presents environmental **risks** and effects as a global structural problem, to which individual or small collective action is irrelevant, an approach that fosters the perception of helplessness. Before the global crisis of 2008, the former dominated the mass media. After the crisis, the latter dominated (Pol, Castrechini, Carmona et al., 2017). This has an effect not only on environmental **behavior**, but also on people's experiences, the dynamics of social relations and power relations, linked to society's capacity for opposition and resilience.

The processes of globalization and structural changes of the last decades, in addition to changes in the form of the city as a habitat for more than half of the world's population, have led to a physical alienation of decision-making organizations (environmental, socioeconomic and political), which increases people's sense of incapacity to make decisions and loss of control, something that seems to foster learned helplessness (Pol, Castrechini & Carrus, 2017). Empowering civil society to address environmental issues and the climate emergency could have the effect of increasing civil society's capacity to respond and oppose the interests of those in power. For this reason, structural actions are often detected that seem to intentionally favor situations that generate learned helplessness. The form and structure of the habitat, which always has a socio-physical dimension (Stokols & Altman, 1987), is an active factor that facilitates or hinders this process.

Legibility – Thierry Ramadier

Spatial legibility is a concept originally proposed by Lynch (1960) to capture the ease with which an individual can recognize geographical features and organize them spatially into a coherent pattern. Overall, it concerns the perceptual quality of the physical dimensions of space and goes hand in hand with a complementary concept, the imageability of places, that is, the quality by which a physical object is likely to provoke a strong image in any observer.

Directly related to **spatial cognition**, legibility influenced much research into the material characteristics of the environment that affect how geographical space is mentally arranged, with the aim of improving understanding of spatial behavior. By distinguishing between easily and less legible layouts, whether by analyzing the urban grid or the location, form and visual aspects of buildings, Lynch has initiated a way of psycho-physicalist research in which the aim is to identify the forms that are most consistent with the individual's cognitive processing of geographical space. The research focuses as much on the individual construction of an efficient spatial representation, as on spatial behavior in situ or in virtual environments. In this model, the function of legibility is to guarantee the construction of landmarks for situating oneself, orienting oneself and for wayfinding. Some authors have criticized the overly cognitive dimension of this concept, which overlooks the affective dimensions of the relationship with space (Taylor, 2009).

In addition to this first proposal, where the notion of representation remains central, a more strictly behavioral approach develops a definition focused on the complexity of the spatial structure. Thus, for Weisman (1981), legibility refers to the ease with which an individual can find his way in a given built environment. This approach is particularly invested in the spatial syntax theory.

A last approach considers legibility as an indicator of the individual's relationship to space, and no longer as an external factor affecting the individual. Thus, the perceptive quality of the physical environment depends on the signs and codes previously internalized by the individual, and on their confrontation with those present on site. This social legibility (Ramadier and Moser, 1998) is also based on the physical attributes of the space, without considering them to be determinants in themselves. Their quality is relational, depending on the individual's geographical trajectory and the sociocultural history of place. Social legibility completes the analyses on the social construction of spatial representations. It is especially mobilized in research on spatial segregation, or on the gentrification of neighborhoods. (Comelli et al., 2018).

Memory of Places – Denise Jodelet

The close connection between space and memory has been, for the first time, emphasized by Halbwachs, inspired by the researchers of the School of Chicago, and later taken up by specialists in collective memory (Brown & Middelton, 2008). Although the natural space is linked to memory as the seat of private memories or as **place** that has been marked by notable historical episodes (for example, scenes of battle), it is about urban space that most of the research on the memory of places has been developed. This trend is due to the fact that the style and history of an era is expressed through the forms of architecture and urban disposition. The spirit of a time becomes that of the places where it deployed its aesthetic, functional and social order. This spirit of the places comes from their ability to perpetuate the atmosphere and the history of a time, elevating some of them to the status of patrimonial spaces established in natural or built environments (sites of cultural value of archeological, historic, monumental or urban type) or organized in museum form. This has led to their designation as 'places of memory' (lieux de mémoire, Nora, 1997) or 'anthropological places' (lieux anthropologiques, Augé, 1994) marked by three characteristics: identity, relational and historical.

Halbwachs has, from his first work on the *Les cadres sociaux de la mémoire* (*social frameworks of memory*) (1925), stressed the role of space, for the following reasons: collective memory always has its seat in a spatial framework; the groups recover their memories in the form they gave to their living environment; there is an isomorphism between the social structure and the material configuration of the city; the ordering of the spatial context delivers, for the group, a sense of stability and permanence.

The interest of studying the memory aspects of space lies in considering the language of identity through which urban and territorial affiliations as well as the affirmation of citizenship are expressed. The link between memory and the city goes, in fact, through identity. This identity takes several forms: identification with spaces, that has been approached in social psychology with the concept of **place identity**; identity affirmations resulting from, on the one hand, the collective arranging imposed by urban development plans that has an effect on the forms of sociability or induces specific and plural **appropriation** of space, and, on the other hand, the intervention of group formations (associations, activists, etc.) which organize citizenship at the local level.

Another reason for examining the relationship between built-up space and memory is also evident from the analyses carried out today on post- and over-modernity. Thus, for Marc Augé (op. cit.), the city is part, with the individual and the religious phenomenon, of contemporary 'worlds' to be interrogated. Contemporaneity would be marked by the extension of the urban fabric, the multiplication of transports and communications, the standardization of cultural references, the globalization of information and images. The over-modernity would correspond to the experience of the acceleration of history, the narrowing of space and the individuation in space. This dual process would change the relationship we have with our surroundings and our community. Thus, the city, favoring individualism and collective abstraction, makes it difficult to create social ties and establish symbolic relations with others. In addition, the problems of the city and the urban area have been made more complex by the development of migrations and the problems linked to the coexistence between communities that are distinct by their ethnic, national or regional origins; by inequalities of status and resources; and by forms of integration in the collective space. So, many dimensions involve, in the forms of living and the relationship to the city, identity and history, and consequently the memory of the groups that invest meaningfully their space of life.

Among the social science works that have dealt with the relationship between identity, space and time (Jodelet, 1982, 1996, 2015), we can distinguish several currents corresponding to scholarly or profane discourses on the city: sacred, political, functionalist, structuralist, semiotic and technological. In these different discourses, the role of memory takes three specific forms: (a) 'factual memory' bearing certain places associated with historical events, or identified by names recalling them; (b) 'collective memory' corresponding to forms of social life (professional, commercial, social, festive, etc.) that once marked these places and whose echo remains in the specific arrangements of their form; (c) 'monumental memory', to use Nietzche's expression, which restores the past as such through objects and structures that are durable but recognizable in their belonging to a past specific era or style.

Taking into account the temporality of memory in which past-present-future interact allows us to examine the psychological and social processes through which: (a) the collective memory inscribes the past in urban places which appear as vehicles of identity because of, on the one hand, their materiality and form and, on the other hand, their settlement and use; (b) the past of the city resonates with the sense of identity manifested in the present of urban existence; (c) the valorization/devaluation of memory-bearing places passes through identification or untying with the groups that occupy them; and (d) the struggle for the future is working on memory, changing the identity of urban places. These psychological and social processes of the construction of the historical sense of the city can be identified through the study of socio-**spatial representations**.

Ménagement – Emeline Bailly

The term 'ménagement' in French comes from the Latin word *mesnage* (derived from *mansio*, dwelling) which means to take care of, arrange, harmoniously arrange one's dwelling, to act with measure, moderation, regard, respect, towards places or persons. It implies a way of acting that is considerate, thrifty, sober and safe from damage. It also refers to the meaning of a household living under the same roof (being in a household) and by extension to cohabitation, living together. Thus, to *'menage'* implies both the action of taking care, with sobriety and economy, and in common, of the inhabited places and beings with whom we live.

'Ménager' was no longer in use in the French language before its rehabilitation, from the 1980s onwards, by several authors interested in urban layout (cf. **urban design**) – that is, the organization and functional arrangement of a space or territory by a collective of various actors in charge of its administration (Zimmermann & Toussaint, 1998) and seeking to propose an alternative.

The French sociologist Michel Marié (1985) uses the notion of 'ménagement' to designate the need for reciprocal adaptation between techniques and societies, between the State's planning logic and the inhabitants in 'ménagiste' logic (motivated by their local values). He defines 'ménagement' as the capacity of planning institutions to self-regulate in order to approach the territory differently through a permanent re-evaluation of the terms of their action according to the forces at work. For him, management is thus an action of conciliation (1996).

At the same time, the urban philosopher Thierry Paquot (1990) also questions the action of planning (which he sees as a technical and administrative procedure that tends to standardize and normalize). He advocates another mode of action: *'ménagement'*. He refers to Martin Heidegger (1958) for whom habitation is linked to a fourfold *'ménagement'*, namely the earth, the sky, the gods and the mortals. For Thierry Paquot, *Ménagement* is linked to habitation and to the art of building bridges and relationships. It involves a flexible, open, discreet, adaptable attitude that respects what is already there and is concerned with the living. It invites us to be gentle with people, things, places and living things (including the earth), in order to make them more amiable (2003). Indeed, for him, tidying also has to do with the hospitality of the habitat. The person who tidies up enters a relationship of hospitality towards urban places, while the hospitality of the places themselves is a matter of welcoming, of amenity. According to him, *'ménagement'* contributes to ecologizing the ways of acting and thinking about territories and the living, by favoring the interrelations between the constituent elements of a single whole. He speaks of an ecology of *'ménagement'* (2021). Following them, several authors are interested in the notion of *'ménagement'* to think differently about our earthly habitation. The *'ménagement'* allows an understanding and an accompaniment of inhabited environments in their intertwining and complexitý to perpetuate the habitability of the world. *Menagement*, thus, introduces a new way of considering the evolution and transformation of inhabited territories. It invites us to take care of what is already there, of nature, of the geographical site and its **landscapes**, of the **places** and constructions built by humans, in other words of the urban and landscape heritage. It stresses the need to act with consideration, sobriety and harmony, to preserve places and living environments and their habitability in the face of **risks**. It activates a sense of living in symbiosis with its inherited, lived, and projected territorial ecology. It calls for common achievements to ensure sustainable pleasure in living. It reconciles human and non-human dwellings with their living environment to offer a quality of terrestrial habitability. This concept is of interest to environmental psychology, as it opens perspectives on understanding the relationships between people and their environment.

Mobility – Sandrine Depeau

Mobility is a polymorphic notion with very labile contours due to the multidisciplinary approach using it and its semantic evolution for more than a century. As an exhaustive definition is futile, let us only take up the two main meanings given by the historical dictionary of the French language (Le Robert). The latter will be discussed in the field of social sciences and environmental psychology. The first one associates it with 'the character of that which changes aspect rapidly' or with 'the essential character that a reality would have of never being identical to itself' (referring here to the idea of change of state). A second one refers to 'the character of what can move, change place or position' (thus translating the capacity to move and to displacement).

More specifically linked to the field of urban research, within which environmental psychology contributes, the notion of mobility (limited here to the geographical meaning) shares some of its evolutionary conceptual currents with sociology (particularly urban). As part of the understanding of the processes of urbanization and the transformation of urban lifestyles, its field of study keeps pace with the various revolutions linked to transport, means of production and communication. The history of this notion is not without inventories in the social sciences (Gallez & Kaufmann, 2009; Lévy & Lussault, 2013), nor without controversies regarding its conceptualization (Borja et al., 2015). However, the latter often leave in the shadows certain theoretical models of environmental psychology furthermore connected to advances in the field of mobilities. If a synthetic definition of the notion is an important achievement, this one cannot be obtained without a detour through the field of social and human sciences, in which a few key periods of its semantic evolution are highlighted here, crossed with the two main meanings (change and movement) understood in the field of environmental psychology.

Mobility in the sense of change

Understood in the sense of change, mobility is apprehended here on a macro scale and in the relationship to places that it helps to link in order to understand the transformations of society. Initially observed, in sociology, mainly through the prism of changes ('ascending' or 'descending') in positions ('vertical' or 'horizontal') in social space (Sorokin, 1927), it only makes sense in geographical space because of the transformations in social and individual organization and in the social structures that are modified. Otherwise, we speak of *fluidity*. Associated with the concept of migration in the ecological conception of the Chicago School, mobility is a descriptor of the transformation of urban spaces and lifestyles, and even personality traits (Sorokin, 1947). Without being fully at the heart of urban ecology, mobility is part of the modernization of societies and urban worlds (Simmel, 1903) in what it reveals about individuals' relationships to time, spaces and social groups, thus marking some of the foundations of the ecological approach in psychology. In this approach, mobility is, indeed, a dimension for defining the individual and the environment in the same dynamic, considering together the spatial and temporal dimensions. This is found, for example, in the work of Gibson and Crooks (1938) that is focused on the safety zone during a car journey (prefiguring the notion of **affordance** based on questions of perception in movement). It is also around the urban behaviors of child populations (Barker & Wright, 1955) that the ecological approach, notably the theory of **behavior settings**, is anchored in environmental psychology. This approach makes it possible to study, in space and time (Barker, 1968), and according to variable levels of involvement, the places frequented by individuals in order to identify behavioral structures. Mobility, understood here on the scale of a territory, conditions access to some places. It is in this logic that Kyttä (2004) will characterize quality environments for children ('Bullerby model').

Beyond its role in the foundations of the ecological approach, mobility, seen here from different levels of spatial and temporal scales (commuting, leisure, residential mobility, migration), colors a large part of the work in environmental psychology, especially on the macro scale of territorial transformations (reticularization, peri-urbanization, metropolization) driven by the revolutions in transportation (especially the democratization of cars) and modes of communication. It conditions, through the play of spatial and social distances, relationships to others, to time and space, socio-spatial experiences and prefigures the logics of living. It is subject to and produces reticular worlds (multi-residentiality, multi-locality), and it transforms the meaning of places, the QoL and urban sociability (Moser et al., 2003).

It also questions the quality and meaning of relationships between living spaces, the strength of ties or **attachments** to territories according to types of spatial mobility (Fuhrer et al., 1993) or even patterns of habitat stability despite residential mobility (Feldman, 1990). Erected (in sociology) as a 'total social fact' (Bassand & Brulhardt, 1980), the concept of mobility has been questioned more widely in the social sciences as a dominant value (the notion of 'generalized mobility' proposed by Lannoy & Ramadier, 2007) in order to better discuss about the resulting inequalities (mobility not only being chosen); even, it can also be understood as a paradigm ('mobility turn' (Urry, 2000) advocating movement and fluidity for the observation of social life through the movement of objects, ideas, individuals, etc. Hence, it becomes a fundamental dimension to interrogate some fundamental dialectics in environmental psychology, such as those inscribed in the local-global, movement-sedentary/fixity relationships (Gustafson, 2009, Lewicka, 2011, Van der Klis & Karsten, 2009) which revisit the concept of **place attachment** (Gustafson, 2014; Di Masso et al., 2019).

In this context, mobility becomes a field of scientific controversy in which the right to the city (Lefebvre, 1968), underpinned by the right to mobility, is confronted with the right to immobility, where the regime of speed is opposed to that of slowness, where the global puts the local in tension, where weak ties question strong ties, where questions of freedom are confronted with those of hardship, etc. Mobility becomes, certainly, a powerful descriptor of the ambivalence of individual-environment relations to understand the reconfiguration of lifestyles (mainly urban), of everyday place experiences and feelings of spatial or territorial belonging, but also, a revisited form to analyze social structures or dispositions that pre-figure displacements (Borja et al., 2015) where "the internalizations of the person are actualized, precipitated and lived" (Borja et al., 2015, p. 224). Finally, by challenging the qualities of residential anchoring, it also reveals, depending on positions in life cycles and in social space, one of the modalities of socio-spatial identity (cf. 'travel identity', Ramadier & Depeau, 2011); it also makes it possible, with certain relational approaches (apprehending places as socially constructed spatial categories), to detect forms of socio-spatial segregation (cf. the notion of replacement, Ramadier, 2010) by focusing on existing analogies between the used places of destination and the configuration of residential space.

Mobility as a movement

More closely related to travel, mobility is a movement between two (geographical) positions marking a departure (beginning) and an arrival (end). Initially, it was mainly studied in the field of transport engineering and economics, and defined in relation to the speed regime and modes of transport (primarily motorized). It is the result of an activity produced (by individuals-agents) that underlies the development of models of flow regulation, the prudential analysis of driving and safety (cf. the creation of the National Institute for Research and Studies on Transport and Safety – INRETS – merged in 2011 with the French Central civil engineering and Transport research laboratory – Laboratoire Central des Ponts et Chaussées). These models tend to reinforce functionalist paradigms and behavioral rationality in the field of social sciences. These paradigms are no longer as dominant as they once were, due to the plurality of disciplines involved.

As a movement, mobility implies a set of conceptual tools most classically related to a decomposed activity (distances traveled, travel motives, time spent, constraints, needs, capacity or skills to move – or motility –situation of the movement) suitable for inspection in space and time, through reported behaviors (cf. travel diaries, geolocalized time-budget surveys, etc.) but also observed in real time, using GPS datalogger. These allow, at the scale of traces, through the places frequented and the modes of travel, to study the daily behaviors often made invisible otherwise (Depeau & Quesseveur, 2014). Studied at various levels of spatial and temporal granularity and from a plurality of bodily, spatial, cognitive, social, but also emotional dimensions (using, among others, sensitive approaches and travel-along interview), travel is similar to a personal and social experience where the regime of slowness (cycling and walking) is also gradually gaining interest in the face of ecological and digital transitions issues.

In this context, the travel choices made through walking or cycling contribute to defining the experienced and traveled **ambiences** or environmental qualities (**walkability**, accessibility, cyclability, etc.) (Brown et al., 2007). In addition, travel observed as a body-testing (drudgery vs. comfort) or as pedestrian journeys made alone or with peers provides indicators of independence or spatial autonomy in the case of populations with reduced mobility (PMR), particularly children (Depeau, 2003) or the elderly (Lord & Piché, 2018). Travel is also defined as a set of behaviors that are acquired and are part of a socialization process (Granié et al., 2018). In this sense, it leads to the notion of habits or routines (Depeau et al., 2017) but also to question the notion of skills with regard to the notion of habitus, and finally, to consider the contexts of travel socialization (family sphere, professional, etc.). From this perspective, travel involves processes of attention (to the environment and to others), risk assessment, spatial cognition and socio-spatial representation, which make it possible to identify factors of accessibility or **legibility** (Lynch, 1960; Ramadier & Moser, 1998) or comfort (Marchand & Weiss, 2009). In the field of public health, active travel as an index of physical activity contributes to the definition of **well-being** (Duncan & Mummery, 2005).

In close connection with urban ecological transition issues, travel is also questioned in terms of its dependence on certain motorized modes and within the behavioral alternatives to be encouraged to contribute to energy sobriety. In this context, travel, reduced to a behavioral intention, is part of a rational behavior explained using different models of the theory of planned behaviors, including attitudes, personal or subjective norms, the perception of control over the situation, and emotions (Passafaro et al., 2014). The results produced from these models contribute to communication and awareness programs (cf., in particular, the staged model of self-determination behavioral change, Bamberg, 2013). Beyond its rational form, mobility (as a travel) as a routine or habit in a given context is also a way of life (Depeau et al., 2017). It is the expression of a relationship with the environment that activates preferences, attitudes and beliefs in different areas of urban life (Van Acker et al., 2016), and in this sense, it is linked to living conditions issues as well as **place identity**. For example, it has been shown that a trip, embedded in a habit, can be hardly understood as a rational behavior to be transformed by applying theories of planned behavior (Verplanken et al., 1994). Finally, the technological developments and devices operated in the field of transport and its infrastructures, by transforming the uses of travel and public spaces, also question the field of driving and the use of mobility assistance tools (Payre et al., 2015).

Nature, a psychological perspective – Henk Staats

What is nature, really? Ultimately, nature encompasses everything we are and are surrounded by, making it a difficult concept to define productively. However, for an understanding of nature from a psychological perspective we can look at a number of cognitive, affective and behavioral dimensions that focus on interacting with the perceptual qualities of the **environment** that is mostly characterized by inanimate matter and organisms, whose creation is essentially not completely dependent on the acts of mankind. This is a broad definition, on purpose, as it clearly includes phenomena that are created or affected by the acts of mankind, for example, cultivated flowers, fields of grain, herds of sheep, and even weather and climatic conditions. This choice stems from the finding that most non-experts tend to include these semi-artificial elements as manifestations of nature. We agree with this, and even from a philosophical standpoint there could be reason to agree. Essentially, it is also in line with current ideas on the evolutionary versus cultural origin of preference for nature, stating that human–nature interaction has always been a matter of mutual adaptation in which notions of unspoiled nature, its beauty and importance, are principally culturally and historically determined (Schama, 1995).

The experience of nature is generally contrasted with the experience of built, urban environments. Important is that generally two literatures on human–nature interaction can be distinguished: the 'good' one, focusing on the beneficial qualities of nature, and the 'bad/problematic' one, dealing with the negative consequences of man's relationship to nature, concerning pollution, **climate change, biodiversity** loss and other ways in which mankind exploits nature in an unsustainable fashion. We will discuss both literatures, to come up with a last section attempting to unify those in a series of concepts that pertain to both.

Beneficial qualities of human–nature interaction

We follow the conceptual analysis by Wohlwill (1983) who distinguished four qualities of the experience of nature in which natural environments are different from built, artificial environments and lead to higher preferences:

- *Stimulus properties*: in general natural environments are less complex, they show more order, an order that can be easily achieved through the way elements are perceived as coherent and fitting yet may contain intricate details providing more richness. Colors are generally less bright and more alike. Sounds are less loud, and more predictable. Movement is less abrupt, and speed is lower. Overall, this makes for a stimulus environment that has lower complexity which is generally considered pleasant, more so than urban environments devoid of natural elements.
- *Growth and change*: the autonomous processes of growth and change, inherent in natural environments arouse curiosity and fascination, and even awe. Realizing that human influence on these processes is unnecessary, limited, or even counterproductive leads to a heightened sense of admiration for nature.
- *No feedback*: being in a natural environment implies the relative absence of other people, especially as compared to most urban environments. This precludes the effects of being continually aware of the responses of others to our presence and behavior. This allows for rest, the absence of continuous vigilance that is present in populated environments.
- *Symbol*: over the course of history nature has been loaded with symbolic meaning. Of innocence, purity, goodness. "People seem to feel that nature is good" (Brown et al., 1986, p. 6). This may especially be the case in western societies in current centuries, a period in which people have become predominantly independent of the perils of nature. Historical research shows that the general image of nature in the Middle Ages was one of evil, horror, and fear (Knopf, 1987).

The outcome of these cognitive and affective processes is the currently dominant view of nature as an environment that promotes psychological restoration (Staats, 2012), and it may increase competence, stimulate physical activity, and inspire reflection on life, thus promoting physical and psychological health (Hartig et al., 2014).

Problematic consequences of man's relationship to nature

Humankind has gradually become more in control of nature, leading to a strongly increased world population, improved health and material affluence, although these benefits are divided in very unequal ways across the world. This has come about with ecological costs that become more and more prominent, of which climate change and biodiversity loss are currently the most pressing problems. These global problems of nature are generally considered the consequence of what is called a social dilemma, the uneven balance of the rewards and costs of nature exploitation, rewards accruing to the individual, costs to the community, described as the tragedy of the commons (Hardin, 1968). Generally, this problematic state of affairs is partly due and at least increased by a value orientation that favors short-term economic affluence. Insight in existing **value** orientations regarding the environment is provided by Dunlap et al. (2000) who developed the **New Ecological Paradigm (NEP)**, a generally used measure to monitor ecological consciousness. However, despite a growing awareness of environmental problems as signaled by studies using the NEP, not nearly enough is done and the state of the environment deteriorates. This has started to become visible, in particular in **climate change** that is salient, grave and dangerous in many ways: rising temperatures increasingly lead to floods, droughts, storms, wildfires and city temperatures that become unlivable. Psychologically, this leads to a fear of natural phenomena, and even to mental depression (Marazziti et al., 2021), for those directly and indirectly suffering from these ecological changes of the world. Under the surface fear of nature has never been completely absent it seems, as illustrated by effects of mortality salience when experimentally induced, leading to lower preference for wild as compared to cultured landscapes (Koole & Van den Berg, 2005).

Combining love of nature and ecological concern, to create a sustainable society

Traditionally, love of nature, as expressed in preference for scenes of natural environments, and ecological concern, expressed as worries about the state of the environment, have been investigated separately. Relatively recent are findings that love of nature can lead to environmental concern and actions to reduce environmental damage (Collado et al., 2013). Currently, the viable concept to describe new ways of interacting with nature, and building on both love of nature and environmental concern is ecosystem services (cf. **ecosystems**), covering technical, medical and psychological uses of nature. To maximize the creation of these services, thus developing what is called NBS, the challenge is to increase the way people include nature into their representation of the self, their identity. Schultz (2002) elaborates the concept of inclusion of nature in the self in three dimensions: **connectedness with nature**, including nature within the cognitive representation of self; caring for nature, feeling close and familiar with nature; commitment to protect nature, the behavioral component, if not consequence, of including nature within the self. An important way to achieve sustainability will be to increase inclusion of nature within the self. "... the only sure path to sustainability is through inclusion – Individuals must believe they are a part of nature" (Schultz, 2002, p. 74).

New Ecological Paradigm (NEP) – Karine Weiss

In 1978, Dunlap and Van Liere questioned the Western way of life in the face of ecological problems. Thus, they oppose, by targeting the contradictory injunctions which we constantly face, the **norm** of consumption to the ecological norm. The first norm corresponds to the growth aiming at prosperity and progress, based on technological evolutions and the liberal economy. This is the Dominant Social Paradigm (Pirages & Ehrlich, 1974). The second norm emerges with the awareness of the limits of growth (Meadows et al., 1972) and rejects an anthropocentric vision of the world for a more ecological vision, which they call the New Environmental Paradigm (Dunlap & Van Liere, 1978). Using the term 'paradigm', the authors hypothesize that these worldviews correspond to a coherent cognitive structure. They then questioned the importance of these ideas in the general population, which led them to develop a specific measurement tool. This is a 12-item scale, which measures the three facets of this New Environmental Paradigm: the capacity of humans to alter the balance of nature, the existence of limits to the growth of human societies and the rights of humans to govern the rest of nature. The results show a strong relationship between scores on this scale and other measures of environmental **attitudes**. They also propose a shortened 6-item version (see Hawcroft & Milfont, 2010).

The evolution of environmental issues over the following two decades led the authors to propose, in 2000, a revised version of their tool, composed of 15 items, and named the NEP scale (Dunlap et al., 2000). They took into account the criticisms of their initial tool, notably concerning the ambiguity of the variables measured, which corresponded rather to 'primitive beliefs' about the individual-environment relationship, or even to "a sort of folk ecological theory of how the world works, the nature of the biosphere, how it functions, and how it is affected by human actions" (Stern et al., 1995, p. 726). Dunlap et al. (2000), however, argue that their scale is an indicator of attitude structure.

Two new dimensions are incorporated into the tool: the notion of "human exemptionism, or the idea that humans – unlike other species – are exempt from the constraints of nature" (Dunlap et al., 2000, p. 432), and the likelihood that environmental change will become catastrophic, which is a measure of the possibility of an ecological crisis occurring. The revised scale shows significant correlations with other measures, such as the perceived severity of environmental problems, support for environmental policies, perceived severity of air and water pollution, and with self-reported PEBs. Being thus linked to environmental attitudes and behaviors, it is rapidly becoming the most widely used tool for measuring not only a "coherent belief system or worldview" (Dunlap et al., 2000), but also environmental attitudes (Hawcroft & Milfont, 2010). However, a meta-analysis (Hawcroft & Milfont, 2010) shows that the NEP scale is used in a very variable way, especially in terms of not only the number of items, but also the number of points on the proposed Likert scales, which is not neutral in terms of the results obtained. In particular, the scores are higher with the short version than with versions with a greater number of items, notably because this short version does not include the part relating to the possibility of an ecological disaster or crisis.

Yet this component currently appears to have the highest score among the NEP scale measures (Ntanos et al., 2019). Furthermore, it also emerges from the 2018 meta-analysis that the socioeconomic characteristics of the samples studied have a significant impact on subjects' responses. In particular, differences are observed when looking at not only groups with very low or very high incomes, but also 'environmentalists', among whom a ceiling effect (Widegren, 1998) is observed, in that their level of agreement with the NEP scale is extremely high (Hawcroft & Milfont, 2010). In addition, rural residents also score higher than urban residents, further marking the importance of environmental sensitivity in the responses obtained (Ntanos et al., 2018).

In their meta-analysis, Hawcroft and Milfont (2010) recommend more consistency in future uses of this scale to make results comparable. In addition, rapidly changing environmental issues raise the question of how reliable and up-to-date the measures are to better reflect current concerns and attitudes. Criticisms of what the NEP scale really measures and the lack of clarity in its structure are, indeed, more than justified in light of this evolution. Reconsidering the paradigm seems to be a relevant alternative, for example, by drawing on three types of conceptions (Bernstein & Szuster, 2018): those of nature (which can be considered, for example, as fragile, or on the contrary resilient), those of technology (which are not only limited to a simple capitalist conception, but can also integrate 'eco-technologies'), and those related to the societal response (characterized, in particular, by the opposition between the importance given to consumption patterns and institutional policies). We are, indeed, at a time when we can probably no longer simply adapt to environmental changes, but rather have to consider how structural changes, that is, profoundly modifying our lifestyles, are possible. Thus, measures of environmental attitudes and concerns should better reflect this evolution.

NIMBY – Patrick Devine-Wright

NIMBY is a discourse used to describe and explain objections to siting new developments that are considered necessary for society (e.g., housing, waste disposal, energy projects, transport schemes), and which are often associated with negative impacts for those living in close proximity. The term NIMBYism originated in the U.S. in the 1980s (Dear, 1992) and is employed by policy makers, industry and the media, particularly in English-speaking cultures, to criticize objectors. NIMBYs are presumed to have the following characteristics or deficits (Devine-Wright, 2011):

- Ignorant of key knowledge or facts
- Irrational and highly emotional, not open to reasoned dialogue or debate
- Selfish – only interested in their own property values and how these might be reduced by development proposals
- Proximate – motivated to act due to the close physical distance of their homes to the site of development

These characteristics are presumed to add up to a general NIMBY attitude of 'put it (i.e., the proposals) somewhere else, just not in my backyard'.

For over three decades, social scientists including **environmental psychologists**, sociologists and human geographers have researched NIMBY discourse. Some have sought to find evidence that spatial proximity explains objection. These studies have captured the opinions of people living at varying distances from the development (e.g., Swofford & Slattery, 2010) but findings have been inconclusive – sometimes, opinions are more favorable at close proximity; at other times, they are not so. Other studies have examined how objectors deal with being labeled as a NIMBY, finding that they often seeking to avoid it due to its pejorative connotations or to reframe it as being less deviant and anti-social (Batel & Devine-Wright, 2021). Finally, many researchers have critiqued the discourse and its appropriateness for understanding siting conflicts, arguing that it is pejorative, inaccurate, evidence of 'lazy thinking' and unfair (e.g., Wolsink, 2005).

In contrast, contemporary researchers explain objections to siting proposals by focusing on issues, including the following:

- lack of trust – in those instigating development or making decisions
- environmental injustice, particularly a sense that procedural (how decisions are taken) and distributional (who bears the costs and benefits of development) justice aspects are unfair and inequitable. These aspects are amplified by power inequalities between developers (often multinational corporations), government decision-makers, local communities and action groups
- **place attachment** – the sense that development proposals are 'out of place', posing a threat to the character of a place or **landscape** and

negatively impacting upon the **identities** of those people who feel attached to that place.

In conclusion, a consensus has emerged that researchers should avoid using the NIMBY discourse but instead focus on it as a topic of investigation (Burningham, 2000). However, this has done little to prevent its continued societal circulation (e.g., by journalists in the media) as a way to describe and understand siting conflicts.

Norms – Paul Wesley Schultz

Short definition: an individual's beliefs about the standards of behavior for themselves and others

The concept of norms has played a central role in the field of **environmental psychology**, and especially in the emerging area of sustainability and PEB. Put simply, norms refer to standards of behavior. From a psychological perspective, norms refer to an individual's beliefs about the standards of behavior for themselves and others. These standards can be beliefs about what people do, or what they approve of doing. In psychological research on norms, it is important to distinguish between personal norms and social norms.

Personal norms refer to an individual's beliefs about their moral obligations to engage in a specific behavior. These personal beliefs are seen as internalized values, and they serve as behavioral self-expectations. For example, a person who believes that they have an obligation to recycle, or to reduce their meat consumption. Note that these are beliefs that apply to oneself and violating these beliefs can lead to feelings of guilt. Personal norms are a key element in the Norm Activation Theory (Schwartz & Howard, 1981), and in the extension of this theory in the Value-Belief-Norm model (Stern, 2000).

Whereas personal norms refer to beliefs about oneself, **social norms** refer to beliefs about the behavior of others. These beliefs can be *descriptive*, in which they refer to beliefs about what other people do. Or they can be *prescriptive*, in which they refer to beliefs about what other people approve of doing. **Descriptive social norms** refer to beliefs about the extent to which individuals within a group engage in a specific action. For example, the belief that 85% of my neighbors put out their recycling bin on collection day; or that 20% of the students at my university are vegetarian. Descriptive social norms can also be about the level or frequency of a behavior. For example, the belief that students living in residence halls at my university take showers that last an average of 8 minutes; or that the average household in my neighborhood uses 800 liters of water per day. **Injunctive social norms** refer to beliefs about the behaviors that are approved or disapproved by others. For example, a person who believes that their neighbors will disapprove of watering their front lawn during a period of drought, or that others will approve of them for riding their bike to school instead of driving a car. Descriptive and injunctive norms are key elements in the Focus Theory of Normative conduct (Cialdini et al., 1990), and research has shown that these two types of social norms exert differential influence on behavior (Göckeritz et al., 2010).

Note that in the psychological research tradition, social norms are beliefs, and not reality. From a psychological perspective, the accuracy of these beliefs is not important, and in fact, there are many programs and interventions that aim at changing or activating these beliefs in order to promote changes in behavior (Nolan et al., 2008). Consider messages that highlight the large or increasing number of people engaged in a specific PEB. For example, Schultz et al. (2008) showed that presenting hotel guests with an in-room placard stating that 75% of guests at that hotel choose to reuse their bath towels resulted in fewer towels getting changed on cleaning day. Similarly, Sparkman et al. (2020) showed that messages highlighting the rising frequency of vegetarian choices on restaurant menus reduced meat orders. In both of these cases, the persuasive message was factually true, but it served to increase beliefs about the level of these behaviors among the target audience.

Research has shown that normative beliefs exert a powerful influence on behavior. Across a range of different PEBs, personal norms, descriptive social norms and injunctive social norms have all been found to correlate with behaviors. In addition, research has shown that persuasive communications that target these beliefs can effectively change behavior – both increasing the frequency of PEBs such as recycling or energy conservation and decreasing the frequency of environmentally harmful behaviors such as littering, eating meat or taking long showers (Bergquist et al., 2019).

Nudge – Christophe Demarque

The verb *nudge* means 'to push against gently'. This term, thus, translates the idea of a friendly pressure. It was popularized by Richard Thaler and Cass Sunstein, an economist and a lawyer, in their 2008 book. It is an umbrella term for any attempt to influence individuals' choices and behavior in a predictable way, but without limiting the initial range of choices or making alternatives more costly in terms of time, effort, social sanctions, etc., based on the assumption that our cognitive limitations often affect individual and collective decision making (Hansen, 2016).

Thaler and Sunstein (2008), thus, defend the idea of a 'libertarian paternalism', a form of governance that aims "to lead the individual to make choices that are in the general interest, without being prescriptive or guilt-inducing" (Oullier & Sauneron, 2011, p. 1). Nudges would, thus, be the tools of active engineering in the service of the 'architecture of choice', seeking to influence decision making while still leaving individuals free. Since the publication of this book, nudges have been widely used, particularly in public policy (e.g., by proposing the most environmentally friendly option by default), even if their contours remain rather vague and their effects over time poorly documented. Based on psychology and behavioral economics, this is a broad concept that encompasses a wide variety of practices under the same label. What they all have in common is that they provide an incentive, but without any direct constraint or reward.

While nudges can be used as levers for behavioral change, a conception of their effects primarily in terms of bounded rationality – which is dominant among the proponents of these approaches – runs the risk of reducing the social complexity of environmental behavior. This could fuel the idea of generic, context-insensitive solutions. In addition, the behavioral change objectives are generally not sufficiently discussed, and may therefore make more or less sense depending on the priorities and issues for the populations concerned.

Nuisance – Dorothée Marchand

Environmental nuisances are defined by Gabriel Moser (2009) as physical environmental conditions that are disruptive or in some cases even harmful to the individuals exposed to them, such as noise, pollution or excessive temperature. The author emphasizes the adaptive dimension of the controllability of a source of **annoyance** on the perception of the nuisance. Thus, the individual's evaluation of his or her ability to exercise control over a situation, his or her environment and sources of annoyance is a determining factor in the perception that he or she has of them.

Levy-Leboyer (1980) shows the lack of consistency between environmental nuisances, their perception and the evaluation made by the individual. For Casal (2006), Casal and Devine-Wright (2014), the factors explaining the expression of environmental complaints are multiple and nuisances must be evaluated by taking into account their context of appearance: the environmental, social and cultural context intervenes in the perception, evaluation and expression of individual complaints. The subjective assessment of nuisances goes beyond the physico-chemical characteristics of the stimuli, and the expression of annoyance is linked to individual sensitivity and, more broadly, the relationship with the environment. The evaluation of nuisances, thus, calls upon a complex field of **attitudes**, **representations** and evaluations that do not only concern the nuisances in question. Indeed, "the annoyance expressed must be placed in the individual's relationship with his or her living environment, of which the nuisance in question is an integral part" (Moser & Weiss, 2003, p. 132).

Perception – Dorothée Marchand & Enric Pol

Perception is a process whose terminology is often confused with that of **representation** and evaluation of an object, a situation or a space. This confusion is more specific in the framework of architecture or geography, that refers to forms, to overall qualities in the apprehension of a **landscape** or a building (Pol, 1993). As Ittelson (1973) explained during his research, it is necessary to differentiate between the perception of 'objects' and 'environmental' perception. 'Object perception' refers to the classical explanation of perceptual processes, focusing on more or less isolated stimuli. 'Environmental Perception' considers the environment as a molar, holistic set of stimuli, which behaves as a perceptual unit (Valera et al., 2018).

Environmental psychology is a discipline in which studies on the perception of space and the representation of places have increased. Four major historical trends have focused on the perceptual process; behaviorism, Gestalt theory, cognitivism, and Gibson's 'ecological theories' of perception.

Behaviorists have considered perception as directly dependent on stimulus control. Stimuli are treated as classes of events for which, not the characteristics, but their equivalent effects are studied (Morais, 1987). The research focuses only on observable elements, behaviors (e.g., walking in the city; cf. **walkability**). The unit of analysis is reduced to stimulus-response, which excludes consciousness, cognitive activity, personality, motivations, etc. In this perspective, living organisms are considered passive with respect to the external environment. Behavior is understood experimentally and considered outside its ecological context.

Gestalt theory introduces the importance of context, especially in the field of visual perception of shapes and configurations of objects. The properties of the stimulus determine the perception (e.g., the configuration of a place, a street). The main idea of this theory is that what is perceived is a whole; its components cannot be dissociated without the perceived whole losing its meaning. Perceptual activity aims at searching for good shapes and in this respect responds to several laws:

- The law of proximity: elements that are spatially or temporally close tend to be perceived as belonging to the same form;
- The law of similarity: similar elements are perceived as belonging to the same configuration;
- The law of symmetry: figures that admit one or more axes of symmetry are more easily recognized as good shapes;
- The law of continuity: a configuration whose elements are oriented in the same direction is recognized as a good shape;
- The law of closure: this designates a propensity to construct configurations that do not contain gaps.

Koffka (1935) distinguishes between the geographical environment (real, which exists outside those who perceive it, and where behavior takes place) and the behavioral environment (which refers to the perceived environment, experienced by the subject). Gibson (1950, 1966) distinguishes between literal perception, which refers to direct experiences, and schematic perception in which the environment is organized into a universe of meanings and is influenced by four factors: early experiences, personal needs, values and attitudes, and social consensus.

With the theory of information processing, the percept takes on a different status. According to the principle of inferential perceptual processing, objects are inferred based on fragmentary information. The organism reacts to situations where sensory information is not or no longer present. These situations go beyond the perceptual system to the system of representations. This is the domain of mental images where the represented object is non-existent but available in the individual's memory through the construction he has made of it, the selection of information he has made about it at the time of perceptual processing, and his experience. The mental image implies an internalization of the perceptual experience. For Morais (1987), perception becomes a stage in the process of knowledge, and it has cognitive and behavioral consequences. The cognitivists give a more preponderant active role to the individual in the perceptual construction. Piaget's work on child development shows that it is by acting on objects and thanks to the feedback that comes from these actions that perceptual construction takes place. The child's first space is the space of action, where the perceived objects are located. Perceptual construction is seen as a subjective construction of the environment. The constructivist approach places experience at the heart of the perception process. The study of perception no longer ignores the expectations of the subjects, their motivations, and the relations maintained with the object or event perceived.

Gibson's Ecological Theory of Visual Perception (1950, 1979) is based on the perception-action process and the concept of **affordance**. It considers that perception is not a process of cognitive processing of the stimuli that the individual receives, nor is it a learning process that allows for the continuous selection of stimuli. As defined by the biologist Uexküll at the beginning of the 20th century (Linask et al., 2015), the person and the environment constitute a whole that cannot be separated; we are interested in the individual-environment unit of analysis. The subject perceives sets that offer him possibilities of action. And it is the behavior that makes him perceive what he perceives. Perception and action are inseparable. The perceptual process is holistic, embedded in an ecological context, and environmental properties are perceived directly as action-relevant set entities. These sets are what Gibson calls 'affordances'.

Contemporary approaches to perception, whether of places, situations, objects or events, emphasize the need to consider perception in relation to behavior, cognitive (representation, memory, etc.), affective/emotional and sensitive processes.

Place – Mirilia Bonnes

The *place* is considered, by mainstream environmental psychology, the main psychological construct of the entire field, also characterizing this domain from other psychological domains as a *place-specific psychology*, with its central postulate that '*people always situate their actions in a specific place*'. Since behavior that occurs in one place would be '*out of place*' elsewhere, the nature of that *place* becomes an important ingredient in understanding human actions and experience.

According to many authors, the *place* should be considered as the main *experiential unit* of individual-environmental experience: the 'main building-block' aimed at overcoming the contrast between the 'objective /physical environment' – or *tangible environment*– as approached by the other scientific and technical domains, and the 'subjective /physical environment'– or *intangible environment*, as considered by the psychological domain.

At its beginning (in the 1960s–1970s), environmental psychology started using the place term as equivalent with that of *environment* [Link] and in particular of that of *physical setting*, initially proposed by Proshansky and Colleagues (1970), as the main construct for the domain; also as a continuation of the construct of *behavior setting*, already proposed by Barker's Ecological Psychology (1968) for explaining individual social behavior in its social context.

The concept of *place* was already largely used by architectural design and human geography domains, which were also philosophically exploring it within the phenomenological perspective, by pointing out several possible dimensions of place-related human experience; when this is considered in holistic terms, on both its spatial and temporal perspectives. The concepts of **topofilia**, of **place appropriation**, or of *sense of place* – as opposed to *place-rootedness* (Tuan, 1980) – were proposed along these perspectives.

According to these theoretical interests, the *place* concept gained increasing relevance inside environmental psychology during the 1980s – within the psychological *transactional theoretical perspective*– by becoming a specific psychological construct aimed at focusing, as far as possible, the entire individual experience – considered in the perceptive-cognitive, emotional-affective and behavioral senses, related to specific socio-spatial units of the daily life environment, as *places*: homes, neighborhoods, schools, gardens, towns, etc.

Several authors made important contributions in this sense, as D. Canter, H. Proshansky, W. Ittelson, D. Stokols, I. Altman, etc. (see Bonnes & Secchiaroli, 1995).

A first systematic definition emerged within early British Architectural Psychology, by D. Canter (1977) who outlined the construct of *place*, by a graphic representation, as a partial overlapping graphic space among three main wider spheres of components : (i) the behaviors/activities related to a given setting, (ii) the physical proprieties of that setting and (iii) the related cognitions and affects concerning both the ongoing behaviors/activities and the physical proprieties of that setting.

Within this general framework, other more specific place-based psychological constructs emerged in the subsequent decades, aimed at further articulating the psychological processes involved in the *place-experience* considered in its perceptive-cognitive, emotional-affective and behavioral aspects. All these constructs could be seen as variously involved in developing that sense of place originally envisaged by human geographers and more recently, some authors started to explore this concept more directly, by considering it as a further place-construct including most of other place-constructs below indicated (Jorgensen & Stedman, 2006).

The construct of *place-identity* was proposed by Proshansky (1978), following the assumption that the *places* where a person lives may contribute to forming his/her self-identity. *Place-identity* is conceived as a sub-structure of self-identity, consisting of a broadly conceived cognitive-affective system about the physical world in which the individual lives. This system is seen as developing, especially by thinking and speaking about familiar places, through a cognitive-affective process of 'distancing' from them, which allows for reflexion and appreciation of the involved places. This construct of *place-identity* has been widely explored, in connections with other place constructs, also emerging in these years, as those of *place imageability, place-dependence* and ***place attachment***.

The constructs of *place imageability* (cf. **Spatial cognition**) and *place dependence* were proposed by D. Stokols and Shumaker (1981), by pointing out the shared meaning and symbolic aspects characterizing the place-experience at both individual and collective levels: the *place* is seen as a material and symbolic product of human action, as well as a symbolic and material context and source of further human actions and experiences; *place-imageability* is the social imageability of a place and refers to the capacity of the place elements to evoke vivid and collectively held social meanings (or *'images'*, or also *'social representations'*). These are supported by both: (i) the *perceptual salience* – based on highly noticeable perceptual features and (ii) the *significance salience* – based on collectively shared, sociocultural meanings related to that place. The interdependence of the person, the social and the physical components of a place are assumed to increase as the place becomes increasingly 'layered 'with sociocultural meanings, that become the 'glue' that binds individuals and groups to particular *places*, by creating *place dependence*. This happens when place occupants perceive themselves as having a strong association with that place, with special attention to sociocultural and socio-functional features of that place.

During the 1990s, the construct of *place attachment* was systematically proposed (Altman & Low, 1992), focused on the possible strong emotional/affective bonds developed, firstly through spatial proximity, towards some *life-places*, as in particular the *residential places*. This was consistent with some early insights by M. Fried (1963/1982) about the feeling of 'grief' found among forced relocated residents, who were showing by this their strong previous *residential attachment*; all this was also similar to the parallel geographer's findings around their concept of *rootedness*.

The construct of place attachment became increasingly prominent inside environmental psychology in the following decades (i.e., Manzo & Devine-Wright, 2021). Firstly studied as a mono-dimensional construct, it is now increasingly considered in a multidimensional sense, tending to include several other place-constructs, as in particular those of ***place-identity*** and *place-dependence*, as well as other possible place-constructs similarly involving positive views and feelings about various aspects of the concerned place.

On the whole, by the focus on the construct of *place* and on its various place-based constructs, the *environment* of environmental psychology can be seen in that *molar*, or meaningful sense (at the individual and collective level), as originally envisaged: the *environment* becomes composed of discrete and meaningful 'socio-physical units', represented by the *places*. These can also be seen as systemically interlinked among them, according to their various linkages of inclusion–exclusion and proximity-distance; often also 'nested' among them, by their progressive inclusion along their spatial scale: from the more circumscribed one to the more extended and inclusive one (i.e. home, neighborhood, town, region, etc., until the widest biosphere); with the possibility of also extending this place-analysis from the *intra-place perspective* to the *multi-place perspective*, until the *inter-place perspective*; thus, a more socio-ecological perspective becomes possible with the environment seen as a *socio-ecological system* (Stokols, 2018).

Within this perspective, the present environmental psychology is further developing in several directions: besides its parallel focus on various *trans-place constructs* – as 'pro-environmental **attitudes**, **values**, world-view, **behaviors**', etc., it also focuses on several specific categories of *places* (traditional and new) as not only *residential-places* (home, neighborhood, town, etc.), *learning-places* (schools, museums, exhibitions, etc.), *working-places* (offices, factories, etc.), *health-care-places* (hospitals, hospices, clinics, etc.), but also *healing-places* – due to *restorativeness* (*cf.* **theory of attention restoration**) *and healing proprieties of* some *places, as green-places (or 'nature-dominated-places', as* parks, wood, mountains or 'natural landscapes'), or *leisure-places* and also some *art-places* – as art exhibitions, museums, *etc.* Also, some *digitalized-places* are now previewed, along with the increasing ongoing digitalization of present human life and related *places* (Stokols, 2018).

Place Appropriation – Andrés Di Masso

Place appropriation is the dynamic process through which the unfolding of spatial practices and experiences articulates meaningful and co-constitutive transactions between people and **places**. It features in the academic literature as 'appropriation of space' (see Korosec-Serfaty, 1976). Conceptual efforts to define appropriation of space tend to describe it as an ongoing process of (re)creation, stabilization and transformation of meaningful and practical people-place bonds, that both reshapes spaces and spatializes subjectivity.

The systematic exploration of the philosophical and anthropological concept of appropriation as a place-related psychosocial process has its scientific origins in the 3rd International Architectural Psychology Conference, an interdisciplinary event held at the Louis Pasteur University in Strasbourg (France) in 1976. The intellectual origins of this concept can be traced back to European Hegelian and, mostly, Marxist critical thought on the human dynamics of exteriorization, objectification and alienation (see Graumann, 1976). It was then developed in the field of Soviet Psychology by Vygotski and Leontiev (Vidal & Pol, 2005) and applied to Environmental Psychology since the 1970s mostly in Germany, France (Lefebvre, 1968), Spain and the U.S., from different epistemological stances (phenomenology in Europe and positivistic pragmatism in the U.S.; see Pol, 1996).

In the Marxist tradition, the process of 'appropriation' involves a metatheory of human self-realization premised on the person's active involvement in transforming the material world around him/her by investing physical and intellectual effort, thereby avoiding alienation (i.e., self-estrangement and lack of self-realization). Hence, appropriation is not merely "the act or process of taking something as one's own or making something one's own" (Graumann, 1976, p. 113), a definition that mistakenly equates it to the legally or normatively improper action of owning things and claiming property. In a psychological interpretation following the Marxist tradition, appropriation is a dialectic and generative process that enables, shapes and regulates the psychological life of the self and the social life of groups and communities through their physical, relational and symbolic involvement and active re-fashioning of the spaces they live in.

Following Chombart de Lauwe (1976), Graumann (1976), Korosec-Serfaty (1976), Serfaty-Garzon (2002), Pol (1996), Proshansky (1976), and Vidal and Pol (2005), place appropriation has the following properties:

- *Temporality.* Place appropriation is not a specific moment or a 'quiet' outcome in the relationship between people and places, but rather a living process that unfolds in longer or shorter periods of time. To appropriate a given place, people must spend time in them, let experiences develop in relation to them and be able to remember them. Thus, appropriation turns place into a mirror of time.
- *Dynamism.* Place appropriation occurs less *in space* than *through space*. Its processual and time-related nature involves that it is not a static phenomenon but an ever-evolving form of relating to space that fluctuates in time as people use, transform, re-imagine, abandon, walk through and talk about the places that are meaningful to them. Through appropriation, people and place constantly interrogate and perform each other, embedding continuity in change.
- *Self-realization.* By means of appropriating places, the person mirrors him/herself in space as the latter becomes dynamically and progressively intertwined with the person's sense of self, personal emotions, group memberships, community bonds and or/cultural belonging, depending on the scale (e.g. bedroom, public square) and nature (e.g. individual, collective) of place. Place appropriation presupposes an individual or collective subject that is partly projected in and refashioned through the personal and shared spaces they actively relate to.
- *Agency.* While spatial property per se does not ensure the actual self-realization of the person, place appropriation demands some form of active involvement of the person in relationship to a given place. Place

appropriation is something that one *does*, and not something that one *has*. Whereas in the form of a creative transformation of a given space or in the form of a strategic or precarious adaptation to its physical and social changes, for place appropriation to 'take place' it must somehow implicate the self-determined will, purposive action or routinized presence of its users.

- *Mastery.* As the person appropriates a place, he/she becomes familiar with it until achieving a sense of mastery close to a feeling of control and competence. Beyond the occupation of a given **territory**, place appropriation involves the skilful domain of specific modes of relating to one place. Constant re-appropriations unfold as new priorities of the person emerge, spatial **affordances** change and the person/group/society itself transform through time.

- *Meaning.* What is actually mastered in place appropriation processes is not only nor primarily the space as a geographical spot, but mostly place as a symbolic field of social meanings and social forces that are materialized and embodied in spatial forms, relationships, social uses, interaction patterns and shared representations of place. Appropriating a place presupposes the person's involvement in a symbolic activity of place making. Such meanings are always historically situated and culture-specific.

- *Dialectical nature.* Place appropriation unfolds in a reciprocal definition between person and space. Material and embodied actions in space shape place-meaning processes, which in turn inform spatial interactions and practices.

Place appropriation can be a means or an end in people's active engagement with their life-environments (Proshansky, 1976). As an end, it tends to connote the physical and/or psychological control, authority, mastery or power over a given space. As a means, several territorial and symbolic modes of place appropriation have been described (Vidal & Pol, 2005). The former include marking, mobility through space, exploitation of nature and urban settings for survival, spatial use and occupation, human-made infrastructures, spatial manipulation or sensory exploration; the latter refer to naming, labeling, categorizing, evaluating communicating and talking about places (Graumann, 1976; Tuan, 1991). Some models of appropriation have highlighted spatial occupation, defense and attachment as its basic territorial components (Brower, 1980). According to other authors, place appropriation encompasses specific psychological functions, processes and experiences beyond **territoriality**, such as personalization, the regulation of privacy and personal space, **place attachment**, urban social **identity**, sense of community belonging, safety, self-distinction or **value** expression (Valera & Pol, 1994; Vidal & Pol, 2005).

Applications of place appropriation range from the design and management of urban parks, the promotion of community cohesion in neighborhoods, participatory planning, design of elders' residences and schools, the analysis of political conflicts and demands on public space, the design of defensible spaces or migrants' re-homing processes.

Place Attachment – Karine Weiss

Place attachment refers to the affective and cognitive bond that individuals develop with a **place**. However, it essentially refers to the emotional aspects of the individual-environment relationship by emphasizing the quality of the bond that individuals form with the various places they have frequented. It is a concept that fully integrates physical and social dimensions of place. Indeed, places most often include people and groups, and also specific activities and experiences, which give them meaning and participate in the creation of this connection (Scannel & Gifford, 2014). Thus, to explain the strength of this connection, some authors emphasize the importance of social relationships that take place in specific places, while others focus on the physical characteristics of places (cf. Hidalgo & Hernandez, 2001). Scannel and Gifford (2014) point out that, most of the time, these emotions are positive, as they reflect the joy, satisfaction and pleasure of returning to or thinking about certain places, but they can also be negative or ambivalent, especially when places have disappeared or undergone changes. However, the predominantly positive aspect of the emotions related to the places of attachment leads us to perceive them all the more positively. Moreover, this positive relationship favors the **well-being** and the physical and psychological **comfort** felt in these places.

Attachment can also refer to imagined places, but time spent in place and individual experience remain the best predictors of the bond that develops with it. Beyond this emotional bond, the cognitive and conative aspects of the relationship with a place are therefore also present when we talk about attachment, as they reflect the mental constructs (e.g., **representations**, memories) and behaviors (e.g., regular visits, pilgrimages) aimed at creating or maintaining this bond (Scannel & Gifford, 2010). The behavioral dimension also refers to the fact that individuals tend to protect the places they are attached to, which involves pro-environmental and place-preserving behaviors (Scannel & Gifford, 2014). Attachment can also lead to dangerous behaviors, such as when individuals refuse to leave places subject to hazards, as may be the case with marine submersion or coastal erosion (Michel-Guillou et al., 2015).

Two complementary models allow for a better understanding of the different dimensions of this particularly rich and complex concept: the tripartite model (Scannel & Gifford, 2010) and the model in tree poles and four dimensions (Raymond et al., 2010).

The first one answers the questions: who is attached? to what? and how? It thus integrates the individual and social characteristics of people, the specificities of places at various spatial scales, and the different processes (affective,

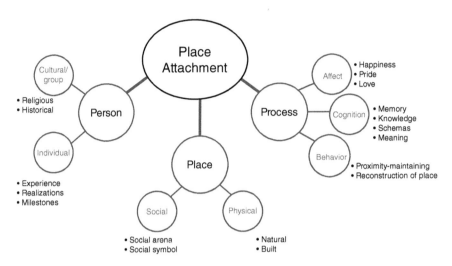

Figure 5 The tripartite model of place attachment (Scannel & Gifford, 2010).

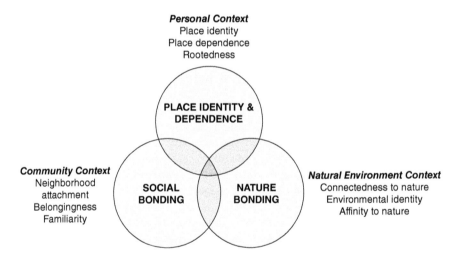

Figure 6 Three-pole and four-dimensional conceptual model of place attachment (Raymond et al., 2010).

cognitive and behavioral) at work in this relationship to places (see Figure 5). We have already described this model elsewhere (Weiss & Rateau, 2018).

The model proposed by Raymond et al. (2010) is, to some extent, similar to that of Scannel and Gifford (2010), but it emphasizes other dimensions of place attachment. Indeed, it specifies the attributes of place by separating its social and natural characteristics and defining social connection and

connection to nature, and the characteristics of attachment related to the individual, through the notions of **place identity** and place dependence. Social connection also refers, in this model, to attachment to the community (see Figure 6).

Both place identity and place dependence can, indeed, be considered as dimensions of place attachment, and the authors define them here as individual connections to places: in simpler terms, we could say that place identity tells us who we are in terms of where we are (a more precise definition is given in this work). As for place dependence, it refers to the way in which the place is likely to fulfill the functions for which we frequent it, by providing the resources necessary for the activities we wish to deploy there. It is, therefore, the functional aspect of the relationship to place.

The use and choice of these models has important methodological implications: while place attachment can be measured with qualitative methods (interviews, observations), many scales are proposed in the literature (e.g., Lalli, 1992; Hidalgo & Hernandez, 2001; Lewicka, 2010). They are constructed according to the dimensions on which the authors who use them wish to focus. For example, Raymond et al. (2010) develop a tool that measures the four dimensions of their model: place identity, place dependence, social connection, and connection to nature.

Place Identity – Marino Bonaiuto & Valeria Chiozza

Place identity: a system of meanings and values associated with a physical environment that contribute to the individual conceptualization of the self, that is, the environment, and specifically the **place** where people live have a profound influence on intrapersonal and interpersonal cognitive and emotional processes, on behavior and on social relationships.

Defining and measuring place identity

Every person in the world 'comes from' and more or less 'belongs' to a place. It can be intended at different geographical and social levels, private or public (such as the house, the neighborhood, or the city); either way, that place shapes the individual by supporting the construction of his/her self-image. While the concept of environment refers to the physical features, the concept of place also includes the evaluations and the activities carried out in such a context by the person (Bonnes & Secchiaroli, 1992).

The concept of 'Place Identity' has been first defined, in modern psychology, by Proshansky et al. (1983). It refers to the link established with a given place that contributes to defining the person: whom the person thinks she/he is, how the person describes herself/himself, how she/he would act towards the location and the people under different circumstances, etc. People attribute meanings to significant places, by means of cognitive and affective features, anchoring their memories and purposes, and developing a sense of belonging. In this way, a precise, significant place supports the formation and maintenance of one's identity, allowing people to identify themselves with their co-habitants and to differentiate themselves from those who live elsewhere, such as being from the countryside rather than from the city, or being from the sea rather than from the mountains, as well as from more specific places. This place-person connection holds both temporal and spatial characteristics: on one side, it reflects experiences and expectations for the future; on the other side, it depends on the objective features of the place. On this basis, individuals create an emotional bond that modifies and influences their identity and perception (Peng et al., 2020).

These processes are then connected to further essential developments in environmental psychology, such as the **attachment** the person may develop with one or more places, which carries cognitive, affective, and conative components and implications. Both constructs require time and complex or memorable experiences to arise (Bonaiuto, Mao, et al., 2016); they crystallize as a person's features, but they formerly emerge as properties of the encounter among a specific environment's features and a person's needs or characteristics (Bonaiuto & Alves, 2012). Once developed, they can significantly affect human behavior by functioning as a part of her/his personal features and identity, including developing a motivational system that regulates the person's reaction to her/his place and the coping strategies with the place's positive and negative events (e.g., regarding natural hazards; see Bonaiuto, Alves, De Dominicis, & Petruccelli, 2016).

Operationally, place identity can be assessed through qualitative and quantitative methods, such as interviews, surveys and standard measurement tools. For example, self-report questionnaires can include identity items such as "I strongly identify as an inhabitant of my city in its entirety" and "I identify more with this city than with others" (Bonaiuto, Fornara, Ariccio, Ganucci Cancellieri & Rahimi, 2015); as well as attachment items such as "It would be very hard for me to leave this neighborhood" (Fornara et al., 2010). Semi-structured interviews can be used to ask people living or working in the study area to describe their place perception and attachment (Polat & Dostoglu, 2017). However, Dixon and Durrheim (2000) highlighted the need to investigate the construct not only by an individual perspective but also rather as a collective construction, considering the sociocultural aspects that contribute to the consolidation of social perception and identification.

The five core functions of place identity

Proshansky and colleagues (1983) defined five core functions of place identity, namely: recognition, meaning, expressive-requirement, mediating change, and anxiety and defense function. The first one (recognition) considers the place as a source of recognition for the individual, where she/he can recognize herself/himself as a member belonging to a particular place and where she/he can assess the environment by recognizing the signs of safety and trust. The second function (meaning) involves the contribution that a specific place brings to determine the meanings by which a person defines herself/himself: it helps in understanding the aims, objectives and functionality of a certain place. Together with the recognition function, this creates a valuable system for context assessment. Thirdly, the expressive-requirement function refers to the situation in which the physical environment does not correspond to the individual's expectations. In similar circumstances, the expressive function intervenes to try to satisfy the individual's preferences by personalizing the environment; in this way, it is possible to reduce discrepancies and discomfort. The fourth function, mediating change, can be understood as the process that mediates the discrepancies between a person's place identity and the characteristics of an immediate physical environment. Ultimately, the anxiety and defense function helps to recognize the threats or dangers present in a given place, defending the individual from feeling anxious or unsafe.

These five functions address choosing one place rather than another, such as a house, office or the places to spend free time. A given place can reflect one's own personality and way of being, and, likewise, the personalization of the same place by the person can reduce pre-existing discrepancies. An environment that meets its inhabitants' physical and emotional needs enhances the feeling of **well-being** and quietness. It is then that one can experience a real connection with that place and have the feeling that the place represents and reflects oneself.

Psychological Distance (theory of) – Oscar Navarro

The theory of psychological distance is an integral part of *Construal Level Theory* (Liberman & Trope, 2008; Trope & Liberman, 2010). According to the construal level theory, individuals mentally represent objects to varying degrees of abstraction. The more the mental representation of an object is construed at a higher level, by relying on imagination to visualize it, the more the object is perceived as abstract. Inversely, the more the mental representation is construed at a lower level (low construal level), the less cognitive mechanisms are used and the more the object is perceived as concrete. A high level of abstraction, therefore, generates greater psychological distance. Psychological distance refers to the distance established between ourselves and an object in cognitive terms and according to its level of abstraction. Psychological distance comprises four dimensions: the social dimension as the measure of space between oneself and others; the time dimension, which describes the distance between the present and a past or future event; the spatial dimension, which refers to the geographical distance between oneself and an object; and lastly, the hypotheticality dimension, which refers to the likelihood of an event occurring (Trope & Liberman, 2003, 2010).

In terms of environmental psychology, this theoretical approach is particularly interesting when dealing with environmental **risks**, including risks related to natural phenomena and, more specifically, **climate change**. Indeed, it is commonly accepted that environmental risks, as objects or stimuli, are represented in a mental space where all the psychological distance dimensions are interdependent. Therefore, whatever impacts one of the dimensions will affect all the others. The literature widely supports this idea (Spence, Poortinga & Pidgeon, 2011). For example, some experimental studies have shown that processing geographically distant information is easier when participants think of similar stimuli, or in other words, stimuli that are socially or temporally distant, which suggests that there is a cognitive correlation. Thus, when participants were asked to concentrate on the details of an event at a low construal level, such as the description of the event, rather than at a high level, such as the explanations of the event, they tended to think that the event was going to take place at a less distant place and time.

Some studies have shown that individuals have a tendency to evaluate the negative impacts of environmental situations as being temporally, spatially (Uzzell, 2000; Gifford et al., 2009; Milfont et al., 2011) and socially distant (Fleury-Bahi, 2008). Where climate change is concerned, for example, individuals are likely to perceive this object as a rather abstract phenomenon (Milfont, 2010). However, one study has shown that a short psychological distance in relation to climate change is linked to both a perception that the risk is high and an intention to adapt behavior accordingly (Guillard et al., 2019). It seems that the extent to which an object is perceived as abstract or concrete leads individuals to adjust their behavior. The above study carried out in France and other studies carried out in English-speaking countries (Spence, Poortinga, Butler, & Pidgeon, 2011) concur that whereas climate change is viewed as abstract, distant or global, and likely in the future, flooding is perceived as a local, real and current phenomenon. The link between the two is not immediately apparent: they are two distinct objects as their construal levels are different. That may explain the difficulty in understanding the causal link between climate change and an increase in flooding events, and ultimately, the reasons for taking steps to adapt behavior and attenuate climate change.

Quality of Life – Giuseppe Carrus, Angela Castrechini, Enric Pol

The notion of QoL in contemporary social and behavioral science has long been debated, from the point of view of different disciplinary, epistemological and conceptual approaches. Typically, trying to define and operationalize the concept of QoL has served the purpose of answering to questions regarding to what extent human beings have been happy during the course of human history, or whether humans can be happy only if living in a wealthy country, or in a rich neighborhood, or for a long lifetime. A basic assumption has been to imply a positive correlation between income, happiness and quality of life.

Organizations like the United Nations or OECD associate QoL to standard living indicators like health, nutrition, working conditions, housing, free time or human rights. The WHO also added a subjective component, with reference to an individual's perceptions of their position in life, **values**, goals, expectations and concerns. Disciplines such as health, clinical, social or positive psychology relate QoL to the possession of the desired material and psychological resources necessary to happiness, but usually with a weak reference to physical settings.

Environmental psychology, on the contrary, has identified the physical conditions of the living environment as a crucial aspect of QoL. This idea can be traced back to the very early pioneers of environmental psychology in the early 20th century (such as Hellpach, Simmel or Tönnies), who were interested in investigating citizens' living conditions and QoL (although without using these labels), in times when socio-political analyses started to address the precarious, unhealthy and inhumane living conditions of life in industrial cities, and new architecture schools attempted to find viable, economical solutions to such a problem.

Thus, a crucial question to be addressed from an environmental psychological perspective is whether and how the characteristics of the physical environment, the interpersonal relations in the environment, and the interaction of individuals with their environments are related to QoL.

A central notion is that of **environmental quality**, assuming that a higher quality of the environment, and the possibility of choosing, controlling and changing it leads to a higher QoL. This assumption can, however, be discussed by taking into account the extraordinary capacity of human beings to adapt themselves to, and appreciate, any environmental condition they have been given, even those that would be judged as extremely bad by the majority of other people. To avoid the risk of environmental determinism, it is also important to consider the concept of QoL in relative rather than absolute terms, and to take into account the asymmetry and inequality of contemporary social structures: what may be a good life for some may not be the same for others.

In environmental psychology, QoL is sought through improved design of residential spaces, housing or urban settings. Environmental psychology relates QoL to the concepts of **restorative environments**, **sustainable development** [Link] and **residential satisfaction**, with a strong emphasis on access to green spaces and **nature** as a fundamental resource to promote the quality of contemporary life. Community life, social cohesion, empowerment and participation are also seen as important to improve QoL. It is assumed that there is not much quality in modern life without participation, citizenship and agency, and that it might be difficult to promote participatory processes if potential participants do not foresee a potential improvement in the quality of their lives: alienation (as opposed to inclusion) and low QoL may, thus, reinforce a negative spiral of individual psychological distress.

In conclusion, promoting QoL and social equality may be possible by an appropriate design and management of inclusive and restorative daily life settings.

Renaturation – Isabelle Richard

From a technical point of view, renaturation could be defined as the fact of recovering a space of **nature** such as it was in its initial state in places where anthropization is maximum. The idea is to find areas dedicated to **biodiversity**, to its conservation and restoration. It would thus be a question of repairing what has been previously degraded by human and/or natural action. This renaturation is an attempt, initiated by the human being, to find, by different means (for example, desoiling areas, sites' depollution, the stop of actions aiming at intensively controlling nature such as the use of pesticides, the massive and regular mowing, the plantation of exogenous species, the monoculture plantations, etc.), an area that comes as close as possible to a natural **ecosystem**. Renaturation is one of the many NBS for adapting to **climate change** by allowing, through its intrinsic qualities, the recovery of essential ecosystem services for the adaptation of territories and populations to the consequences of climate change (stronger **resilience** of territories to flooding, reduction of heat islands by creating cool islands, preservation of biological diversity, preservation of pollinators, etc.).

From the point of view of environmental psychology, renaturation could be understood as the restoration of meaning, sensoriality and social ties in highly anthropized environments that have been degraded on a natural and social level, through the reintegration of floristic, faunistic and human life. In this respect, the term renaturation could be similar to that of restorative spaces, as they are described in environmental psychology, in that these spaces allow individuals to reduce tensions, allow leisure activities, a reconnection to nature, etc. In sum, renaturation would allow an improvement of the overall **QoL**, including health, by connecting individuals directly and more frequently to nature and by confronting them with its complexity. In this sense, renaturation, through the very connection to natural elements, could also transform **practices** and **behaviors** towards more sustainability. We thus return, with renaturation, to the idea of a transactional approach as described in environmental psychology.

Restoration would, thus, be a doubly beneficial action for human life and for biodiversity by allowing nature itself and ecosystems to regain their place, their functions for humans and their right to exist for what they are: neutral spaces, having their own functioning and being elements of a natural system of which humans are a part but only a cog.

Residential Discrimination – Ghozlane Fleury-Bahi & André Ndobo

Discrimination can be considered as the concrete acting out of hostile sentiments (prejudice) and negative beliefs (stereotypes) of individuals or groups towards other individuals or groups (Dovidio & Gaertner, 1986). Within the same town, there can be marked differences from one neighborhood to another in terms of the quality of the residential environment. Certain areas can have a combination of several problems: few shops, a non-existent or unsuitable transport network, a degraded or polluted environment, issues of insecurity that engender a poor reputation and stigmatization, and socioeconomic precariousness of the populations. Residential segregation and the socio-spatial disparities that are characteristic of these areas constitute a major social and political issue in that they do, indeed, reveal how social inequalities are imprinted spatially in society.

Because these phenomena of socio-spatial segregation are characterized by the differential distribution of groups in space and variable possibilities for interaction between individuals of a group or differentiated groups, they can generate phenomena of residential categorization and discrimination. What holds for all social categorizations is true for residential categorizations, that is, that people tend to identify positively with their place of residence (cf. **place identity**) compared to other residential areas. Based on this intergroup polarization, some people may tend to stigmatize the members of other residential areas. Therefore, the notion of residential discrimination refers to a discrimination anchored in the socio-spatial division of residential space. This division has institutional causes, mainly linked to the inequality of public investments and the presence of the state in these areas. Research studies show that this division also has psychosocial consequences in terms of perception of the discrimination, identification with the place of living and **appropriation** of this residential space, together with consequences in terms of self-esteem and **well-being** (Schulz et al., 2000; Schmitt & Branscombe, 2002).

Residential Satisfaction – Marino Bonaiuto & Valeria Chiozza

Residential satisfaction: experience of pleasure or gratification deriving from living in a specific place, that is, general evaluation inhabitants report with their housing, which can be considered at various levels of geographical scale (house, building, neighborhood).

Defining residential satisfaction

The residential environment (i.e., house, building, neighborhood) represents the urban space where the individual measures himself/herself daily; it can impact mental health and psychological **well-being** through physical characteristics and social processes. For these reasons, residential satisfaction is perceived by the inhabitants to represent one of the main components of people's overall **QoL**, concerning the pleasure or gratification deriving from living in or inhabiting a given place. The environmental evaluation provided by inhabitants is called 'naïve' or 'subjective' and it reflects the experiential dimension felt by the individual. The assessment of the residential place includes the three main components of the psychological construct of attitude: (a) the affective component, which can be equated to **place attachment**: residents can develop an attachment bond that prompts a motivation to care for it, improve it and not abandon it, and it may intervene in many relevant aspects related to residential satisfaction (e.g., Fornara et al., 2018, 2019); (b) the cognitive component, which reflects the assessment of the different aspects of the environment (i.e., physical, social, functional, contextual; see Bonaiuto et al., 1999; Fornara et al., 2010; Bonaiuto, Fornara, Ariccio, Ganucci Cancellieri & Rahimi, 2015); and (c) the behavioral component, based on the habits and activities conducted in the setting (e.g., Bonaiuto et al., 2004).

Residential satisfaction can depend upon different kinds of factors, depending on the person (e.g., personality traits, various socio-demographics, and residential features such as age and length of residence), her/his social network (e.g., relationships with neighbors, participation in community activities), and the physical characteristics of the residential place (e.g., availability of green spaces and walking paths, building aesthetic features). The effects of such factors can be simple and direct. However, their effects can sometimes depend upon other variables (moderation effects): for example, the perception of the indoor and outdoor architectural style tends to vary with the cultural background of the inhabitants and, in general, residential satisfaction tends to increase when the place of residence meets cultural expectations, probably due to identification processes and complementary behavioral patterns (Bonaiuto & Fornara, 2017). In other cases, cumulative effects could be at play: where the single residential physical factor does not have a relevant impact on residential satisfaction, the cumulate effect of several factors can significantly affect the inhabitant's residential satisfaction. For example, the perception of urban risk factors in the neighborhood produces negative effects in terms of residential safety and well-being (considered as proxies of residential satisfaction) only when at least about four or five of them cumulate in the resident's experience (Bilotta, Ariccio, Leone, & Bonaiuto, 2019).

Measuring and explaining residential satisfaction

The assessment of the inhabitants' residential satisfaction implies the investigations of multiple quality indicators belonging to different areas: architecture and city planning features, social relations, various services and general context features. So far, two main methodological approaches have been adopted to describe inhabitants' perception and evaluation of the residential place. The first one is an inductive approach that usually privileges qualitative techniques such as unstructured or semi-structured interviews or small group discussions where inhabitants talk about their residential environment in the presence of one or more researchers. The second type is deductive, and it privileges quantitative methods such as administering to a large sample of residents a (preferably standard and already validated) questionnaire including items about the residential environment. In this second case, participants are usually asked to respond using a scale ranging from 'not at all' to 'completely' to items such as 'How satisfied are you with the house' or 'building' or 'neighborhood'. However, as mentioned before, the evaluation of the residential place includes the affective, cognitive and behavioral dimensions, and these areas can be addressed by using specific standard and validated scales already tested in the literature. Statistical analyses to be carried out on the inhabitants' responses can allow, on the one side, to test if people assign different degrees of importance to various aspects of a residential place, depending on multiple personal factors such as socio-demographic characteristics, personality traits, homeownership, social **norms** and **values** shared by a group (Zwarts & Coolen, 2003). On the other side, such a test can ascertain if the evaluation is based on social or residential factors too. For instance, building aesthetics, the presence of preserved green areas and flat size are usually positively related to neighborhood satisfaction, whereas an inverse relation is generally detected in circumstances of home crowding (Bonaiuto & Fornara, 2017). Some studies (Bonnes & Bonaiuto, 2002) have pointed out that the cognitive assessment of residential satisfaction involves and integrates different environmental dimensions. For example, the perception of a high density of built space (physical-spatial dimension) tends to be associated with an equally high human density or crowding perception (social dimension). Specifically, applied research needs to use standard measurement tools where every indicator can measure a single specific feature of the residential place (e.g., a certain physical, social, functional or contextual feature). However, for more basic research purposes, the evidence highlights a psychological fusion of different urban characteristics. Thus, in the 'eye' of the inhabitant, the single indicators mentioned above are merged and considered all together when assessing the residential place.

The residents' global evaluation represents a valuable source of information about the appropriateness and quality of the environment and should be carefully considered to achieve a complete environmental–psychological evaluation of the residential place. The psychological and experiential dimensions brought by the residents into the assessment are critical to improve and to implement residential designs, or simply to assess them, for example, within a post-occupancy evaluation approach (e.g., Bonaiuto et al., 2019).

Resilience – Ricardo García Mira

The concept of resilience refers to the ability of a person or a community to resist or recover quickly from a stressful or traumatic event or an adverse circumstance that entails danger or **threat**. Luthar et al. (2000) refer to the term as the ability to positively adapt to **stress** or trauma. A disaster, a catastrophe, an illness, an accident, the death of or separation from a loved one are some examples that can appear to challenge our experience. Although we are born with a basic system to face up to certain difficulties, we do not come equipped with an instruction manual to know exactly how to do this. While some people develop a good capacity to confront these difficulties individually or collectively, developing a positive adaptive response to the situation and moderating or avoiding negative consequences, others do not and show more dependency or **vulnerability**.

Psychology has referred to resilience as a process of adaptation to the threat posed by a stressful or traumatic event. Being resilient means developing the ability to cope and adapt throughout this process, in order to recover and develop the capacity to overcome threatening circumstances, solve the problem and re-establish a certain normality in the interaction of the individual with the environment. We can distinguish between the role of the individual who develops this capacity and the role of the situational context that favors or hinders adaptation to interaction. Thus, resilience as a process makes sense by integrating the analysis of the set of personal and situational factors that interact with the individual in the development of their capacity to face the threat.

Resilience, however, goes beyond the individual level. The community of individuals that make up a group, a city or an entire state, can become resilient through programs that promote resilient environmental behaviors, within a process of socially responsible learning and innovation in the face of threat. For Hegney et al. (2007), resilience is the ability to learn from the past, be open to change and have an inclusive disposition, with a sense of purpose. Similarly, resilience can be built up with policies that drive changes in social awareness and collective behavior. The determination of policies and policy combinations that can activate social changes in the face of climate, mitigating the impact of **climate change**, for example, has been an issue that has recently been explored in relation to sustainable lifestyles (García-Mira et al., 2017; Vita et al., 2020).

Swim and Whitmarsh (2019) highlight the value of responsibility for action that can be encouraged in the community through the use of own resources to promote social learning and group activities that contribute to generating climate resilience. For example, the stimulation of changes in the choices of type of food, transport or consumption can contribute to mitigating the most negative impacts (see García-Mira, 2014, 2017; García-Mira et al., 2017). Activities can prepare the population for the impact, through adaptation programs, helping to reduce **vulnerability** and increase community resilience.

Both the concept of resilience and that of vulnerability have helped define the framework in which we understand how communities respond and adapt to social and environmental challenges (Adger, 2006; Folke, 2006). Regarding risk, Böhm and Tanner (2019) analyze how certain psychological responses can reduce perceived **risk** by reducing vulnerability and enhancing resilience. The transformation of cities to face the risk of climate change and reduce its impacts is a topic that addresses resilience by promoting NBS. Nature not only improves cognitive functioning and fosters social relationships, reinforcing general resilience (Wells & Phalen, 2018), but also plays a role in urban contexts. Cities today face a series of social and environmental challenges that seek to increase climate resilience through local action plans.

Finally, regarding the measurement of resilience, it is usually carried out using the Connor – Davidson Resilience Scale (Connor & Davidson, 2003), a self-reporting scale that comprises 25 items that measure resilience. A shorter version, with 10 items on the same scale, has also been applied in numerous studies (Campbell-Sills & Stein, 2007).

(Revitalizing) Interlinkings – Chris Younès

Edgar Morin has made the concept of 'interlinking' the keystone of complex thought. It concerns "the work of links", "the act of linking and being linked and its result", as set out in *La Méthode*, which is presented in six volumes published over three decades, from 1977 to 2000. The last volume, titled Éthique (Morin, 2004), is more explicit and advocates the concept of 'interlinking'. Morin considers that this notion, initiated from a theoretical and practical point of view by the sociologist Marcel Bolle de Bal in relation to the psychosociology of human ties, fills a conceptual void by giving a substantive nature to what was only conceived adjectively and by giving an active character to this noun: the adjective 'linked' is passive whereas the noun 'interlinking' is activating. Morin goes so far as to make this an epistemological and methodological imperative as well as an ethical and political one: "We must, for each and every one of us, for the survival of humanity, recognize the need to interlink, to interlink with our own, to interlink with others, to interlink with the Earth as a homeland".

Faced with a certain modernity that has favored separation, this the ecology of interlinking constitutes a paradigmatic change inviting us to weave together heterogeneous constituents – both complementary and antagonistic – to face **uncertainty**. Whether it is a place, a biotope or planet Earth as a whole, the challenge is to understand the interactions between the elements and the living beings that characterize them. Indeed, as soon as attention is brought on an inhabited milieu, dynamics of interpenetration, interdependence and inter-engendering are observed holding together the parts and the whole. This is achieved through limits that distinguish, spacing which imposes distance and through the porosities between things and beings.

It thus amounts to deconstructing the dualism established between the two major universals, nature and culture. From modern times, the dominant view was the opposition between humans and nature following the representation initiated in the 17th century by Galileo, Bacon and Descartes of an external nature that could be mastered. This representation has been challenged out of fear due to the devastation of ecosystems, the awareness of the finitude of the planet and of the vulnerability of the community of living beings. This change of perspective began with the ecological account presented in 1866 by Haeckel in his work 'General morphology of organisms' as a science studying the relationships established between living beings and their environment. Darwin is a major figure in that he deals with the complex chain of competitive and cooperative interactions between organisms that co-evolve with their milieu. A century later, Félix Guattari committed himself to an ecosophy that he defines as "an environmental ecology that is at one with social and mental ecology, through an ecosphere of an ethical-political character" (Guattari, 1989).

Current interrogations in the context of sustainable development aiming at associating the viable, the livable and the equitable are so many ways of considering how everything interpenetrates and exchanges. Devices of alliance and metabolisms between humans and non-humans, solidarities and crossbreeding, cooperation, landscape continuities and hybridizations, these various natural-cultural resiliencies do not remain a simple juxtaposition in pacified relationships. Symbiotic relationships are sought without ignoring the power of wild nature. A holistic and dynamic vision, thus, resurfaces in the prism of regenerative ecosynergies, tending to harmonize the metamorphoses in their co-cycles and co-rhythms of life.

Risk – Karine Weiss & Marie Bossard

Risk is the probability that a hazard will occur, or more precisely that a hazard will create this situation of danger and cause damage. This damage concerns both human and non-human issues. It is, therefore, commonly accepted that risk is the result of the intersection between the hazard and these issues. In the human and social sciences, the **vulnerability** and the capacity of populations to respond are integrated into this equation, which, in turn, highlights the vulnerability of individuals and communities. These elements allow us to emphasize the human factor, particularly through the perception of risk and vulnerabilities. Indeed, it is the subjective aspect that is at stake in the problems of prevention and protection in the face of risk: what is the acceptable level of risk? What is the desired degree of protection and what measures are we prepared to take to achieve it? These questions are linked to two major components: the level of **uncertainty** associated with the probability of occurrence of each type of risk, and the severity of the potential damage. This is what the expected value paradigm proposes, allowing the calculation of gains and losses for each action chosen to face the risk (cf. Kouabenan, 2007). This analytical approach to risk ('risk as analysis'), which involves decision making based on logical and reasoned calculation, is complementary to the more emotional approach, which emphasizes intuitive reactions based on affect and experience ('risk as feeling'). A third, political, dimension can be added to these two approaches, insisting on the socially constructed character of risk: "Risk is by nature subjective and represents a mixture of science and important psychological, social, cultural and political factors" (Slovic, 1999).

In psychology, several complementary approaches address the issue of risk: a clinical approach, which focuses on the consequences for the health of individuals of the actualization of a risk; a cognitive approach, more specifically centered on cognitive biases in the perception of risks and their behavioral consequences; and a psychosocial approach, integrating **perception** in a broader way, including **social representations**, 'risk awareness', and even 'risk culture'.

Environmental risks

Environmental risks are a specific category of risks: they have a collective character, in that they affect a large number of individuals, but also because they are the result of general action and/or inaction and because their mitigation also requires the action of many people (Steg & De Groot, 2019). They are associated with a high degree of uncertainty, are perceived as having a high level of danger, and are associated with a low sense of control. Environmental risks can be broken down into two categories: those with multiple, and most often invisible, temporally and spatially distant consequences, such as pollution (of air, water or soil), or climate change and the loss of biodiversity and natural resources. The second category corresponds to natural disasters (e.g., floods, tsunamis, storms, etc.), which have immediate and direct consequences on populations and territories. Many of them, however, are related to the effects of climate change, as highlighted by the IPCC report. In addition, environmental risks raise ethical issues insofar as those who cause them are not necessarily those who have to suffer the consequences (Steg & De Groot, 2019). Also, the population has very little confidence in public action in the face of this type of risk and attributes little credibility to the information made available to it (IRSN, 2016).

Emerging risks

The term of emergence places a certain number of new or poorly known risks in a specific context of controversy, uncertainty and/or lack of understanding of the dangers to health and quality of life (OECD, 2003). In the absence of a consensus on their subject, emerging risks can be understood according to their nature (physical, biological, chemical, psychosocial or a combination of several of these aspects), or by what characterizes their novelty: it may be a totally new risk (e.g., new materials or new technologies), or it may be a risk that is not yet known. It can be a completely new risk (e.g., new materials or technologies), a risk that is already known but which appears in a new context (e.g., an industrial installation on a new site) or an object that is already known, but whose perception of its risky nature is changing (e.g., vaccination) (Roig & Brocal, 2018). The adjective of emerging is, therefore, essentially associated with the new and evolving aspect of the risk, which explains the insufficiency, or even non-existence, of scientific knowledge about it. This gap makes it difficult to describe scientifically and can cause significant concerns for exposed populations, who then construct representations of it from eclectic and very often irrational elements (Marchand, Weiss, & Zouhri, 2017). In addition, media information, most often sensationalist, substitutes for this lack of scientific information, reinforcing some of these representations, generating contradictions and seeking to arouse strong emotions, such as fear.

A risk considered as emerging must be apprehended by an interdisciplinary approach, in order not only to produce knowledge about it, but also to better understand how the populations concerned interpret it and act about it. From a social psychology perspective, the following question is crucial: for which group(s) does this risk become emergent, and under what conditions? Particular attention must, therefore, be paid to the contexts (whether social, political, historical or spatial) in which these new risks are embedded, in order to better understand the emergence of possible representations of them in the groups concerned.

Risk perception

The characteristics of the risk as well as the characteristics of the perceiving individual shape risk perception (Kouabenan & Cadet, 2005). Regarding the characteristics of the risk, three variables are identified by Peretti-Watel as the main components of risk perception: perceived severity, perceived frequency and declared fear of the risk (Peretti-Watel, 2003). Regarding the characteristics of the individual, risk perception depends on the way the individual characterizes the risk based on social representations, value and belief systems or previous experiences. Therefore, from a psychosocial perspective, risk is understood subjectively (Slovic, 1987). The integrative model of risk perception (Renn & Rohrmann, 2000; Renn, 2008) groups the factors involved in risk perception and their interaction: (a) heuristics and biases, which act during the formation of individuals' judgments and allow for the selection and analysis of risk-related information; (b) cognitions and affects, which influence the perception of risk properties, based on the selected information; (c) social influence and institutional policies, which incorporate into risk perception individuals' trust in institutions, their values, organizational cultures, social and political structures, and the socioeconomic status of the perceiver; and (d) cultural determinants that condition how lower levels interact and influence the individual's risk perception (ibid).

Representation of risk

According to a sociocultural approach, risk is an objective danger, but the relationship that individuals have with risk is dependent on the social and cultural context. Risk is characterized as such according to this context. According to a constructivist approach, there is no objective danger, which is also the product of a social construction. Risk cannot, therefore, be defined outside of this context (Lupton, 2013). This is why we sometimes speak of risk representation rather than risk perception. Indeed, by representation, we mean the reconstruction of an object by the individual, of its characteristics, in an active way (Joffe, 2003). With the notion of representation, it does not matter whether the risk is real or imaginary, since it exists in the individual's representational universe (Peretti-Watel, 2003). When we speak of risk representation, the latter is considered a social construction. The use of the term 'representation' makes it possible to imply common sense thinking by conceiving the activity of perception as a construction of common sense knowledge dependent on symbolization relationships, dependent on social reality and social knowledge (Joffe & Orfali, 2005).

Risk culture

Risk culture corresponds to "the awareness of risk, and to the body of knowledge that enables actors and citizens to anticipate the impacts of a situation and to adopt appropriate behaviors in the event of a disaster" (Courant et al., 2021). The term 'culture' may seem inappropriate because culture not only corresponds to the acquisition of beliefs, but also includes law, morals, art and all the customs and habits that form the basis of communities. The culture of risk therefore envisages that risk, and especially the ability to cope with it, becomes an integral part of the way of life of the populations in the territories concerned. This form of knowledge is necessarily based on collective memory, even if we know that memory-related processes distort and select information, which has a strong impact on risk perception. Nevertheless, in regions where certain types of risk are highly recurrent (e.g., the risk of hurricanes in the West Indies), risk is anchored in everyday life and corresponds to a form of shared culture: education of schoolchildren, information in public places, behavioral habits during hurricane seasons, etc.

However, for some, risk culture is a questionable term because it refers to a negative notion, that of 'cultivating risk' (Blesius, 2013). In other parts of the world, such as Quebec, it is preferred to use the term civil safety culture: the focus is on safety rather than risk, which gives it a more positive connotation.

Sick Building Syndrome – Dorothée Marchand

Sick building syndromes are described as crises that occur in specific contexts and are expressed through individual, social, organizational and health disorders (Bulletin d'épidémiologie hebdomadaire, 2007; Kermarec & Dor, 2010;

Marchand et al., 2010; Marchand et al., 2014). The environmental quality and mental health of people living in indoor spaces are equivocally implicated in understanding collective contagions.

As remarked by Marchand et al. (2012), sick building syndrome (SBS) is classified as an idiopathic environmental intolerance (Sparks, 2000; Crasson, 2005). From an environmental health perspective, these intolerances refer to symptom clusters associated with environmental factors that are tolerated by most people and not explainable by other known psychiatric or medical disorders (Sparks, 2000). This category focuses on **emerging risks** such as SBS, electrosensitivity, chemical odor intolerance syndrome, etc. SBS has been a matter of public concern since the 1980s, when the WHO sought to qualify the health problems associated with indoor air quality. SBS is defined as a condition affecting a higher-than-expected proportion of people in the same establishment. It is manifested by aspecific symptoms or discomforts (headaches, skin irritations, ENT disorders, nausea, fatigue, etc.) without any identified cause. Although the etiology of these symptoms and discomforts is undetermined, a number of factors have been identified since the 1980s as increasing the risk of SBS. These risk factors are related not only to the building itself, to indoor air quality, but also to individuals (WHO, 1983). Their most frequent contexts are communities and tertiary spaces, more rarely residential spaces. Marchand et al. (2010) point out that for several decades, due to a lack of suitable research protocols, several names have reflected the lack of knowledge and understanding of these crises: collective irritant syndromes, collective hysteria, unexplained collective symptoms, collective health syndromes, collective psychogenic syndromes, etc., all terminologies that have attributed this collective and singular expression of a malaise to psychosocial factors. The scientific uncertainties that characterize SBS have relegated the phenomena to the register of the irrational, sometimes confused with the psychopathological or even the psychogenic. In 2010, the sociologist Barthe denounced a trend towards 'psychologization' in the field of environmental health (Barthe, 2010, p. 371), which is based on an a priori attribution of psychological causes to certain complaints or claims.

An interdisciplinary exploration of SBSs led us to adopt the term 'sick building syndrome' to highlight the salience of the environmental dimension of these syndromes (Marchand et al., 2012). In the cases of SBS studied, our investigations have shown that their origin lies in an environmental pathology that explains the emergence of a **crisis**. The consideration and management of complaints and symptoms then explain the evolution of the crisis, the individual and social environmental malaise felt. The psycho-environmental approach has shown that the expression of the crisis and the evolution of the syndrome are linked to the crisis management and its representation, as well as to the representation of the environment and the disease, the perception of **risk**, the communication process and the management of **stress**.

Social Dilemma – Robert Gifford

Social dilemmas (Dawes, 1980) are a family of three similar problems that share two main properties. The first is that each participant receives more (or is penalized less) for a self-interested choice than for a public-interest choice. The second is that the participants benefit more if most or all of them choose to act in the public interest than if most or all choose to act in self-interest.

Commons dilemmas

The first of these three problems, commons dilemmas (also sometimes called resource dilemmas) was described by William Lloyd (1837) and Garrett Hardin (1968), but was first used as a term by Robyn Dawes (1973). Commons dilemmas are about choices made by individuals or groups who have access to a limited supply of replenishable natural resources. The dilemma is that one is not only tempted to take much of the resource, but also understands that if other harvesters do the same, the resource (and therefore one's own chance for larger longer-term gains) might be ruined.

Social trap

The second type of social dilemma is called a social trap. These dilemmas are about time, that is, when individuals (or societies) succumb (or not) to gratifying short-term rewards that have some built-in and gradual cost that eventually becomes very large. Classic social traps include over-indulging in food or drink, smoking and the use of some pesticides. The dilemma is about,

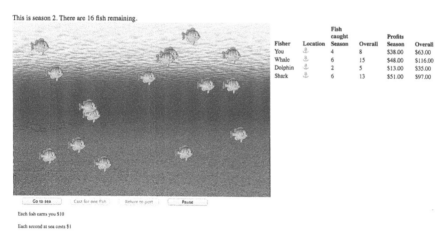

Figure 7 Fishers in the microworld – **Gifford**.

for example, having another piece of cake, another drink or cigarette, or using a damaging amount of pesticides to kill every weed on one's property.

Public goods problem

The third type of social dilemma is called a public goods problem. In this problem, the dilemma is about one's choice to contribute (or not) to something that would benefit the community as a whole (such as donating blood or donating to a fund to purchase parkland), but would also benefit the donor. The dilemma in a public goods problem is an ethical one: if you never donate blood, should you ask for it later if you need a blood transfusion? Should you use that park that you did not help purchase, when asked for a donation to build it? Those who use such a social benefit after refusing to help bring it into existence are called free-riders.

The image below is from FISH, a microworld created to study commons dilemmas (Gifford & Gifford, 2000; Gifford, 2014). Fishers in the microworld have the option to take many fish early, thereby enriching themselves, or to harvest fish slowly and cooperatively, in a sustainable way. Their dilemma is that taking many fish early endangers their possibility of greater gains from long-term harvesting over many seasons, coupled with the fear that perhaps others will harvest many fish early so that their reward might be very small because others take most of the fish.

Social Ecology – Daniel Stokols[5]

Naturalistic field observations of the relationships between organisms and their physical habitats conducted by biological ecologists were later applied to the study of human populations residing in large urban areas. Led by scholars such as Park et al. (1925) at the University of Chicago, research on the relations between people and their urban **ecosystems** came to be known as *human ecology*. The Chicago School of human ecology emphasized biological and economic processes of human adaptation to environmental resources and constraints. A major focus of their research was the geographic distribution of health and behavioral problems across different spatial zones of urban regions (e.g., from low-income districts of the inner city to more affluent suburban areas located further away from the urban core).

An important limitation of the Chicago School's concentric zone theory of human ecology is that it overemphasized biological and economic dimensions of human ecosystems while neglecting sociopolitical, legal and ethical considerations (e.g., environmental justice concerns; cf. Bullard, 1990) as well as the material and symbolic influences of environmental design on **behavior** and **well-being** (Michelson, 1970). Firey (1945) contended that environmental

5 Adapted from Stokols (2018).

features of human ecosystems convey symbolic as well as material meanings that exist independently from and sometimes in contrast to their economic and locational **values**. Alihan (1938) offered a broad critique of the Chicago School of human ecology and called for the establishment of a more integrative interdisciplinary approach to the study of human communities, combining the concerns of bioecology and economics with those of sociology, psychology, anthropology, law, ethics, urban planning and other fields.

Alihan (1938), Emery and Trist (1965), along with scholars such as Bookchin (1996), Binder (1972), and Moos (1979), referred to this broader, transdisciplinary conceptualization of human-environment relations as *social ecology*. Rooted in these cumulative scholarly efforts, the term 'social ecology' is now widely used to denote a broad-gauged transdisciplinary approach to the study of people-environment relations that integrates the diverse perspectives of multiple fields (such as geography, sociology, psychology, economics, law, anthropology, architecture, urban planning, and public health; cf. Stokols, 2018).

Key features of contemporary social ecology

Social ecology examines how environmental contexts from local to global scales affect human health, behavior and the sustainability of our surroundings. Contextual influences on these phenomena emanate from at least *four environmental spheres*: (1) the *natural environment* comprising the plant and animal species living in a particular area, abiotic features including geologic and climatic conditions, and various resources produced through nature-based rather than human-initiated processes; (2) the *built environment* including physical resources designed and produced by people, such as their buildings, vehicles and tools used to create other products: (3) the *sociocultural environment* encompassing organizational and institutional entities, political and economic structures, social **norms**, legal codes, and the social activities that people perform as members of groups and communities; and (4) the *virtual environment* composed of computing and mobile communications equipment, the *World Wide Web*, the *Internet of Things*, social media, virtual reality and other digital technologies (see Figures 8 and 9). This partial list of features within each environmental sphere is not exhaustive but it conveys the variety of circumstances that influence people's interactions with their surroundings. A major challenge in social ecological research is to identify from among myriad contextual variables those that are most crucial for understanding particular health, behavioral and sustainability outcomes.

Rather than viewing social ecology as a distinct discipline (or subdiscipline) tied to a delimited body of knowledge or 'facts', it is more aptly construed as an over-arching (or *meta-analytic*) perspective for framing scientific and societal problems in relation to alternative spatial, temporal, sociocultural and virtual contexts. This process of analyzing problems contextually is helpful in identifying underlying causes and characteristics of complex

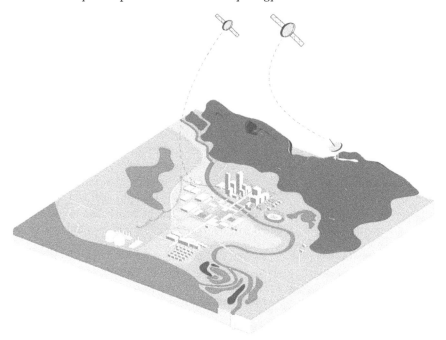

Figure 8 A human community: composite of natural, built, sociocultural and cyber
spheres of the environment.

phenomena, whether the focus is on understanding the poverty, violence,
climate change or factors that affect residents' health in a particular region.
Social ecological approaches to analyzing these and other complex problems
are organized around certain fundamental principles – conceptual and methodological guidelines that can be used in combination with each other to
broaden our understanding of humans' transactions with their surroundings
at local, regional, and global scales.

The transdisciplinary, integrative vision of social ecology offers a dynamic
analytic framework – a *conceptual mapping system* or *problem-framing device* –
that can be used to enlarge the scope of theory development and research
design – and just as importantly, to assist the translation of research findings
into strategies for resolving societal problems. Viewing social ecology as a
transdisciplinary analytic framework permits a broader understanding of environmental and social challenges, and more innovative solutions to them,
than can be achieved through less integrative approaches.

The rapid rise of digital information and communication technologies –
our *virtual ecology* – has wrought widespread and dramatic changes in both
the material structure and latent qualities of human **environments**. Whereas
earlier discussions of human and social ecology have focused predominantly on
people's interactions with the natural, built, and sociocultural environment –
especially the combined impact of economic and political forces, depletion of

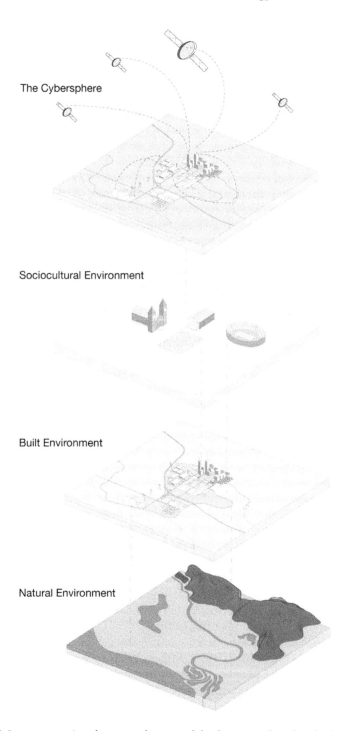

The Cybersphere

Sociocultural Environment

Built Environment

Natural Environment

Figure 9 Interconnections between the natural, built, sociocultural and cyber spheres of environmental influence in human communities.

natural resources, and pollution on environmental sustainability – they have given less attention to the rapidly expanding *cybersphere* – a fourth domain environmental influence that emerged in 1980s as a byproduct of digital information technologies. The *natural, built, sociocultural*, and *virtual* domains of our surroundings are thoroughly intertwined and interdependent with each other (see Figures 8 and 9). It is important to recognize both their unique and synergistic impacts on health, behavior and global sustainability.

Core principles of social ecology

First, all branches of ecology assume that *environments are made up of multiple interdependent features*. Biological ecologists study the relationships between living and non-living components of plant and animal biomes. The immediate locale of a plant or animal includes members of its own species as well as other life forms. Plants and animals also must adapt to non-living (or 'abiotic') features of their environs like geological and climatic conditions. Human ecologists studying urban environments pay close attention to geographic and economic influences on **behavior** and health. The environments that social ecologists study comprise material and symbolic features, physical and sociocultural components, natural and built (designed) elements, and place-based as well as virtual domains. These features of human environments exert a combined or *synergistic influence* on behavior and **well-being**.

Second, *ecological analyses include multiple geographic, social, and temporal scales for understanding health and behavior*. Environments are viewed as part of a *nested structure* where local situations and settings are embedded in larger, more remote regions (e.g., classrooms within schools within neighborhoods). Also, *environmental participants vary in the complexity of their social structure*, ranging from individuals, groups and organizations to larger communities, societies and international entities. From a temporal perspective, *people's encounters with their surroundings can be studied over short or long periods* (e.g., from observing children at noisy elementary schools to re-testing them years later to see if they developed adult hypertension). A *multi-level contextual approach* is essential for understanding the many sources of environmental influence on the behavior and health of individuals, groups and populations. Yet because multi-level analyses of people's relationships with their surroundings over extended periods are so broad, they pose significant challenges. Investigators must decide which contextual variables to include and how broadly to draw the spatial, temporal and sociocultural boundaries of their research when analyzing human-environment transactions.

Third, *social ecological research relies heavily on the concepts and assumptions of systems theory* (Bertalanffy, 1950; Miller, 1978) to explain how environmental structures and people's reactions to their surroundings change over time. The organization and functioning of environments continually evolve in response to both biospheric and behavioral forces (e.g., geologic and climatic shifts, humans' consumption of fossil fuels, development of new technologies, buildings and transit systems). Environments and their inhabitants are dynamic systems where individuals and groups react to changes in their surroundings and, in turn, actively modify the environment to better suit their needs. Individuals' ability to cope with changing conditions depends on whether their personal attributes (e.g., genetic heritage, analytic and behavioral skills, perceived control over the environment) are well matched to the demands of the situation. When the fit between people and their environment is lower than desired, they experience physical strain, emotional stress and other kinds of *negative feedback* (Katz & Kahn, 1966). In some cases, individuals fail to achieve a state of balance with their surroundings. Instead, the negative impacts of environmental demands become more severe through a process of *deviation amplification* (Maruyama, 1963). Chronic exposure to environmental **threats** in those situations can lead to exhaustion and ultimately death (Selye, 1956). Deviation amplification is an inherent property of both individual-environment and population-environment transactions.

Fourth, because ecological research spans so many categories and levels of environmental influence, it is *inherently transdisciplinary* in its approach to understanding people's encounters with their surroundings. In addition to combining concepts and theories from multiple fields, ecological studies use multiple methods and measures to study environment and behavior. Many of these investigations emphasize the transformative goals of social ecology mentioned earlier, in that they are intended to *improve society* as well as to promote *scientific discovery* (Becker & Jahn, 2006). Translating scientific knowledge into solutions for complex problems (e.g., reducing the impact of school noise on children through improved classroom design; public policies designed to reduce fossil fuel consumption and promote greater use of renewable energy sources) requires collaboration between scholars and community members representing diverse disciplinary, professional and citizen perspectives. Social ecology emphasizes a *transdisciplinary action research* approach (Stokols, 2006) where academic and non-academic perspectives are combined to better understand and manage environmental challenges.

Relationship between social ecology and environmental psychology

Although there are certain overlaps between social ecology and environmental psychology, they are different in key respects. A widely used textbook in environmental psychology defines the field as "...*the study of transactions between individuals and their physical settings*" (Gifford, 2014), where the term transactions refers to the reciprocal relationship between people and their everyday environments. Social ecology adopts a broader purview by considering not only individuals' but also groups' transactions with sociocultural and virtual as well as physical features of their environment. Social ecology's concern with the structure, functioning and transformation of human environments at micro to macro scales extends well beyond a psychological perspective on *individuals'* relationships with their surroundings.

Social Representations of the Environment – Patrick Rateau

In a broad sense, social representations can be defined as systems of opinions, knowledge and beliefs specific to a culture, a category or a social group and relating to objects in the social environment. They are, therefore, presented as an undifferentiated set of 'cognitive elements' relating to social objects.

This set has four main characteristics (Abric, 1994; Rateau et al., 2011):

- First, it is *organized*. It is not a chaplet of elements placed end to end, but a 'structure'. This means that these elements have relationships, links, which make them interdependent. These relationships are themselves the result of a certain 'vision of things' of the members of the group.
- Secondly, this set is *shared* within the same social group. However, this consensus is always relative because it depends on both the homogeneity of the group and the position of its members in relation to the object. Thus, the consensual character of a representation is generally partial and often localized to a small number of elements of the representation.
- Thirdly, this set is *collectively produced* in a global communication process. The pooling of the elements at the origin of the formation of the social representation – and thus the sharing of these elements – is closely dependent on inter-individual exchanges as well as on exposure to internal and external group communications.
- Finally, this set has a fourth characteristic which refers to its purpose, which is to be *socially useful*. Firstly, because social representations constitute grids for reading, deciphering and therefore understanding the reality with which groups are confronted. Secondly, because they constitute guides during social interactions and are massively used during exchanges with other groups. Finally, social representations provide criteria for evaluating the social environment which make it possible to determine, justify or legitimize certain behaviors. In this perspective, they fulfil a function of orientation of social practices and constitute systems of expectations or anticipation which allow the adjustment of behaviors. Moreover, they also intervene *a posteriori* in the sense that they constitute systems for justifying our behavior and that of others.

From all these points of view, representations are, above all, 'social' and cannot be reduced to a purely intra-individual process of perception which would mediate the relationships of individuals to the environment. However, many studies conducted in the field of environmental psychology often focus on how individuals perceive their environment as a function of their emotions or their life experiences, thus remaining centered on intra-individual processes or on objective environmental contexts. The attention given to collectively shared meanings, thus, remains in the background. However, several studies show how social representations of environmental phenomena are conditioned more by general beliefs about the environment than by objective characteristics of exposure to these phenomena (Castro et al., 2010).

For example, a study in France sought to identify the social representation of atmospheric pollution and its effects on health (Fleury-Bahi et al., 2015). Residents of three cities were surveyed: two polluted cities and one unpolluted city according to an objective air quality index. The results indicate the existence of two common and structuring dimensions of representation: that of the causes of pollution (traffic, transport and industrial activity) and that of its effects (respiratory diseases, allergies and cancer). These results show that although atmospheric pollution is a major health and social concern, it is not linked to objective exposure to polluted air: the groups considered as such by the health authorities share a social representation of air pollution similar to that of the group living in a non-polluted area. The only difference linked to the objective context lies in the degree of importance attributed to the source of the pollution: road traffic in one of the polluted cities and industrial activity in the other.

Taking social representations into account in the field of the environment, thus, allows the identification of the knowledge, beliefs and values that groups share with their living spaces (Navarro, 2016). It, thus, makes it possible to enrich the description of the objects studied, to diversify the methods of approach and to develop new questions related to the processes of emergence and transformation of social representations.

Socio-spatial Categorization – Pierre Dias

Categorization refers to a cognitive process that simplifies, classifies and orders the information processed by an individual (Piaget & Inhelder, 1959). All the objects (physical and social) that make up the sensory, perceptual and cognitive environment of people undergo a treatment which classifies them into classes according to their 'nature'. The objects are grouped according to their similarities and constitute ordered classes which generalize the characteristics of the elements which compose them. We understand that categorization is based on a principle of simplification. The treated objects lose the complexity of their characteristics to be assimilated more easily to classes, and the classes induce generalization of the properties which define them to the objects which compose it.

Tajfel (1981) shows that categorization leads to distortions in the processing of information by two processes: the exaggeration of the contrasts between two categories, and the exaggeration of the similarities between the objects of the same category. If these processes exist in all individuals, the criteria which guide them depend on a social construction. Thus, the categorization process actively participates in an identity function by expressing the position of the individual in his physical and social environment. Attributing certain characteristics more than others to an object is not trivial and refers directly to social thoughts and judgments (more or less stereotypical because based on a simplification) which are based on the **norms** and **values** of the social group to which they belong.

In this sense, the categorization of geographical space consists of ordering spatial information according to criteria of socially constructed assimilations and contrasts. It makes it possible to understand the way of conceiving a territory while making the link between the social and geographical order (Debarbieux, 2004). We note that spatial categories are not specifically based on physical boundaries which generally help define spatial units (Aldhuy, 2003). This process takes place from the social understanding of spatial elements. Social meanings have particular importance in the existence of spatial categories. It is, therefore, the individual-environment relationship that is at the center of this process (Dias & Ramadier, 2016). To put it another way, the socio-spatial categorization explains the different relationships to geographic space, and at the same time, it strengthens belonging to a social group by expressing this relationship.

The process of socio-spatial categorization can ultimately approach an unconscious socio-cognitive segregation which allows individuals to position themselves in struggles for the **appropriation** of geographic space, and which contributes to socio-spatial fragmentation in its morphological application.

Socio-spatial Representations – Denise Jodelet

The current research on socio-spatial representations, inspired by the theory of social representations (Moscovici, 1961, 1986), has developed since 1976 (Jodelet & Milgram, 1976), in the fields of environmental psychology and of the study of the imaginary in social psychology (Moliner, 1996; Arruda & de Alba, 2007). This movement, of an international character, is interested in the ways of conceiving and presenting, verbally or in writing and drawings, the space according to the occupations, activities, uses and human arrangements that give meaning to its various forms, particularly in the urban sector.

This perspective meets various contributions that, in the social sciences, were interested in images of the city (see, among others: Lynch, 1960; Ledrut, 1973; Proshansky, 1978; Maffesoli et al., 1979; Bourdieu, 1980; Simmel, 1984; Choay, 2006; Gieseking & Manglod, 2014; Hall, 2017), as well as in relations between men and the environment (Lewin, 1936; Barker, 1968; Altman, 1975; Proshansky, Ittelson, & Rivlin, 1976; Levy-Leboyer, 1980; Stokols, 1978; Moser & Weiss, 2003; Moser, 2009).

The peculiarity of this current of research (Jodelet, 1982, 1987, 1991, 1996, 2015a) is to insist on the social conditions that mark the modes of **appropriations**, use and evaluation of living spaces. It, thus, records a convergence between the social sciences and psychology to address the question of the way meaning is attributed to the space considered as a place of life involving those who are attached to, take place, and develop their activities there. Indeed, this current goes beyond the traditional perspectives of the relationship to space and the way meaning is given to it. Namely: the objectivist perspective, posing a mechanical influence of physical space on individuals in limited contexts; the subjectivist one, relating the meanings of material space to the role of imaginary and emotional projections of individuals; or, the semantical one, treating the living environment as a non-verbal system of significant elements linked to other cultural systems of meaning. On the other hand, the study of socio-spatial representations focuses on transactions between man and his environment and takes into consideration the meanings invested in space, its images and representations, due to a process of social semiosis involving the temporal dimension of transactions.

In the transactionalist perspective, introduced by Altman (1975), individuals and the environment are mutually defined in interdependence. This leads to filling in environmental psychology, a social vacuum, because the transaction thus postulated implies the consideration of the social in two ways: the environment becomes 'socio-physical', the individual 'social subject', an actor marked by his affiliations, enrolment and social relations. To say that the environment is socio-physical is no longer to consider it only as a set of forces affecting the conduct, but as a material and symbolic product of human action (Stokols, 1982). The elements of the ecological environment are conceptualized in spatial terms. This approach is accompanied by the recognition of their social dimension, expressed in terms of meanings. Thus, for Stokols, the socio-physical environment is a compound of material and symbolic traits whose study demands the apprehension, in a single analysis, of the so-called 'subjective' and 'objective' elements. It is the occupants of the various spatial frames who make them pass from the status of mixing of material elements to that of a symbolically significant site.

The symbolic value of material space that integrates the meanings produced by human action is also emphasized by one of the founders of environmental psychology, Proshansky (1976, 1978), for whom it must become "a science of socio-historical behaviour". This is the beginning of a consideration of the social subject, the individual being defined by his topological or situational identity. This identity is established, according to Proshansky, in response to the physical environment through a complex set of conscious and unconscious ideas, beliefs, preferences, feelings, **values** and goals, behavioral tendencies and skills relevant to this environment.

Here are the lineaments of an approach to a social subject. To go beyond this, we need only ask ourselves where the individual gets his ideas, beliefs, etc. relating to the environment in which he is located. Transactional models do not do this because, although they affirm that the influence of society and culture on spatial cognitions ensures their common characteristics, allowing to aggregate them into distributed representations or to generalize their processes, they are unable to account for this influence, both empirically and theoretically. There is a limit that can be overcome by the approach in terms of socio-spatial representations that, inspired by the theory of social representations and integrating the contributions of other social sciences, provides an account of how the meaning comes to the site.

The approach of the psychological and social phenomena that develop during the transactions between the individual and his environment has for a long time presented another limit: it has focused, above all, on the immediate relationship, the causal or significant interactions existing between built space and those who live, work in it and pass through it, without taking into account the temporal dimension of these interactions, nor the memory games that structure them. It is only tardily that environmental psychology has dealt with the relationships between memory, meanings and **place identities** (Arisidis et al., 1992). For this it has been necessary to recognize that the meanings of space are marked by culture and history and that the subjective meanings attributed to it by its occupants have to do with their biography and the history of their group.

It is at this point that the approach to socio-spatial representations is fruitful in that it makes it possible to identify the psychological and social processes of the historicized construction of places, especially urban places. In this case, the space is considered as expressing, in its organization, a social order, and thus lends itself to the game of interpretations that can be analyzed through the representations constructed by the social subjects. In these representations, material forms and social marking of spaces are closely intertwined. The links existing between the physical appearance of a city and its human elements emerge as well from the affirmation of the specificity of lifestyles, the social climate and the activities that give their uniqueness to the materiality of places, as from the registration of the social characteristics of the inhabitants, which ensure the identity of urban settings and modulate their physical value.

These phenomena have been largely illustrated by studies carried out as part of a research program on a number of cities: Brest, Mexico, Nantes, Rome, Vichy (Jodelet, 1996, 2015; Hass; 2002; de Alba, 2010). The same methodology, based on the commented drawing of urban spaces, has made it possible to draw up, for each of these cities, a map of known and unknown places, appreciated or rejected ones, and to compare them with indicators considering their history and characterizing their type of settlement, in terms of activity, socioeconomic level and social, ethnic or racial affiliation. In addition to the already widely recognized role of spatial arrangements and practices in the formation of urban images, it has thus been possible to highlight the importance of identification and memory. In this way, a wide field of investigation is constituted, which makes it possible to unite, under the same glance, the private, social and historical dimensions of the mental construction of urban living spaces.

Solastalgia – Dorothée Marchand

The concept of solastalgia was proposed by the philosopher Glenn Albretch (2007). It is derived from the English word 'solace' meaning comfort, and 'algie' meaning pain.

Solastalgia results from a negative emotional state linked to the degradation of nature by human activities and the threat or loss of places to which a person, a group, a society is intimately attached, and which constitute a basis of identity: "Solastalgia is the experience of negative changes in the environment. It is similar to the concept of nostalgia, a sort of homesickness experienced by someone who is far from home, but for solastalgia, the person is already at home, it is their place that is leaving them" (p. 57). Development operations, tree felling, fire, etc. can generate solastalgia.

Solastalgia refers to a state of profound helplessness and distress caused by the disruption of an ecosystem, "the feeling experienced in the face of stressful and negative environmental change" (p. 11). Albrecht points out that this is accompanied by negative emotions in the relationship the person builds with the world, but that emotional reparation is possible. This reparation would open up the symbiocene, a term he proposes for a positive era, positive emotions and thus a future:

> To imagine a new period in Earth's history, it is necessary to move away from the anthropocentric individualism of the Anthropocene... The symbiocene begins with the recognition of vital interdependence as the concrete foundation of all thought, policy and action.

The conceptual challenge is to reconnect with the living, the vital and to overcome the (eco-)anxiety provoked by our relationship with our environment.

This concept can be compared to **eco-fatigue**, which expresses a weariness linked to an excess of information or pressure relating to ecological issues. This fatigue is accompanied by a feeling of being overwhelmed, of no longer having control over the situation and can lead to very negative emotional states, to **eco-anxiety**. The conceptual exploration of solastalgia is based on the analysis of the emotions experienced in the relationship with the Earth and their role in the individual construction. All the experiences and emotions accumulated since childhood – which build the relationship between the individual and his environment – constitute a system of influence that Albrecht calls 'sumbiography'. Relationships to nature are central to Albrecht's analysis.

Space – Space Psychology – Bernardo Jiménez-Domínguez & Rosa Margarita López Aguilar

The concept of space in social sciences refers to social space. For the *Oxford Dictionary of Geography*, social space is the use and **perception** of space produced by social practices as opposed to personal space. According to Castells (1996) in *The Information Age*, space as an expression of society is crystallized time and in reality, it is society itself. Time and space cannot be understood separately from social action. For Massey (2005) in *For Space*, time is the dimension of succession and space is the dimension of simultaneity and the dimension of multiplicity as contemporary plurality, in which different trajectories coexist. The space is always under construction, never closed or finished. In this sense, space is a social product; as such, it is imbued with power, it refers to the relationships between people and it has social effects.

Kaminski (1976) clarify from the *Umweltpsychologie* that every social system has a historicity that is symbolically manifested in the physical environment. This is valid not only for buildings, but also for **nature**. The complex environment that **environmental psychology** talks about is a human and historical environment; it is a socioculturally modified space. In *Psychology and the Environment*, Lee (1976) emphasizes that beyond the relationship with the **environment**, environmental psychology deals with the various concepts created by man as representations of space. The social scheme would be the normative perception of the way in which people organize themselves in space without distinguishing between physical and social relationships in their local context but rather as a synthesis or socio-spatial scheme.

Moles's psychology of space (Moles & Rohmer, 1972) stems from his interest in everyday life based on the influence of Bachelard (1958) first and Lefebvre (1968) later with whom he had a direct relationship. His theory of space is a phenomenological analysis of actions in the framework of people's daily lives in an anticipated transdisciplinary framework. The space exists only from its perception by the person situated in a broader environment with which it interacts and that modifies the perception of it. Moles sees space as a metaphor for the social system, which makes possible diverse perspectives for a psychosociology of space. Moles understands everyday life as the relationship of the person to society and also recognizes the influence of Lewin's concept of the topological field and the phenomenology of time and space of German philosophers such as Husserl and Heidegger. This is part of his urban psychology research in Ulm in 1964, based on which he created his concept of shells of existence as concentric domains that allow differentiating the psychologist's perspective of phenomenological analysis from individual perception and the perspective from the outside that corresponds to the rationality of the architect. Moles assumes the complexity of this relationship assuming the dialectic between the private and the collective and the freedom of indeterminate and relative personal action. Derived from this, ways of doing research are being generated, overcoming the traditional separation between objective and subjective properties, incorporating imaginary and imaginable properties to study the public space, including the concept of the labyrinth. Moles, despite the vast and extensive of his multidisciplinary contributions, recognizes not only his collaborator and co-author Rohmer, but he also does so with other authors who according to him were working in the psychology of space on important issues, such as Fischer, Ekambi-Schmidt, Korosec, among others and also the urban psychology that was already done in other countries with whom they met in 1976 to talk and share their work in the congress of architectural psychology in Strasbourg coordinated by Korosec on the key issue of the appropriation of space.

There are several books that appear around the same time on the subject of urban and architectural psychology, such as that of Canter (1974b) who designed for his psychology courses for architects a pioneering text *Psychology for Architects* in which he proposes how to solve the dialectic between the person who will be the user of the architect or designer's work and the response of the building. Architects are expected to understand the psychological impact of the built environment so that they can apply it in their designs. Mercer (1975) publishes *Living in Cities*, in which he welcomes the review of well-known colleagues in the field such as Canter and Lee and criticizes the late arrival of psychologists to a space in which urban planners, architects, geographers and sociologists have already contributed to his understanding from these disciplines and emphasize that the rapid growth and technological advance of cities alters the experience and raises the need to respond to the question about what his own self-creation is doing to the life of the urbanite. For his part, Fischer (1976) in the same vein proposes in his book *The Urban Experience*, a social psychology of urban life on the experience of being an urbanite and how social relations are influenced by the urban scene and the consequences that this entails has in its own being and personality. For his part, Mikellides (1980) publishes a book in which psychologists and architects write jointly with the title of *Architecture for People*, in which he begins by clarifying that what architectural psychology asks is why people respond differently to buildings and at the same time why some buildings are to your liking and others not. As long as users do not make their own contributions and are part of decision making, inhabited spaces are opposed to their well-being and at the same time become a serious problem for the economy. To debate and respond to these issues, a large number of contributions were shared and presented at the European Conferences on Architectural Psychology from 1969 to 1976 in the cities of Dalandhui, Kingston, Lund, Surrey, Sheffield and Strasbourg. The continuity of these congresses currently occurs in the biannual congresses of IAPS, and those of EDRA, as well as in its publications and bulletins.

The terms 'space psychology, architectural psychology, ecopsychology, urban psychology, urban psychosociology ended up subsumed in that of environmental psychology, which was assumed to be more general, although this use of the word 'environmental' only occurred in psychology and in the rest of the social sciences the urban term predominated. This was in keeping with what Lefebvre (1968) anticipated as the urban society. However, in Latin America, the concept of the urban persisted in the discipline in some authors who use the term urban psychosociology, as is the case of Aguilar in Mexico whose transdisciplinary work since the 1990s has been carried out in conjunction with anthropologists, sociologists and urban geographers. In addition, as of the year 2000, a task force of urban psychology appears among the divisions of the APA, as a development of the Committee of Urban Initiatives of the APA, whose stated purpose in a very complete and updated report is the understanding and improving the problems of urban life through research and practice for the well-being of people (see *Toward and Urban Psychology: Research, Actions and Policy*).

Spatial Cognition – Thierry Ramadier

Research on spatial cognition encompasses a breadth of studies on the cognitive operations involved in the mental construction of the spatial arrangement of geographical objects memorized by an individual or group of individuals. Downs and Stea (1973) proposed the generic term 'cognitive mapping' and initiated the first interdisciplinary studies bringing together psychologists and geographers. They investigated two main areas of research: spatial practices, analyzing for instance how individuals find their way, and spatial representations, then referred to as cognitive maps, analyzing the correspondences between these representations and the physical reality in the field, based on the production of images or discourses on space. More broadly, research on spatial cognition posits that cognitive processes and their outcomes are intermediary variables that orient spatial practices and the resolution of everyday spatial problems. We will also see that in some cases it draws on the understanding of the symbolic **appropriation** of places.

The first study published outside the field of philosophy focused on analyzing 'imaginary maps' (Trowbridge, 1913). Research by Tolman (1948), which decisively influenced and renewed the behaviorist approach of that time, showed the impact of cognitive processes on spatial practices. Yet, Lynch (1960) remains arguably the most stimulating driving force for environmental psychology research into these topics. His work on the composition and organization of images of the city gave new momentum to a psycho-geographic approach while adhering to the bio-physicalist principles established during the interwar period. Since then, many disciplines, including cognitive geography, linguistics, neuropsychology, cognitive psychology, the cognitive neurosciences and computer sciences, have taken up the study of spatial cognition. They share a functionalist premise which holds that spatial cognition steers behaviors in space, in the way that a geographic map works. Other disciplines, such as sociology, social psychology, history and political science, address spatial representations not so much to grasp the cognitive processes involved in their construction as to evidence their impact. Historically, environmental psychology has drawn on both of these approaches in its development. Since the early 1970s, the models of cognitive psychology have been combined with those of social psychology for the purpose of understanding how social significations relate to spatial representations and contribute to their diversity. This sheds light first on individuals' relationships to geographic space, and second on their impact on inter-individual or inter-group relationships and ultimately allows for developing a socialized conception of cognition and more specifically of spatial representations.

Stokols (1978) proposed to distinguish spatial cognition (the analysis of the arrangement of memorized geographic elements) from environmental cognition (the analysis of the significations associated with the elements of spatial representation), thereby clarifying a dichotomy in research on spatial cognition that has endured to this day, as there has been little dialogue between cognitive approaches centered respectively on social relationships and on individuals. However, we now have at our disposal some scientific findings that attest to the relevance of reconciling the two approaches, albeit all drawing on a localist perspective on geographic space (Ramadier, 2020). Indeed, the various approaches to spatial cognition mainly rely on the division of space into places that are defined and analyzed in and out of themselves. There are a few relational approaches looking into how places relate to other places or comparing the spatial distributions of social groups. The localist approach tends to favor the understanding of geographic arrangements by comparing them to geographers' representations. Below, a brief overview of various approaches in spatial cognition will single out their respective advances and limitations.

The strand of research that considers spatial cognition strictly as an intermediary process and product facilitating behaviors of navigation in geographical space is currently largely dominated by scholars in neurocognition. By investigating the construction and functioning of 'spatial abilities', a first group of research has evidenced 'place cells' (singling out an association between a place and neuronal activity in the hippocampus). The interactions between different place cells form a cognitive map (O'Keefe & Nadel, 1978). On the other hand, psychologists and geographers have pointed out the importance of spatial scales in the construction of these physiological activities. While numerous types of scales have been proposed, they are all centered on the individual and the individual's body, in a way that is reminiscent of Moles's 'shells' (Moles & Rohmer, 1972), albeit complemented by the idea of a space for navigation (Loomis et al., 1999). While each of these spatial scales relates to different cognitive treatments, research by Hegarty et al. (2006) and Meilinger et al. (2008) has demonstrated that they are interrelated, and that having mastered one helps mastering the others. This neurocognitive approach has, however, considered the individual's relationship to space. Scholars have evidenced two relationships to space – referred to as a reference frame: an egocentric one, in which the organization of space is constructed based on the individual's position in space, and an allocentric one, in which the observer's position has no bearing on the organization of objects in space (Berthoz, 1991). These two relationships to space are reminiscent of psychology research on field dependence (Witkin, 1959), with the caveat that with the concept of personality taken out of the equation, the two reference frames cohabit in the same person (Kozhevnikov & Hegarty, 2001), even though they relate to different neurocognitive treatments. Studies on the development of spatial skills in children have also evidenced these ego- and allocentric reference frames in their spatial reasoning (Acredolo, 1978), previously discussed by Piaget and Inhelder (1948) in terms of decentering.

Cognitive psychologists have also shown a keen interest in navigation in space, much as environmental psychologists have, but they have seldom problematized individuals' relationships to space and often drawn on artificial intelligence for collaboration. The resulting 'computational' models tend to reduce the cognitive map to a directory and a network of memorized trips (Kuipers, 1978). However, cognitive psychology emphasizes spatial representations, envisioned as individual representations that relate to the physical features of space. In that perspective, environmental psychology has accumulated a wealth of knowledge on mental activity in relation to the structuring of spatial representations, on the physical determinants of space that affect representations, and on the dimensions of individuals' relationships to space that come into play in their spatial representations. In the first paradigm, three significant processes have been highlighted. First, the relationships between **places** are not only topological. They are grouped hierarchically depending on their location and/or function. This cognitive categorization of geographic space produces spatial distortions: distances within a category are underestimated, whereas distances between categories are overestimated (Hirtle & Jonides, 1985). As a result, any kind of geographic rupture, physical barrier or symbolic border will also produce overestimations of distance. Then, some geographic elements acquire the status of prototypes (typical representatives) of a given spatial category, also referred to as 'reference point'. Their spatial relationship to other elements in the category is asymmetrical: when the reference point is the starting point for the estimated distance, that distance is underestimated, whereas when it is the arrival point, it is overestimated (Sadalla et al., 1980). Lastly, the overall spatial structure of representations is divided into two large families: representations are either more or less interconnected as route-map, or topological relationships between the represented entities, as survey-map (Appleyard, 1970). Numerous physical characteristics are involved in the formation of spatial categories, reference points and spatial structures. The most extensively studied are the shape and complexity of the urban layout (e.g., in a grid, radiating in concentric circles, etc.), ruptures in geographic space (paths, obstacles, changes in topography, function, design or population, etc.), the salience of geographic elements (size, architectural form, contrast with surrounding elements, etc.) and their location (at an intersection, offering a perspective, etc.). Likewise, individuals' relationships to space affect their spatial representations. The main factors in play here include spatial practices (mode of travel, places visited, etc.), familiarity with places (frequency and duration of visits), the use of navigational tools (maps, etc.), lifestyles (tourist/resident, social class, age, sex, etc.) and the value attributed to places (enjoyed, rejected, etc.). The subjectivist approach that dominates the study of the impacts of relationships to space on spatial representations focuses on individual experience as it relates to social conditions, thereby ruling out the idea of a socio-cognitive construction of these representations. This field of research examines the way in which language contributes to structuring the division of geographic space (Denis, 1997), especially through linguistic operators and spatial prepositions, and their ability to allow individuals to communicate, to gain awareness of spatial relationships or to imagine them.

The cultural approach to spatial cognition addresses space almost exclusively from the angle of **representations**, with the exception of Barker's (1968) work on ecological psychology. The spatial cognition versus environmental cognition dichotomy in research is not as clear-cut in these ethnographic investigations. Here, significations associated with space play a central role in the analysis. The physical features of space are not considered in and out of themselves but as contextual variables (Heft, 2013). The idea of representation as a cognitive tool in the service of spatial practices is more nuanced, given that these two facets of relationships to space are envisioned as interrelated. There have been two main strands of research partaking in this approach: one consisting of evidencing the cognitive processes associated with orientation, navigation and the structure of language in various cultures, and the other focusing on comparing the spatial representations of different sociocultural groups residing in the same places. The approach looking into the social representations of space differs from the cultural approach in that it is not so much immutable, inherited values that orient spatial cognition as a construction shared within social groups in their dealings with a space that is also itself socially marked (Jodelet, 1982). Also drawing on the transactional approach of environmental psychology (Altman & Rogoff, 1987), this model posits that the significations of space are not filters through which spatial cognition passes through, but actively contribute to the elaboration of these cognitive processes. The histories of individuals and the histories of places both serve as the basis for representations, allowing this approach to move beyond an analysis focused on the individual's immediate relationship to geographic space and to evidence the effects of collective memory on spatial cognition (Haas, 2004). Still, it concurs with the cultural approach in arguing that divergences between spatial representations feed social conflicts. Lastly, another social and cognitive approach to spatial cognition highlights the issues and social relationships involved in the construction of spatial representations (Dias & Ramadier, 2015), based on the Durkheimian hypothesis of a correspondence between social structures and cognitive structures. Spatial representations are not only considered as generating conflicts over the **appropriation** of space stemming from sociocultural differences, as social conflicts and issues are shown to themselves contribute to the differentiation of spatial representations. The cognitive representation of space becomes an indicator of social and spatial stances.

As a result of this variety of approaches, multiple theoretical models of spatial representation have been suggested. Kitchin (1994) has identified four main types of models. The first is the literal model of the mental map in neuroscience, wherein spatial representations are elaborated on the basis of first-hand or second-hand geographic experiences and transposed to a neuronal network. The second is that of the analog and functional mental map based on a double coding of information available in the memory (Paivio, 1971): geographic information is first stored in the memory in the form of concepts, which are then used to draw a mental map based on subjective distances between memorized geographic features. These distances are directly related to the distances of geographic space in this model; the closer the mental map to the geographic map, the more efficient and reliable it is for everyday practices. The third model uses the mental map as a metaphor. The cognitive processes at work are the same as those described previously (double coding), except that there are no geographic metrics in the image produced. Here, spatial relationships are topological (above, farther than, etc.) and linked to relationships to space rather than to space itself. Lastly, the fourth model approaches spatial representations as hypothetical constructions. At odds with the first model, it sees spatial representations as conceptual representations. The idea of image is absent, and internalized spatial relationships are neither Euclidian nor topological. They are also conceptual (involving for instance the time and cost of a trip). More broadly, spatial cognition is characterized by a controversy between two theoretical approaches: a neo-behavioral one focused on thought without image (Pylyshyn, 1973), and another on imaged thought (Kosslyn & Pomerantz, 1977), foreshadowed by Piaget and Inhelder (1963), who had emphasized the relationship between actions and cognitive operations.

Spatial Meaning – Kevin Clementi

The term *spatial meaning* refers to the process of construction of sense based on the decoding of spatial *signs* – or systems of signs – by individuals who inhabit a specific environment. Taking up Peirce's definition, Eco (1989) defines the sign as something that – for someone – replaces something else. For example, a nodding of the head can stand for the concept of affirmation or negation. A *spatial sign,* therefore, is a sign conveyed through a significant that is a geographical element (e.g., a monument) or a spatial system (e.g., a neighborhood).

According to the structuralist semiology of the 1960s, the signifying character of the city can be identified by analyzing it to the same degree as a text, as a system of signs (e.g., Barthes, 1967). One could argue that an environment has a language. For instance, having integrated a linguistic code – French – we will be able to talk with others with whom we share this code. Thus, the integrated configurations of spatial codes allow us to read and decode the space. Therefore, this approach permits to move from the simple identification of the signifying and symbolic character of space – which for Barthes (1967) refers to, for example, the work of Lynch – to a true analysis of the process of spatial signification.

Post-structuralist theories highlight the active role of the 'reader' of the space in the processes of signification. For instance, the same element can have different meanings for different individuals according to their internalized codes – for example, based on specific social positions or residential trajectories. Meaning also varies along with socio-historical contexts and situational frames. For instance, the processes of meaning-making will differ depending on one's position: *Place de la République*, in Paris, has distinct meanings for residents of the neighborhood, for a foreign tourist, for one who is there during a demonstration or when the place is deserted in the early morning. Finally, there is *interpretative cooperation*, more or less fruitful, between the sender of a message and its reader (Eco, 1989). If one considers the city or its developers as the sender, the 'meaning' of a district for its urban planners will not necessarily be the same as for its inhabitants.

Psychosociological studies focusing on the spatial inscription of memory provide rich examples for the analysis of spatial meanings from the theoretical perspective of social and socio-spatial **representations** (e.g., Haas, 2004). These studies emphasize the role of space in the processes of collective re-construction of memory, especially by identifying the social issues and conflicts related to different spatial perceptions and interpretations.

Stress – Gary W. Evans & Kalee DeFrance

Stress is used in two different ways within environmental psychology: first, as a biopsychological outcome measure and second, as a characteristic of environments.

First, stress is an outcome influenced by the physical environment independently. Stress can also occur when certain physical characteristics interact with various psychosocial and personal characteristics. Stress occurs when environmental demands exceed or tax individual resources to respond or cope. Stress outcomes are often measured by survey indices of negative emotions such as feeling overwhelmed, under pressure, unable to control circumstances, stress, or tension, and often accompanied by anxiety and arousal or feelings of nervousness (Cohen et al., 1995). Stress is also assessed by examining biomarkers indicative of heightened sympathetic nervous system activity (e.g., blood pressure, epinephrine, norepinephrine, skin conductance), increased hypothalamic-pituitary axis activity (e.g., cortisol), increased inflammation (e.g., C-reactive protein, IL-6) and alterations in metabolic activities (e.g., weight gain, higher levels of lipids) (Contrada & Baum, 2011). A more recent innovation in physiological stress measurement is called allostatic load. Allostatic load is a composite index of multiple biomarkers of stress. Allostatic load predicts long-term morbidity and mortality better than any single biomarker (McEwen, 2012).

It is also possible to measure stress levels by observing nonverbal behaviors, including facial expression, repetitive object-play, fidgeting, self-manipulation such as scratching or touching face, as well as use of **personal space**, defensive body postures, and other nonverbal behaviors to minimize social interaction (Cohen et al., 1995).

Stress can also manifest in impaired cognitive performance, but this relation is complex. Tasks that demand higher cognitive capacity are more sensitive indicators of stress. These include tasks requiring attention to multiple sources, tasks with high levels of difficulty or tasks that persist over a long period of time (Cohen et al., 1986).

Finally, there is evidence that when people are exposed to adverse physical environments that are uncontrollable or unpredictable, this can induce diminished motivation indicative of **learned helplessness** (Cohen, 1980; Cohen et al., 1986). For instance, following experiences of congested commuting, individuals are less persistent in solving challenging puzzles (Cohen, 1980; Cohen et al., 1986). Stress is not the same as mental health but clearly can influence psychological distress.

The second way stress is used within environmental psychology is to refer to environmental conditions (i.e., stressors) that can cause stress outcomes such as those described above. The most common examples of these have been noise, crowding, traffic congestion, pollutants, thermal extremes (primarily high temperatures), disasters (including **climate change**) and chaos (Evans, 1982; Evans & Cohen; 1987; Bilotta, Vaid & Evans, 2019). Chaos refers to properties of environmental experiences that are intense and unpredictable; often characterized by noise, crowding, interruptions, lack of structure or routines, and instability of residential, school or work setting. Though less common, stress has also been used to refer to characteristics of designed settings as well as products and technology (Evans, 1982, 2003). A common example of stressful design would be a place where one is readily disoriented (e.g., many primary care hospitals). At a different scale, trying to use technology or a product that is unfathomable causes stress.

As an illustration of how physical, psychosocial and personal factors can come together as sources of stress, consider noise. At a given level of noise, if you are trying to complete an important task that demands concentration, it will be more stressful than if you are simply disturbed while listening to music. Moreover, if you are noise sensitive, the same noise level during the same task will cause more stress. The physical parameter, sound level, plus the psychosocial environment, behavior engaged in, along with the personal characteristic, noise sensitivity, come together to affect stress outcomes (Cohen et al., 1986; Evans & Cohen, 1987; Bilotta, Vaid & Evans, 2019).

Finally, stress has contributed to environmental psychology by helping researchers think about underlying processes that link the physical environment to human responses. When people are faced with environmental demands that challenge adaptive capacities, they try to cope with those demands. For instance, children in noisy homes or schools appear to cope by tuning out or ignoring auditory stimuli. Unfortunately, an unintended, negative side effect of this coping strategy is that children become less attentive to speech. Speech perception is a fundamental building block of reading acquisition. One of the primary reasons why noise causes delayed reading acquisition is because of deficits in speech perception. Importantly, the pathway linking noise, speech deficits and reading acquisition is not explained by hearing loss, as several studies have shown the above pathway among children with normal hearing. Furthermore, the levels of noise sufficient to produce reading delays are far below those necessary to cause hearing damage (Cohen et al., 1986; Evans, 2021). Noise and other environmental stressors can also affect children's caregivers which, in turn, can affect children. Teachers in noisy schools, for example, experience fatigue, more job stress, and have less speaking time; all with implications for student learning. Parents in crowded homes tend to be less responsive to their children's needs (Evans, 2021).

Stress reduction theory – Roger S. Ulrich

Roger Ulrich's *Stress Reduction Theory* (SRT) provides a detailed and logically consistent explanation for why **nature** exposure can be expected to reduce psychological and physiological stress, enhance cognitive functioning or performance, and promote improved health outcomes. The theory generates several testable hypotheses and has the important strength of establishing tight direct links between theoretical arguments and objective psycho-physiological measures of stress and **restoration**. SRT emerged from Ulrich's *psycho-evolutionary theory* (1983) which postulates that immediate, unconsciously triggered and initiated affective responses – not 'controlled' cognitive responses – play a central role in the initial level of responding to nature, and have major influences on physiological responding, attention/intake, and conscious processing. A basic argument is that this multimodal process of responding quickly motivates adaptive behavior. The emphasis on affect was informed in part by Ulrich's early empirical finding (1979) that stressed that people assigned to view nature settings evidenced a much larger increase in positive affect and greater reductions in negative emotions (fear, anger) than those who viewed urban scenes. SRT holds that people benefit most from encounters with nature when they are stressed, but even unstressed people evidence more positive responding to nature than environments lacking nature (Ulrich, 1983). The theory tends to use the terms 'stress recovery' and 'restoration' interchangeably, although restoration is interpreted as a broader term that can also apply to recuperation from understimulation and boredom.

As a carryover from evolution, modern humans have a highly developed capacity for responding with stress and physiological mobilization to demanding or threatening situations. SRT maintains that the immediate benefits for early humans of stress responding and adaptive behavior when encountering challenging situations or sudden threats could be great (survival), but they came with costly effects such as energy-draining physiological mobilization and strongly negative emotions (fear, anger). If a threat or challenging situation were resolved, and an individual then encountered a natural setting favorable to ongoing well-being or survival, SRT proposes that the adaptive need would be for recuperation or a 'breather' from stress. (See Ulrich, 1993, for a detailed discussion of favorable/unthreatening in contrast to unfavorable/threatening characteristics of nature settings.) SRT contends that a capacity for restorative responding to nature enhanced survival chances because of its role in promoting rapid recovery from fatigue and deleterious psychophysiological effects of stress, and regaining the capacity to engage in vital activities. The theory proposes that a capability for rapid recuperation from stressful episodes was so advantageous for early humans that it favored the selection of individuals with a partly genetic proneness for readily acquiring stress-reducing responses to nature settings (Ulrich et al., 1991; Ulrich, 1993). This argument holds that modern humans, as a genetic remnant of evolution, have a proneness to quickly and readily acquire restorative responses to nature content and settings (vegetation, flowers, water) but have no such proneness for most built or artifact-dominated settings and materials (such as concrete, metal, glass). Ulrich suggests that restorative responding should not appear spontaneously or in the absence of learning. Rather, some learning or conditioning may be necessary to elicit a capacity for restorative responding to nature that is characterized by easy acquisition and resistance to 'extinction' or forgetting. The SRT proposition that a proneness for acquisition of restorative responses is in the human gene pool supports the hypothesis that stress-reduction benefits of nature tend to be evident across different cultures and diverse locations.

SRT advances the general hypothesis that recuperation from stress should be faster and more complete when people are exposed to most nature settings, in contrast to built environments lacking nature. The theory predicts that following a stressor, restorative influences of exposure to nature should involve a broad shift in feelings towards a more positively-toned emotional state, changes indicative of stress reduction in different physiological systems (such as the autonomic, neuroendocrine, skeletomuscular) and that these changes are accompanied by mild to moderate levels of sustained attention. The theory contends that a critical element in restorative responding to nature is a quick-onset positive affective reaction that plays a central role in shaping the positive character of changes in psychological and physiological states, and behavior or functioning (Ulrich, 1983). A positive initial affective response comprising liking and moderate interest should produce increased levels of positive feelings, reduce negatively toned or stress-related emotions such as fear and anger and motivate attention and perceptual intake.

SRT explicitly predicts that this combination of positive influences should be associated with rapid reduction (within seconds or minutes) of deleterious physiological mobilization (blood pressure, heart activity). Regarding influences on the autonomic nervous system, the theory holds that stress recovery should be evident in reduced sympathetic (fight/flight) activity and increased parasympathetic activity indicative of 'rest, digest, and recharge' (Ulrich et al., 1991; Ulrich, 1993). Because SRT contends that restoration is evident in central nervous system indicators, the theory was early in predicting that such effects are also expressed in the endocrine system as reduced levels of stress hormones, and in the immune system as enhanced functioning. SRT, thus, identifies credible pathways by which stress-reducing effects of nature can foster improved health outcomes.

There is much evidence that responding to stressors is often accompanied by declines in working memory and cognitive functioning. In sharp contrast to the *Attention Restoration Theory*, SRT contends that increased cognitive performance and attention restoration are effects of stress reduction, and that cognitive performance gains are mediated primarily by affect, not attention (Ulrich et al., 1991). This position is bolstered by meta-analyses showing that the effect of nature on emotions is much greater than its effect on attention. Consistent with emotion/cognition theory and research, SRT proposes that positive emotions elicited by nature foster increased performance on high-order cognitive tasks requiring flexibility in thinking, making remote associations, and creative problem solving (Ulrich, 1993). However, positive affective responses are not expected to reliably increase performance on low-order tasks that require a narrow and inflexible focus of attention and rejecting or suppressing associations with other material.

Many studies have replicated and extended Ulrich's original findings (1979; Ulrich et al. 1991) that restorative influences of brief nature exposure involve a rapid and broadly positive shift in emotions together with physiological changes indicating stress reduction. Meta-analysis has supported the reliability of emotional influences and found that the effect size for positive affect is quite large; the effect size for reduced negative affect is smaller but still robust. It is noteworthy that both randomized laboratory experiments and well-controlled field studies (in cities, parks, forests, hospitals) have consistently shown that nature exposure quickly reduces stress indicators in different physiological systems. In this regard, studies have confirmed the specific SRT predictions that restoration is evident in reduced sympathetic activity and increased parasympathetic activity indicative of rest and recharge. A practical design implication of SRT is that designing built environments with prominent nature may harness therapeutic influences that are carryovers from evolution, resulting in more stress-reducing and healthful settings. Beyond environmental psychology, SRT research has had widespread influences on urban forestry, **landscape** architecture, architecture and public health studies of the benefits of nature in urban contexts.

The positive emotional and physiological states elicited by nature are a plausible mechanism underlying the finding that hospital patients recovering from surgery had more favorable recovery courses, including lower intake of potent narcotic pain drugs, shorter hospital stays, and more favorable evaluations of their emotional states, if their windows overlooked trees rather than a brick building wall (Ulrich, 1984). This study has stimulated a great deal of research on health-related benefits of nature in medical settings, including randomized trials showing that nature exposure lessens patient pain, reduces anxiety and physiological stress, and increases satisfaction and perceived quality of care. The research suggests that the effectiveness of nature exposure in reducing pain is enhanced if it is high in realism and involves nature sounds as well as visual stimulation. Other studies have found that hospital patients and healthcare staff who use well-designed therapeutic gardens report improved emotional well-being and reduced stress. Regarding healthcare workers, stress and burnout are prevalent and serious problems that worsen work performance, care quality and patient safety, and elevate rates of costly staff turnover. Thus, it is notable that a well-controlled study based on SRT found that nurses working in hospital intensive care units had significantly reduced burnout when they were assigned to take a daily work break for 6 weeks in a leafy garden, in contrast to attractive indoor break rooms (Cordoza et al., 2018). SRT research findings have been extensively applied to inform the design of hospitals and other healthcare facilities internationally, have influenced healthcare architecture design guidelines issued by governments and professional societies, and played a pivotal role in bringing nature into many billions of dollars of new construction.

Sustainable Behavior – Víctor Corral-Verdugo

Sustainable behavior refers to actions aimed at meeting human needs while, simultaneously, protecting the socio-physical resources of Earth. This means that sustainable actions help both the satisfaction of people's needs and the conservation of the environment. Sustainable behavior is the main subject of *conservation psychology*, one important branch of **environmental psychology**. The original goal of conservation psychology was to investigate *pro-ecological behavior* and its instigators. Pro-ecological behavior allows people to effectively face the degradation of the natural environment caused by humans. Environmental problems have a social component that simultaneously affects and is impacted by the deterioration of nature, but this component had not necessarily been considered in the study of pro-ecological behaviors. Indeed, the original studies of pro-ecological behavior focused primarily on actions of natural resource conservation without consideration of their social implications. With the emergence of the concept of *sustainability*, that linked bioecological problems with social issues, an expansion of the idea of pro-ecological behavior was developed, leading to the concept of sustainable behavior. This idea established that human development should consider both the satisfaction of people's needs (social conservation) and the protection of the biosphere (environmental conservation). A way of achieving such an ideal was through sustainable behavior.

A recent classification includes three dimensions of sustainable behavior: self-caring, pro-social and pro-environmental behaviors (Corral-Verdugo, Pato, & Torres, 2021), implying that sustainable behavior is about protecting oneself, others and the natural environment.

Self-care is the most basic sustainable behavior; its actions allow achieving and maintaining own physical and mental health, psychological growth and general **well-being**. Sustainability begins with caring for oneself, before caring for others and the biosphere, because no one can protect other people and the environment if self-preservation is not practiced in advance. Exercise, eating healthy food, practicing positive thinking, regular visits with a physician or other medical professional to check health condition, meditating, and nurturing affectionate relationships with people close to the individual are examples of *self-care* behaviors.

Caring for others, in turn, is practiced through *altruistic* and *equitable* behaviors (i.e., prosocial actions). The physical environment cannot be protected if the satisfaction of all human beings is not met and inequalities among individuals, social groups and nations are not decreased.

Prosocial actions aid the satisfaction of those human needs, particularly for the less advantaged; they provide fairer access to resources and promote the empowerment of minorities and disadvantaged groups. More specifically, altruism implies assisting others without expecting reciprocity and is manifested through actions such as supporting charities, helping – economically and emotionally – others in need, volunteering for diverse prosocial causes, donating blood and visiting the sick, among many others. Equitable actions, in turn, promote respect, fair distribution of resources, and the avoidance of discrimination based on ethnic origin, gender, social class and other demographic characteristics. Inequity is one of the most noxious manifestations of the absence of sustainability; that is why humankind must fight against this social threat by stimulating equitable behaviors and practices in individuals, social groups and corporations.

Finally, *caring for the* **biosphere** implies the protection of the natural world, including all living species and the ecosystems that nurture those species. *Pro-ecological* and *frugal* actions are part of these PEBs. Pro-ecological behaviors are aimed at conserving natural resources and the integrity of Earth's ecosystems. These behaviors have a direct impact on the preservation of plants, animals, and the organic and inorganic substrates that allow life on the planet. Water conservation, protection of biodiversity, composting, energy saving and **climate change** mitigation activities are instances of pro-ecological behaviors. Frugal behaviors, in turn, consist of actions directed at reducing human impact on ecosystems through the minimization of consumption and avoidance of waste. Their impact on the preservation of resources is indirect, yet not less important. These behaviors include reuse of products, decreasing meat consumption, opposing consumerism and waste of products, and, in general, practicing a way of living focused on reduced consumption. Consumerism, along with inequity and overpopulation are considered the most important causal factors of the current ecological crisis. Frugal behaviors are crucial in facing and solving problems caused by consumerism.

These three sets of sustainable behaviors (self-care, care for others, and care for the biosphere) are significantly interrelated, according to research results, and are expected to reinforce one another. Self-care, for instance, not only results in maintenance of own health but also results in benefits for the social and physical environment. Physical exercise like walking and biking, eating healthy food, and avoiding meat consumption benefits one's own health as well as decreases the negative environmental impact of transportation by car, and carbon and methane emissions that lead to climate change. Moreover, caring for others is usually a motivation for engaging in environmentally responsible behaviors, as revealed by the pertinent literature. People who practice pro-ecological and frugal behaviors think of other people, because they know that environmental conservation is a prerequisite for human wellbeing. Therefore, altruistic and equitable individuals tend to engage in PEB because of their anthropocentric concerns. Those same individuals practice self-caring behaviors because they know that caring for others is not possible if they do not care for themselves in the first place. The evidence reveals that sustainable behavior is a higher-order factor shaped by diverse facets of behavior (self-care, caring for others and caring for the biosphere). Furthermore, despite being unique and differentiated, these facets interrelate and reinforce each other. To solve the serious environmental crises facing the planet, it is necessary to promote a global citizenry that practice sustainable actions in their everyday activities. These actions should be practiced in the three facets previously mentioned, simultaneously, to be effective as they are all necessary for the purpose of achieving a sustainable world.

Therefore, identifying what makes possible the interrelations of those apparently independent sets of sustainable behaviors is of enormous importance. One avenue of research examines the role of pro-sustainable *deliberation* in the display and maintenance of sustainable behaviors and in enabling the interrelation between their different facets. Results indicate that people who develop intentions to act in a pro-sustainable way are more likely to engage in sustainable behaviors. Evidence suggests that pro-environmental actions and, in some cases, pro-social behaviors result from avoidance of punitive measures, as occur in the case of resources conservation to avoid fines or money expenditure. However, these motivations are not necessarily connected to a prosocial or pro-environmental goal (but rather, a purely egoistic goal) and are not considered driven by an interest in pro-sustainability. As such, to develop a sustainably oriented way of living, individuals should *direct their actions* specifically towards the goal of protecting humans (oneself included) and nature. By doing so, the pre-existing differences between self-care, caring for others and caring for the environment are minimized and an orientation towards pro-sustainable action emerges.

Similarly, human *motives* for conserving the socio-physical environment are highly important. Certainly, egotistic motives (conserving the environment for one's own benefit) may help the goal of sustainability but being altruistically oriented and developing a concern for the integrity of nature are also necessary and important for this purpose. The positive consequences one can obtain from environmental and social conservation are also fundamental motivations of sustainable behavior. It has been suggested that altruistic and equitable individuals experience hedonistic well-being from engaging in prosocial actions, and pro-ecological behaviors are often accompanied by increased levels of subjective well-being (happiness). It is necessary to investigate why some people experience these positive psychological states while others report opposite experiences (discomfort, feelings of sacrifice). Yet, the fact that many individuals obtain psychological gratification from practicing sustainable behaviors offers interesting and useful clues for further research and intervention.

Other research avenues involve examining the influence that human capacities, including abilities and competency, have on sustainable behavior. Individuals need to be effective (i.e., skillful, competent) to produce sustainable behaviors. However, before becoming socially and environmentally competent they must obtain information regarding environmental and social problems and knowledge about how to solve them. Knowledge of environmental and social issues is a necessary condition for solving social and environmental problems, but knowledge alone is not sufficient. The ideal scenario for the display of effective sustainable behavior is the development of *competency for sustainability* (CS). CS can be defined as the possession of abilities to respond to pro-environmental and pro-social requirements. Those abilities imply the proficiency necessary to engage in self-care, altruistic, equitable, pro-ecological and frugal behaviors, whereas requirements are those demands imposed by society and oneself that lead to being a pro-sustainable person. As such, abilities or skills must meet the imposed requirements in order to effectively address social and environmental problems. The central concept is that abilities or skills must match the requirements asking for a solution of social and environmental problems.

Pro-social and pro-environmental **norms** are instances of social pro-sustainability requirements. The unwritten rules regarding how members of a group should behave in the face of environmental or social issues often determines individual action. If those norms can activate the skills required to solve a problem, they function as pro-sustainability requirements and, in conjunction, social norms and skills produce a competent action. Other types of social pro-sustainability requirements are included in the goals explicitly declared in educational programs. They can assume the form of goals for pacific coexistence, civic behavior and proenvironmental acting. Students and the public receive information regarding prosocial and pro-environmental behavioral expectations. They are also asked to display the necessary skills to achieve those goals.

Pro-environmental requirements are also embedded in personal psychological factors (traits, **attitudes**, beliefs, **values**) that lead individuals to act in a pro-sustainable way. Believing in the seriousness of environmental problems and the need to solve them, having pro-ecological and prosocial attitudes and values, being oriented towards the future, having a pro-sustainable personality, and experiencing affinity for nature and people predisposes individuals to develop pro-environmental and prosocial skills. The combination of those skills and personal requirements also produces pro-sustainability competence.

Finally, the **environment** itself can be a powerful driver for sustainable behavior. The contextual configuration (physical design, naturalness, diversity, etc.) may guide an individual to act in a prosocial and pro-environmental way. For instance, previous research suggests that people are less likely to litter if their surrounding environment is free of garbage and that individuals living or working in a sustainably designed building are more likely to dispose of their food waste in a more sustainable way. It is also known that settings containing high degrees of naturalness and other restorative components not only increase well-being in children, but also promote prosocial interactions. In adults, restorative experiences in nature may lead to the protection of the physical environment with a significant amount of pro-ecological behavior variance explained by those restorative experiences in **nature** (cf. **Theory of attentional restoration**). Moreover, contextual configurations of the built environment, such as compactness and social diversity of cities, positively influence prosocial and proecological activities; these results provide clues for the planning and (re)design of cities.

In recent days, the idea of *positive environments* (also recognized as 'sustainable environments') has emerged as a plausible explanation for sustainable behaviors. A positive environment is defined as a setting that (1) provides resources that satisfy needs, (2) enables the individual to face environmental challenges and (3) requires the individual to conserve resources for future needs (Corral-Verdugo, Corral-Frías, Frías, Lucas, & Torres, 2021). This implies that positive environments *give* resources and *ask* for the conservation of those resources. From this theoretical perspective, a positive environment contains enablers and instigators of environmentally responsible behaviors. *Social norms* – previously discussed here– *social models* (individuals of higher reputation that display expected responsible behaviors), and prosocial and pro-environmental *affordances* are examples of these enablers and instigators.

Affordances are properties of the person-environment interaction that induce effective actions. Sustainable behaviors are effective actions, that is, they are competent behaviors such that examining affordances that result in sustainable behaviors is of enormous importance. Prosocial and pro-environmental affordances signal the opportunity for, and enable individuals to engage in actions of conservation of the socio-physical environment. They are also conceived as alternatives or solutions for socio-environmental problems enabled in a physical or social environment. Researchers are implementing strategies based on affordances of products that, when used, result in the conservation of energy, water and diverse natural resources. Others are designing artifacts affording waste separation for recycling.

In conclusion, by protecting oneself, others and the biosphere, sustainable behaviors promote the dual purpose of meeting the needs of *all* humans while simultaneously protecting the resources of Earth. Environmental psychologists have studied factors leading to the instauration of sustainable behavior in individuals and societies. Results of those studies demonstrate that the three facets of sustainable behavior reinforce each other through deliberation and motivation to act in a sustainable way. Additionally, evidence suggests a competency for sustainability is required, which matches social and personal pro-environmental requirements with skills. Furthermore, there is evidence that shows that the environment contains clues that enable or instigate sustainable behaviors. In combination, the evidence can inform ways of converting environmentally depredatory behaviors of individuals into a more sustainably-oriented life.

Sustainable City – Tomeu Vidal

A city committed to sustainability involves the care of the environment and the **well-being** of its citizens. A sustainable city furthers the **QoL** of its inhabitants, social justice and the well-being of future humanity, without destroying the natural capital. The variability of this commitment depends on the interpretation of sustainability (weak or strong) on which it is based. Weak sustainability postulates the full substitutability of natural capital. Strong sustainability is based on the preservation of the irreplaceable 'existence' of critical natural capital to human existence and well-being and for future generations (Palen et al., 2015).

One of the fundamental challenges for sustainability in cities is the integration of its economic, social and environmental dimensions, as noted in the 17 SDG's proposed by the United Nations. Making cities more inclusive, secure, resilient and **sustainable**, as proposed by SDG 11, requires an integrated governance model and inclusive and participatory implementation (Valencia et al., 2019). On the other hand, the effects of inclusive and participatory policies are observable in city spaces. In this sense, growth management, connectivity and accessibility to services and affordable housing are the principles that the New Urban Agenda proposes for a spatial sustainability, in addition to paying attention to spatial equity and spatial density (UN-Habitat, 2020). City governments are best placed to tackle many of these issues. However, an international response is also required. The well-known expression 'think globally, act locally' is complemented with 'think locally, act globally' in several sustainable urban development initiatives (UCLG-United Cities and Local Governments, C40 cities, Eurocities, etc.).

From Environmental Psychology and People-Environment studies, this approach is summed up in the way that the shape of cities can help achieve greater social, economic and environmental well-being. Another main challenge for sustainable cities is about changes in beliefs, behaviors and lifestyles that enable more just relationships among people and a better connection between humans and biophysical environments to promote a real sustainable behavior.

Sustainable Development – Karine Weiss

Since the Brundtland report, sustainable development has been defined as "development that meets the needs of the present without compromising the ability of future generations to meet their own needs" (Brundtland, 1987). Even if the question of the sustainability of our modes of production and our societies had already been raised since the 1960s, this report, 'Our Common Future', constitutes one of the founding documents of sustainable development and defines its main principles: the principle of solidarity between peoples and between generations, the precautionary principle with the possibility of going backwards in case of random or unforeseeable consequences of our actions, and the principle of participation, with an emphasis on governance. However, this text does not, strictly speaking, constitute a definition of sustainable development: at best, it specifies the aims of a development that would be sustainable, without it being clear what kind of sustainability we are talking about: sustainability of growth, of resources, of societies, or of all three. Thus, we have already pointed out elsewhere (Weiss & Girandola, 2010), the difficulty of basing such a definition on 'needs', with the latter being poorly identified, in terms of both limits (anthropocentric or biospheric?) and specifications (primary needs limited to survival, or material needs, leading to overconsumption?). Moreover, the Brundtland report does not specify the means to achieve sustainability, but rather the points of attention, emphasizing first the inequalities of development throughout the world, then the limits of environmental resources. However, it constitutes a basis for reflection, first for the Rio Summit in 1992, and then for governments that should be moving in this direction. The concept has evolved over the course of the major international conferences: while the Brundtland report emphasized the contribution of societies and their evolution to sustainability, in particular through education and equality of peoples, the issue quickly became essentially environmental and, as a result, economic.

Many authors have highlighted that the large number of different definitions of sustainable development have little in common, apart from the 'three pillars' of this development scheme: economic, social and environmental (cf. Weiss & Girandola, 2010). Based on this observation, organizations are now working on the sustainable development goals, which, according to the 2015 United Nations General Assembly Resolution, are broken down into 17 objectives for the 2030 horizon:

1 Eradication of poverty throughout the world
2 Fight against hunger and promotion of sustainable agriculture
3 Access to health and promotion of well-being for all at all ages
4 Access to quality education and lifelong learning opportunities
5 Gender equality and empowerment of all women and girls
6 Access to safe water and sanitation in a sustainable manner
7 Access to reliable, sustainable and affordable modern energy services

8 Promotion of sustained, shared and sustainable economic growth with access to decent jobs
9 Resilient infrastructure, promotion of sustainable industrialization and innovation
10 Reduction of inequalities within and across countries
11 Resilient and sustainable cities and communities
12 Sustainable consumption and production patterns
13 Combating **climate change** and its impacts
14 Sustainable use of oceans, seas and marine resources
15 Preservation and restoration of terrestrial **ecosystems**
16 Promotion of peace and access to justice
17 Global partnership for the achievement of the Sustainable Development Goals

When reading these 17 goals, we find the complexity of the issues related to sustainable development, already raised by Real-Deus (2010). Since the late 1960s, research in social and environmental psychology has focused on the study of factors that can explain how individuals can adapt their behaviors to environmental changes and modify their behaviors with a view to sustainability (Steg & De Groot, 2019). Initially focused on local issues referring to events that are more easily perceived by humans (e.g., air pollution, noise, environmental stress), research has gradually turned to consumption and environmental resource conservation behaviors. Although they exist in the background, the social and economic objectives of sustainable development are left aside by the vast majority of authors. Moreover, the difficulty of establishing a link between these individual behaviors and the stakes of sustainable development persists. Today, these issues are concentrated around climate change. However, the links between individual actions and their impacts on the climate are neither direct nor apparent, which does not facilitate an emotional understanding of the phenomenon. In this respect, the field of psychological research remains open.

Territory, Territorialities – Marie-Line Félonneau

One might have thought that during globalization, the concept of territory would lose its pertinence. On the contrary, it seems that the notions of territory, territoriality and territorialization remain more relevant than ever. But the use of the term territory is sometimes perilous, on account of its extreme polysemy and its use across many fields of research. Strongly marked by ethology and biology, which associate 'territory' with stereotyped behavioral responses based exclusively on genetic and biological bases, the notion, in its symbolic dimension, remains deeply contaminated by ideology.

In environmental psychology, the term is generally defined as an area controlled by a person or group. Overall, it can be said that the notion of territory directly implies the control of a given space over which a right of possession, real or symbolic, is more or less explicitly exercised. It is a control zone with which one can identify, and which materializes the boundaries of the self and the group to which one belongs. Thus, practices of territoriality refer to a set of spatial behaviors inseparable from a feeling of possession and control linked to psychological and cultural meanings, and thus resulting in codified social uses (Fischer, 1992).

Since human territoriality develops from a chain of territories of the Self (Goffman, 1973), from a nesting of shells (Moles & Rohmer, 1972) or from a succession of bubbles (Hall, 1966), it can be conceived as a dynamic process of **appropriation** that expresses the relations between the individual and the group(s) within a given physical space.

Although the most private territory corresponds to the borders of the Self (Altman, 1975), the reference territory is most often that of the endogroup. Thus, one could say that the boundaries of the territory of life are also those that separate the endogroup from the surrounding exogroups, whatever the spatial scale, from housing to the nation to the continent.

By embodying both the boundaries of the Self and the boundaries of the group, the territory and the related territoriality behaviors function as identity markers which may generate conflicts. Nearly a century ago, sociologists from the Chicago School (Burgess, 1925, in particular) explained the process of urban organization by the dynamism of the most vigorous elements that appropriated the most favorable ecological zones. Thus, the delimitation of a territory is a powerful indicator revealing, a cause and a consequence of, intergroup tensions, conflicts and domination.

Over the course of several decades, psychologists and sociologists (Paluck & Esser, 1971; Bourdieu, 1979, 1993) have shown that the socio-spatial setting of individuals and groups is linked to their position in the social hierarchy at a given time and in a given context. It has been extensively demonstrated that the higher one climbs up the hierarchy of social positions, the more likely one is to increase one's territorial hold and free oneself from spatial constraints; conversely, the lower one goes, the more one is subject to one's perimeter of life. This mechanism of territorial assignment is as widespread as it is documented, from the school playground, where gender defines the position of pupils, to the neighborhood where the social position of the inhabitants dictates their possible territorialities.

If the notion of territory is no longer systematically central in the current literature, psychological research continues to investigate person/place relationships in order to uncover the emotional ties existing between the individual and his or her territories. To do so, environmental psychologists have extensively investigated the concepts of **place attachment** (Hidalgo & Hernandez, 2001), **place-identity** (Proshansky et al., 1983), **appropriation**

(Morval & Corbière, 2000; Pol, 2002) or **topological identity**, as an emotional consciousness of belongingness to a **place** and to other people who inhabit it (Félonneau, 2004).

More recently, with the emergence of the question of **climate change** and the problems arising from it, we are rediscovering the heuristic scope of territorial anchoring in its subjective dimension for understanding the environmental behavior of individuals and groups. Indeed, the literature reveals the links between the feeling of belonging to a territory and the type of relationship the subject has with his or her environment. Since research on the NIMBY effect, environmental psychologists have shown that the territorialization of identity, operationalized by measuring the individual's attachment or identification with his or her place of life, is likely to modify environmental perception and evaluation (Sullivan & Young, 2020). The **nuisances** (pollution, incivilities) of the place with which one identifies are, therefore, often underestimated by individuals; most likely in the effort to safeguard a positive self-esteem and maintain a feeling of control over one's territory (Bonaiuto et al., 1996). Similarly, numerous studies show that the perception of environmental **risks** is highly subject to spatial and temporal biases, particularly spatial optimism (Gifford et al., 2009) which, once again, results in the underestimation or even denial of the seriousness of risks perceived in close proximity to home, compared to those located at a greater distance.

More broadly, recent literature demonstrates that environmental concern is strongly linked to the territorial anchoring of individuals and that a territorialized reading is likely to shed light on the relationship of individuals to **climate change**, its causes as well as its consequences. By varying the territorial scales (neighborhood, city, region, country, planet) that function as identity anchors, Devine-Wright and Batel (2017) show that the social acceptance of certain infrastructures depends on the spatial level to which individuals are attached; their research demonstrates that individuals attached to a global scale, as opposed to local and national scales, are more concerned by climate change.

In conclusion, as the notion of territory remains fundamental for myriad studies in human and social sciences (sociology, history, geography), it has, for environmental psychology, a major and renewed relevance regarding ecological issues. However, this is on the condition that the individual's territory of reference is considered plural and dynamic, and that it is not limited to an overly strict localism.

Indissolubly linked to the concepts of **place attachment**, **appropriation** and **topological identity**, the notion of territory remains relevant for understanding the extent to which an emotional consciousness of belonging to a place, and to the others who occupy it, is an explanatory variable in the perception of environmental threat and a predictor of environmental **attitudes**, beliefs and **behaviors**.

Therapeutic Environments – Kevin Charras

According to the European charter on environment and health: "1. Good health and **wellbeing** require a clean and harmonious environment in which physical, psychological, social and aesthetic factors are all given their due importance. The environment should be regarded as a resource for improving living conditions and increasing wellbeing; 2. The preferred approach should be to promote the principle of 'prevention is better than cure'; 3. The health of every individual, especially those in vulnerable and high-risk groups, must be protected. Special attention should be paid to disadvantaged groups; 4. Action on problems of the environment and health should be based on the best available scientific information".

Architectural psychology, that will later become 'environmental', takes its roots from the reflections between architects, medical doctors and psychologist concerning therapeutic characteristics of environments. As for any human activity, whatever period and clinical discipline in which it took place in, architectural design has proved to be a support of care.

Architectural trends are closely related to scientific knowledge and public health ambitions. When Church provided care, architecture of *Hôtels Dieu* followed ecclesiastical precepts, whereas medical techniques took a back seat. Alienists of the 17th and 18th century carefully observed the impact of the environment on mental health and came with the idea that architecture was part of the healing process. In the 19th century, to avoid proliferation of miasmas by evacuating polluted air in general hospitals architects provided high ceilings, thus indicating that architectural design of hospitals responds to immediate beliefs and concerns of an era. Opening up of cities and the sanitation of urban spaces contributed to the eradication of pathogenic sources. The anti-psychiatric movement and discovery of pharmacological therapies enabled to take a step towards urban care and sectored psychiatry. The actual inclusive movement is no exception to this rule, since one of the major societal issues is the design of adapted housing, for it to contribute to independence of people in vulnerable situations living there.

History shows that, when engineering and medical knowledge find their limits, architecture becomes an unavoidable support and is approached as an instrument participating to cure and care. Incurable diseases, indeed, require a very particular attention. Hence, when diseases involve behavioral, emotional or cognitive symptoms, architecture becomes a central element of care.

Therapeutic characteristics of the environment are not always addressed distinctly in scientific literature and are sometimes amalgamated, without precising its therapeutic virtues, technical and architectural treatment, or uses made of it by professionals. Among therapeutic environments, scientific, clinical and architectural literature allows us to distinguish three main categories:

- *Design of care spaces for therapeutic uses*, approaches architecture in a technical and objective aspect with the aim of facilitating acts of care and enhancing comfort of patients. Hospital architecture is the most representative of this type of environment, and provides an important empirical and scientific corpus. This category of therapeutic environment concerns characteristics such as lighting, ventilation, physical and visual comfort, odours, size and surfaces, materials...

– *Design of the environment as a support for care* consists in structuring the space in such a way to serve care agendas of vulnerable people and to answer instrumental, and sometimes therapeutic, aims of daily life. This concerns, for example, settings such as care or living units for people with progressive neurocognitive or developmental disorders.

– *Healing characteristics of environment* addresses interventions involving environments whose very characteristics have therapeutic or healing values or which are intended to promote health. Use of gardens for their restorative attributes are a good example of healing environments, although their landscape dimension can also relate to the previous category. Multisensory rooms are also good examples.

With the advent of inclusive approaches, design of urban spaces tends to fall into this category and the arrival of technologies such as virtual reality and augmented reality open new perspectives.

Threat – Sofia Payotte & Sabine Caillaud

The concept of threat is specifically relevant when it comes to environmental issues because, contrary to risks, threats are unpredictable and inevitable and they provoke a transcendental change in our living conditions (Drozda-Senkowska, 2020). Threat is "the anticipation, by a group or an individual, of a negative outcome associated with perceived insufficient resources for facing this outcome" (Milburn & Watman, 1981). Thus, threat has two dimensions: a cognitive one (beliefs about an outcome, about resources) and an emotional one (fear). Threat is constructed and transformed during interactions, bringing into play one who is perceived as threatening (an object, an individual or a group) and one who is threatened (Jodelet, 2017). Thus, the concept refers to both a content and a process. As a social construction, threat expresses the group's interest (Drozda-Senkowska, 2020), so that analyzing the context in which threat appears helps to understand its functions and shapes. Thus, the concept allows to catch social, identity and cultural issues which contribute to the construction of environmental issues.

Time Perspective – Christophe Demarque

Individuals' relationship to time is largely determined by their interrelations with the social context. In psychology, temporal experience is studied in particular through the construct of 'Time Perspective', initially proposed by

Kurt Lewin. For Lewin, the time perspective encompasses the totality of an individual's points of view, at a given moment, on his psychological future and on his psychological past. It thus refers to the three temporal registers, determining the meaning that a situation or an event will take. This conception underlines the importance of the subjective experience of the environment and its constitutive role of situations. The temporal experience, thus, appears as an essential structuring element of the psychological field.

From this point of view, time perspective can then be defined as "the result of a socially regulated cognitive process of representation which allows a subject to apprehend in his life space, at a given moment and depending on the context, the past, the present and the future. Contributing to the structure of this living space in a dynamic relationship of interdependence with the environment, it determines the perception of situations and the meaning assigned to them by the subject, as well as his or her behaviors" (Demarque, 2011, p. 65).

Time perspective is a multidimensional construct, often studied through three dimensions (Apostolidis & Fieulaine, 2004): temporal extension, which refers to the past or future depth in which the individual projects himself; predominant temporal orientation, which indicates the preferred temporal register in which the individual thinks and acts; and temporal attitude, that is, the valence (positive or negative) attributed to the different registers that make up time perspective.

In environmental psychology, there is a predominance of studies on future temporal orientation (Bonnefoy et al., 2014). One reason for this is the characteristics of many of the ecological challenges we face. For example, **climate change** is not readily discernible through immediate sensible experience. Adaptation to a phenomenon of this nature, therefore, requires anticipatory representations to guide our behaviors. Thus, positive links are observed between future orientation and pro-environmental attitudes, as well as with different behaviors (for a review, see Milfont & Demarque, 2015).

While time perspective is determined by relatively stable interindividual differences, acquired via cultural and social belonging factors, it is also determined by situational characteristics. For example, the choice to use public transportation results from the interaction between several psychological factors – including future temporal extension – and situational factors (service quality, low-cost access) (Collins & Chambers, 2005). It is necessary to take these contextual variables into account in the study of PEB; otherwise, a reductionist view of the construct may be taken, overlooking the dynamic nature of the time perspective and its interdependence with context.

Topological Identity – Marie-Line Félonneau

The psychological literature concerning the spatialization of identity (cf. **Place identity**) has been a homogeneous and extremely rich theoretical field. By postulating that topological identity must be approached from the motivational processes underlying other identity processes (Breakwell, 1992), we can conceive of it as part of self-identity, comparable to gender, political or ethnic identity (Proshansky et al., 1983; Lalli, 1992). One must incorporate components of group identity, while also keeping in mind that topological identity is based upon both the physical features of a place and its social characteristics. With this perspective, we therefore define the topological identity as the propensity to feel an emotional consciousness of belongingness to a place and to other people who inhabit it, not only as a function of personal dispositions and personal references, but also as a function of collective, culturally marked, ways of thinking about the environment (Félonneau, 2004).

Numerous studies show that **residential satisfaction**, environmental assessment, and even the perception of **climate change** are often predicted by the topological identity of individuals. In general, it is observed that a strong identification with place leads to an underestimation of nuisances and environmental threat. Nevertheless, topological identity, like other spheres of identity, must be considered and conceived through both its particular dynamics and the different environmental scales that fulfill specific identity functions.

Strongly rooted in the tradition of environmental psychology and inextricably linked to the concepts of **place attachment** and **appropriation** without being synonymous with them, topological identity is gaining renewed interest with the emergence of environmental issues. Indeed, it is already proving to explain environmental attitudes and **behaviors** and is therefore likely to be used to initiate behavioral change.

Topophilia – Cristina Garcia Fontan

Topophilia consists of two words from the ancient Greek τόπος (tópos, 'place') + -philia (love). The term fuses the concepts of feeling and place and it reflects the affective bond between people and place. It was coined by American poet W.H. Auden (1947), used by French phenomenologist Gaston Bachelard (1958), and made popular by geographer Yi-Fu Tuan in his essay and book *Topophilia* (1961 and 1974). In the book *The poetics of space*, Gaston Bachelard defines it as "the determination of the human value of the spaces of possession, of the spaces defended against adverse forces, of the spaces loved, to their value of protection...". In this sense, the author has conferred a poetic category of the spirit, where the perception of space is mediated, not only because of the sensory experience but also because of the imaginative burden we place on it.

It is also related with the environmental perceptions and values at different levels: the species, the group and the individual. The Chinese geographer Yi Fu-Tuan elaborates his own definition of the concept of topophilia, relating it to a feeling of attachment (emotional-affective relationship) that links human beings to those places with which they feel identified. Such a feeling would exalt the symbolic dimension of human habitation and express a powerful instinct of belonging to the world.

Umwelt – Hartmut Günther

The German dictionary of Jacob and Wilhelm Grimm (2021/1854) defines *Umwelt* as the "world surrounding, enclosing a human being". Subsequently, the essential meaning of the term was extended to any number of relationships between individual(s) and the world surrounding them.

Uexküll, a biologist, is generally credited with using the term *Umwelt* for the first time in a scientific text, *Umwelt und Innenwelt der Tiere*, published in 1909, dealing with the reaction of invertebrates to external stimuli. Subsequently, Uexküll (1921, 1936; Uexküll & Kriszat, 1956) extended the analysis to include humans; yet the emphasis continued to be on the impact of the environment on the organisms' reactions on their respective, specific *Umwelten* (plural).

The first to associate *Umwelt* and psychology was Willy Hellpach (1924), in a handbook chapter titled *Psychologie der Umwelt*. Hellpach argued that the *Umwelt*, to the extent that it impacts the human psyche, relates to three distinct 'circles' or dimensions. Humans are surrounded by 'nature', that is, ground/soil, air, light, weather, forest, mountains or plains, bodies of water (rivers or lakes), etc., which he named 'geopsychic' factors (1924, p. 110). Furthermore, they are surrounded by other humans, they are constantly part of a human society, which may be summarized as 'socialpsychic' factors (ibid., pp. 110–111). Finally, humans live in a world, created in conjunction with fellow humans, that is, 'culture' that consists of books, laws, dogmas, states, buildings, which are closely related with the socialpsychic factors and are called 'culturepsychic', historical or *zeitgeist* (ibid., p. 111). Hellpach expanded on these three dimensions in subsequent publications, *Geopsyche* (1911b, 1950), *Sozialpsychologie* (1951) and *Kulturpsychologie* (1953). Hellpach touches on the reciprocal nature of the human–environment relationship in the section on social psychology, when he refers to Simmel (1908) and speaks about *mitseelische* (spiritual) relationships, that is, the mutual influences of one individual upon the other (Hellpach, 1924, p. 150). While not explicitly using the term 'reciprocal', referring to the social psychological issue of mutual influences, and seeing this in the context of his second dimension into which the individual is embedded, it is safe to infer reciprocity. As to the three dimensions or circles, as referred to by Hellpach in his 1924 text (p. 110), he stated, "one can recognize three circle that, even if they overlap now and then, they essentially … allow to be noted in their essential difference".

As far as 'multiple' perceptions of and interactions with a same environment are concerned, Martha Muchow (1935) very nicely demonstrated how a given environment can provide distinct **affordances** (of course, she did not use that term, only anticipated the phenomenon) in different individuals under varying circumstances. At the same time, while Muchow was at the University of Hamburg as part of the William Stern's research team, Uexküll was part of a different laboratory at the same university.

Today, we can clearly see the correspondence to proximal, distal and global perspectives of Environmental Psychology. Without directly establishing this correspondence, it can be inferred from Graumann's (1999) considerations of the implications of Hellpach's three levels of environmental psychology. Later, we can find some echo on Bronfenbrenner and Morris (2006) when they talk of concentric circles with the individual in the center and ever-expanding circles of environments with which (groups of) individuals stand in a reciprocal relationship.

Uncertainty – Dorothée Marchand

The concept of uncertainty is part of the field of **risk** perception and man-agement. Environmental risk refers to a factor in the environment that repre-sents a danger to a number of health or environmental issues. It indicates the probability of a hazard occurring and raises the question of the severity of its effects. Risk does not necessarily imply a causal relationship between an ob-jective factor and a consequence on health. Bourg et al. (2013) define the risk landscape according to three characteristics: manufactured, uncertain and global. Since risks are the product of human activities, modernity, industrial-ization and new technologies, they are uncertain. Emerging hazards, whether health, environmental or climatic, complicate the levers for reducing uncer-tainties into calculable risks. They reveal ignorance about these threats and introduce the notion of uncertainty into scientific debates to qualify uncer-tain risks. Arciszewski and Drozda-Senkowska (2006) show, in the context of GMOs (genetically modified organisms), that the threat comes not so much from the knowledge of a hazard as from the uncertainty of its unknown con-sequences or those perceived as insufficiently studied. For Borraz (2008), risk is no longer what science shows, but, on the contrary, what it does not show. Sociologists emphasize the extent to which uncertainty has penetrated envi-ronmental health issues (Chateauraynaud & Torny, 1999; Callon et al., 2001; Barthe & Jouzel, 2005), particularly with the recurrent health scandals since the 1990s (asbestos, bovine spongiform encephalopathy, contaminated blood, neuromediators, etc.). More recently, it has also widely penetrated the issues relating to climate change and the hazards that accompany it.

From a psychological point of view, this new relationship to risk, in which ignorance of the danger is put into perspective with intolerance of the un-certain, of the absence of knowledge, can become a source of anxiety. Defays (1991) defines uncertainty as "a state of ignorance or indeterminacy of a system, an individual, a situation, an assertion". This concept has inspired nu-merous works in health psychology (Mishel, 1988), work psychology (Karnas,

2000) and experimental psychology, particularly in relation to theories of decision making and intolerance to uncertainty (Ladouceur et al., 2000). The absence of certainty or even simply of knowledge about an identified source of risk can make the context particularly insecure and be a source of ill-being and anxiety. With the observation that the relationship between the individual and his environment is impacted by the representation of danger and behaviors in the face of risk, environmental psychology considers the dimension of uncertainty in risk management and the analysis of environmental controversies (Marchand et al., 2017).

Urban Crime – Elena Sautkina

Urban crime includes attacks directed against individuals or their property and ranging in their degree of violence.

Cities have higher crime rates compared to suburban or rural areas. A high socioeconomic divide and diverse social and physical characteristics of urban environments create criminal opportunities. Crime is unequally distributed across cities, forming 'hot spots', due to specific environmental (physical and social) characteristics required to commit specific types of crime.

Fear of crime is an apprehension about becoming a victim of crime. It is a subjective evaluation by lay people, and is determined by individual (e.g., emotional) and social (e.g., informational, representational) factors. Environmental characteristics such as signs of social disorganization, low surveillance or poor lighting are triggers of fear of crime. Hot spots of actual crime do not always match geographically with hot spots of fear of crime.

Urban Design – Dorothée Marchand

In France, the town planning code (article L 300–1) indicates that "development actions or operations are intended to implement a local housing policy, to organize the maintenance, extension or reception of economic activities, to promote the development of leisure and tourism, to provide public facilities, to combat insalubrity, to safeguard or enhance the built or non-built heritage and natural areas".

Thus defined, planning is envisaged as a set of objectives. In environmental psychology, urban planning is part of the field of spatial planning and the dysfunctions that accompany it. The development of large housing estates since the 1950s, urban sprawl, sustainable development, metropolization (...) make the urban space an environment in constant transformation, which generates as many psychological involvements. Several fields of research have been developed in environmental psychology to study them; for example, environmental stress (Moser, 1992), environmental assessment and **management**, and **residential satisfaction**.

Development programs promote 'quality' approaches from a technical and qualitative angle that neglect the qualitative dimension of **places**. The observation that urban quality [Link]is deteriorating, a situation that has been exacerbated by the Covid pandemic, calls for redevelopment strategies to restore **QoL**, **well-being** and social cohesion (Bailly & Marchand, 2019, 2021). Considered from the angle of the opportunities offered by places **affordances** and their **restorative** potential, more or less concerted and participatory development projects can thus restore urban quality by taking into account psychological dimensions; the development of walking paths, green spaces, public spaces, etc. are all development vectors that lead to the notion of '**ménagement**'.

Values – Goda Perlaviciute & Thijs Bouman

Values are desirable, general goals or ideals that transcend specific situations. Values serve as guiding principles in the life of a person or other social entities, guiding their decisions, attitudes and behaviors (Schwartz, 1992). Values are considered universal, meaning that all individuals and social entities are believed to endorse them to some degree. Yet, the importance individuals and social entities attach to each value varies, where more strongly endorsed values typically influence decisions, **attitudes** and **behaviors** more strongly.

Schwartz's value theory (1992) introduced a taxonomy of values structured along two dimensions. One dimension distinguishes values that focus on the interests of others, society and the environment (self-transcendence values) from values that focus on self-interest (self-enhancement values). Another dimension distinguishes values that focus on openness to new things and ideas (openness to change values) from values that focus on tradition and conformity (conservatism values). Depending on their alignment along the different dimensions, different values may represent compatibility of conflicting goals or ideals (see Schwartz et al., 2012 for the refined motivational structure of values).

Two types of self-transcendence values – biospheric and altruistic values – and two types of self-enhancement values – egoistic and hedonic values – are particularly relevant for people's environmental attitudes and **behaviors** (Stern, 2000; De Groot & Steg, 2008; Steg et al., 2014; Bouman et al., 2021). Biospheric values reflect caring about **nature** and the **environment**, and altruistic values reflect caring about the **well-being** of others and society. People who endorse altruistic and, especially, biospheric values more strongly are generally more likely to adhere to pro-environmental attitudes and behaviors because acting pro-environmentally benefits the environment and society. Egoistic values reflect caring about personal resources, such as money and power, and hedonic values reflect caring about one's pleasure and **comfort**. Egoistic and hedonic values are typically negatively related to pro-environmental attitudes and behaviors because acting pro-environmentally can be costly (e.g., price premium for pro-environmental products) and/or not pleasurable and inconvenient (e.g., taking shorter showers, giving up riding a car). Yet, some PEBs may also have egoistic or hedonic benefits (e.g., using less energy at home reduces the energy bill, eco-friendly food may be perceived as tastier and healthier), in which case stronger egoistic and hedonic values may promote engagement in such behaviors.

Because values are abstract constructs, they typically guide environmental attitudes and behaviors indirectly, via other variables. The VBN theory (Stern, 2000) postulates that people are more likely to engage in pro-environmental actions when they feel a personal obligation to do so (i.e., pro-environmental personal norm). People have stronger personal norms to act pro-environmentally when they believe that things they value are threatened (i.e., awareness of consequences) and that their actions can prevent or promote the threat (i.e., ascription of responsibility). Accordingly, people with stronger biospheric values are likely more aware and concerned about environmental problems, are more aware about what they could do to mitigate the problem, and accordingly feel a stronger pro-environmental personal norm to act, which motivates concrete environmental actions. The fact that the relationship between values and environmental actions is mediated by specific beliefs, such as awareness of consequences and ascription of responsibility, means that environmental behavior can be influenced by shaping those beliefs, for example, through science communication and the media (Stern, 2000).

Another variable by which values guide environmental attitudes and behaviors is environmental self-identity – the extent to which people perceive themselves as someone who acts pro-environmentally (Whitmarsh & O'Neill, 2010; Van der Werff et al., 2014). People who strongly endorse biospheric values typically have a stronger environmental self-identity, which motivates them to consistently engage in multiple pro-environmental actions (Van der Werff & Steg, 2018; Balundė et al., 2019; Zeiske et al., 2020). While biospheric values form the stable core for individuals' environmental self-identity, environmental self-identity may also be influenced by individuals' past actions. Reminding people of their past PEB may, therefore, be an effective way to strengthen environmental self-identity and to promote PEB (Van der Werff et al., 2014; Van der Werff & Steg, 2018).

Vulnerability – Oscar Navarro

Vulnerability can be defined as the possibility or likelihood that an individual or group of individuals will be negatively impacted by a natural or human-induced event which threatens their well-being or existence. This possibility, likelihood or propensity varies according to certain pre-existing characteristics or living conditions at the time of the hazard event. The notion of vulnerability evokes two sides of the same coin: the material and objective conditions of individuals; and the perception of individuals of their own vulnerability. Vulnerability is said to be caused by social, spatial, economic and political inequalities, which make individuals susceptible in a hazardous situation and less able to cope. It is also shaped by **inequalities** in terms of housing, the quality and level of urbanization, and the economic growth rates and dynamics of an area.

Vulnerability is, therefore, a combination of three things: differential exposure to hazards and nuisances, differential sensitivity (susceptibility, predisposition) to such hazards and nuisances, and differential preparedness to respond, adapt and recover from the impacts (Downs et al., 2011; Rossignol et al., 2015).

This inequality or disparity in relation to hazards is based on not only objective conditions, but also subjective ones that are inherent to the social and cultural category to which individuals belong. From an environmental psychology perspective, vulnerability also includes perceived vulnerability, or how individuals judge their own vulnerability. Although this judgment is based on the aforementioned objective conditions, it is also influenced by socio-cognitive mechanisms that contribute to shaping judgment and action, as well as by the contextual and social factors that condition such mechanisms. The level of vulnerability perceived depends on five key factors (Moser, 1998; Navarro & Michel-Guillou, 2014): (1) the judgment of the exposure to a **risk**; (2) the sense of control or the belief that effective means of protection exist; (3) the sense of anticipation in relation to negative outcomes; (4) the causal attributions, beliefs and naive theories used to explain hazard events; and (5) familiarity with the environment and/or the hazard because of physical, social and temporal proximity. Perceived vulnerability is shaped by a feeling of not being in control of the situation, not being able to prevent the effects of the event or protect oneself from the event, and not being able to recover from the event easily. An individual thus evaluates his or her own resources and his or her capacity to control and manage things before, during and after the disaster event. Perceived control refers to how much individuals feel they can influence the environment.

Walkability – Julie Roussel

This term, used by Jane Jacobs (1961), was sometimes used in the work of urban planners, sociologists and architects (Gehl, 1987) until the early 2000s. This period marked the starting point of a craze for walking in urban environments (Winkin and Lavadinho 2010; Lavadinho, 2011) – even if some researchers did not wait for this time (Augoyard, 1979).

This concept 'Walkability' has been developed mainly in the U.S. and Canada, and then more widely in Anglo-Saxon countries, and quickly became part of the desire to evaluate the 'walkable' potential of a space, based essentially on objective and physical indicators.

This concept, mainly associated with an urban environment (although it is not exclusively reserved for it), assumed that walking requires specific environmental (spatial) conditions to be practiced. While tools for assessing and characterizing pedestrian potential such as PEDS (Pedestrian Environment Data Scan) or MAPPA (Marchabilité Pour les Personnes Agées) provide a certain number of indications on the functional and safety characteristics (in the sense of road safety) of the walking environment, other factors such as its atmosphere (cf. **Ambiance**) should not be ignored (Amphoux, 2002; Thomas, 2010), nor should we exclude the affective and cognitive relationship that links an individual to a space. The risk would then be to have an approach with a flow logic management [Link urban design] which considers the individual walker only as a vehicle and denies him as a sensitive being who belongs to the environment he perceives (Ittelson, 1973; Thibaud, 2008). It could, therefore, be harmful and incomplete not to consider the experience of walking in its multidimensionality.

The walkability of a space is, therefore, not limited to a set of physical criteria (which, nevertheless, represent – for some – a prerequisite for the practice of walking, for example the presence of a pavement or any space dedicated to pedestrian movements). The walkability of a space also depends on a set of subjective criteria linked to psychosocial processes of interpretation such as perception [Link] (Marchand & Pol, 2021) and/or individual/social representations which are involved in the emergence of the feeling of urban comfort [Link] (Roussel, 2016). In order not to be reduced to the assessment of physically measurable indicators, walkability must be analyzed through the prism of the individual's relationship to the space and all the psychosocial mechanisms at work in this relationship (Moser & Weiss, 2003).

Wayfinding – Sergi Valera

Wayfinding is an adaptive function which allows to move by the space in an easily and straightforward manner. That implies to know about where you are and what is your destination, to identify the best route for arriving – even, occasionally, the way to get back – as well as the recognition of the arrival point. Among others, wayfinding involves sensory processing, as well as environmental **perception** and cognition. Thus, spaces ought to provide information that facilitates understanding the place, how to orient yourself and take decisions about how to navigate by the environment. In a broad sense, wayfinding is viewed as the most common means of acquiring place knowledge (Golledge, 1992).

Some scholars such as Carpman and Grant (2002) view a successful wayfinding as an outgrowth of a 'wayfinding systems' composed of three types of elements:

– *Behavioral elements,* involving move toward destinations, follow paths, and use mental images or cognitive maps.

- *Design elements*, involving the presence of signs, landmarks, maps, lighting, or facility layouts.
- *Operational elements*, involving terminology, wayfinding training or wayfinding systems maintenance.

Moreover, Gärling et al. (1986) describe three characteristics of physical environments that affect wayfinding:

- *Degree of differentiation*. That is, the degree to which certain parts of the environment are perceived as equal or, on the contrary, have the property of distinguishing themselves from the rest.
- *Degree of visual access*. That is, the possibility that different parts of the environment can be seen and located from advantageous points (for example, watchtowers, places with a certain elevation or external points).
- *Complexity of the spatial distribution*. That is, the amount and difficulty of information that must be processed to move around an environment. Excessive complexity makes both navigation and spatial learning difficult.

You-are-here-maps

This is one of the most useful tools to facilitate wayfinding in complex environments. It is based on the triangulation between your own position and definite landmarks located in the map. However, on some occasions, the violation of a set of simple rules leads to confusion and inefficiency. These rules are (Levine, 1982):

- Optimal localisation for providing asymmetric perspective of the environment
- Structural matching, or correspondence between the environment and its map representation.
- Forward-up equivalence, in the case of a vertical placing.

Desire Lines

Humans have the ability to recognize environmental cues that lead to finding the best path for going from one place to another. However, in some cases, environmental design gets in conflict with natural wayfinding. In these cases, people tend to transgress the environmental layout and use their own obvious pathways. The term 'desire lines' derives from Gaston Bachelard's 'les chemins du désir', and it relies on the human basic need to get from one place to the next, promoting **walkability** (Furman, 2012).

Well-being – Barbara Bonnefoy

In psychology, well-being is used in both fields of health and the environment. The term 'well-being' has its philosophical roots in the teachings of ancient Greece: the hedonic and eudemonic traditions. In the hedonic tradition, the term 'well-being' is closely related to Epicurean views that the ultimate goal of life is to maximize pleasure – hedonia – and minimize pain (Waterman et al., 2008). In contrast, the Eudemonic view of the well-being derived from Aristotle's philosophy (The Nicomachean Ethics) captures the essence of the two great Greek imperatives: first, to know oneself, and second, to become what one is. The latter requires discerning one's unique talents (the *daimon* that resides within each of us) and then working to realize them. (Waterman et al., 2008). Although wellness research has tended to distinguish these traditions, there is, nonetheless, considerable overlap between the two.

Specifically, contemporary conceptualizations oriented to the hedonic view suggest that well-being is composed of two factors: an emotional component characterized by affective balance, and an evaluative component characterized by overall life satisfaction and satisfaction in specific and important life domains such as work, personal life or family life. Together, these two components are referred to as subjective well-being (Diener, 1984; Kahneman et al., 1999). Hedonic well-being consists of the pursuit of two elements: pleasure, that is, positive emotions, pleasant sensations and positive feelings; and **comfort**, such as relaxation, ease and freedom from pain. A hedonic orientation, therefore, consists of seeking what is subjectively pleasant.

Physiologically, hedonic well-being is a pleasurable physiological sensation caused by neurochemical responses in the dopaminergic system in response to external stimuli that have rewarding properties (e.g., food, drugs, sex or music) (Lachaux, 2013). Thus, people have a natural propensity to increase their happiness by experiencing stimuli that trigger the release of dopamine in the brain – the so-called reward system.

In the field of environmental studies, the notions of **quality of life**, **environmental satisfaction** and well-being are often synonymous (VanKamp et al., 2003), but they are conceptualized differently.

Modern conceptualizations of well-being based on eudemonia focus not only on attention to authenticity and personal excellence, but also on actions taken to actualize this potential. They focus more on the meaning of life, the essence of human nature and the deeper purposes of the person than on personal pleasure.

They also draw their history from the current of humanistic psychology initiated by Abraham Maslow (1968) and Carl Rogers (1961) in particular. Eudemonic theories situate well-being more in the process of working towards goals that are meaningful to the person than in the final affective and emotional states. From this perspective, well-being emerges from engagement in activities that lead to personal growth and development of one's potential (Waterman et al., 2008), rather than in the search for immediate pleasure. Carol Ryff (1989) and Martin Seligman (2002) offer interesting perspectives to consider a conceptualization of measurable indicators of this type of well-being. Carol Ryff characterizes eudemonic well-being through six fundamental and interrelated dimensions: autonomy, mastery of one's environment, personal growth, positive relationships with others, life goals and self-acceptance (Ryff, 2013). Autonomy emphasizes the qualities of independence, self-determination and self-regulation of self-actualizing individuals. Autonomy experienced by a person is also the ability to not seek approval from others, to possess personal opinions, to freely express one's opinions. The mastery of one's environment refers to the ability to choose or create environments adapted to one's psychological needs and reflects a kind of adequacy between the external and internal worlds of a person. More concretely, it can be not only about mastering one's time, but also about knowing how to arrange one's home or work space to feel comfortable. Personal growth is about self-realization and the fulfillment of one's personal potential. It is, therefore, a dynamic aspect of positive functioning that evolves continuously over time. The person seeks to learn new skills, to progress, to improve certain aspects of their personal life. Positive relationships with others concern all of a person's social relationships (family, friends, etc.). For example, it is a matter of developing empathy, meaningful and lasting friendships, supporting one's loved ones and feeling supported by others, loving and being loved. Life goals are what characterize the beliefs that give meaning to life. These beliefs evolve throughout life and allow us to give meaning to our lives. Finally, self-acceptance is experiencing a positive self-image, knowing one's limits and strengths.

The perspective envisaged by Seligman (2002) makes a distinction between the pleasant life – a life that successfully pursues positive emotions; the committed life (using one's strengths to carry out activities that make us feel good and obtain satisfaction) and the meaningful life (using one's strengths and virtues in the service of something much greater than oneself, a cause for example.) – and between the five components of well-being that allow for a happy life: positive emotions, commitment, meaning in life, positive relationships and personal fulfillment. Experiencing and seeking positive emotions is related to living well and hedonic well-being. Commitment refers more to the notion of flow developed by Csíkszentmihályi (1990), that is, a commitment to an activity that absorbs the person in a task, making him forget the passing of time and allowing him to excel in his abilities. Finding meaning in one's life, cultivating positive social relationships such as experiencing great love, feeling empathy, helping others and accomplishing oneself in one or more areas of one's life are other indicators of sustainable well-being.

Subjective well-being and eudemonic well-being, far from being in opposition, complement each other and offer a relatively rich conceptualization of well-being. These two aspects of well-being are particularly used in environmental psychology, which approaches a person's well-being through his or her **connection to nature** (Mayer & Frantz, 2004; Nisbet et al., 2011) and the restorative properties of the natural environments that he or she inhabits and travels through (Kaplan, 1995), particularly because restorative environments reduce **stress** and restore people's attentional capacities (cf. **TRS**).

Another angle that approaches well-being is also related with **comfort** of spaces (habitat, workplace, institutional spaces, public transport etc.). The places we frequent and inhabit, whether built or natural, are closely related to human well-being. Finally, on a global scale, the notion of well-being is an interesting indicator to evaluate the state of health of a nation, to promote sustainable global development. Health and well-being are, indeed, one of the 17 goals supported by the United Nations for sustainable world development.

Various scales have been developed to measure each of the proposed concepts. Some of the most popular in the study of well-being are the Positive and Negative Affective Schedule (PANAS, Watson & Clark, 1999), the Satisfaction With Life Scale (SWLS, Diener, 1984), the Psychological Well-being Scale (PWS, Ryff, 1989).

Work Environment – Eva Moffat

Work environments are spaces in which workers accomplish their missions, develop formal or informal social relationships and thus experience a greater or lesser level of satisfaction. They are individual and social territories in which work is carried out and experienced (Moffat, 2016).

Previously focused on the workstation, our conception of the work environment has gradually evolved over the years, as it has always been strongly influenced by the development of science and technology. Today, the work environment is not limited to the frontiers of the organization, but involves larger areas such as the district, the city and/or the international space (Moffat et al., 2016). In this way, we consider the work environment as a system composed of four interacting environments (workstation, office or production space, work space and district) within a local, national or international context (from Moffat, 2016):

- *Workstation*. This is the space closest to the employee, the one in which the person has the material resources to do his/her work. It is the space in which the employee spends most time.
- *Office space*. From the individual office to the open space, office spaces have been deeply modified by work practices arising from the emergence of NTIC. Currently, several types of office layouts can coexist, depending on the sector of activity. Whatever the type of office space, it remains a space inhabited, occupied and experienced by the person who works there (NippertEng, 1996).
- *Work space*. This includes the workstation and the office space but also formal spaces, informal social spaces, and circulation spaces.

- *District.* By locating in a district, a company marks it, shapes it and gives it a visible identity in space. Indeed, the district often develops by creating green spaces or transportation infrastructures, for example. Shops can also be set up.
- *The city.* Many cities support organizations in their economy, management, and employee mobility. For example, Nantes Métropole is developing the use of sustainable modes of transportation such as public transport, carpooling and cycling for work or home-to-work trips.
- *The region.* The region is the seventh of the concentric zones that Moles and Rohmer (1978) called 'man's shell'. It participates in the development of the working environment of companies located in its area. For example, the 'Grand Paris' is a development project for Paris and its agglomeration, which will involve the expertise of organizations and stimulate employment, integration and training.
- *The world.* In France, many laws have influenced the organizational spaces of companies. One example is the anti-smoking law, which came into effect on February 1, 2007, banning smoking in the different spaces of the company.

At the international level, the United Nations also participates in the development of Moles' final 'shell' with its sustainable development objectives: facilitating economic development, cooperation in international law, international security, human rights, social and human progress, within a context of world peace.

References

Abrahamse, W., & Matthies, E. (2018). Informational strategies to promote pro-environmental behaviour: Changing knowledge, awareness, and attitudes. *In* L. Steg & J.I.M. de Groot (Eds.), *Environmental psychology: An introduction* (pp. 261–272). New York: Wiley.

Abric, J.C. (1994). *Pratiques sociales et représentations.* Paris: Presses Universitaires de France.

Acredolo, L.P. (1978). Development of spatial orientation in infancy. *Developmental Psychology, 14*(3), 224–234.

Adger, W.N. (2006). Vulnerability. *Global Environmental Change, 16*(3), 268–281.

Aizlewood, C.E., Raw, G.J., & Oseland, N.A. (1996). Decipols: Should we use them? *Indoor & Built Environment, 5*, 263–269.

Ajdukovic, I., Gilibert, D., & Labbouz, D. (2014). Confort au travail: Le rôle de l'attachement et de la personnalisation dans la perception de la qualité de l'espace de travail. *PTO, 20*(3), 311–327.

Albrecht, G. (2007). Solastalgia: the distress caused by environmental change. *Australasian Psychiatry, 15*, S95–S98.

Aldhuy, J. (2003). Identité, catégorisation socio-spatiale et mobilité: être urbain et se penser rural? *Travaux de l'Institut Géographique de Reims, 115*, 45–58.

Alihan, M.A. (1938). *Social ecology: A critical analysis.* New York: Cooper Square Publishers, Inc.

Altman, I. (1975). *The environment and social behavior privacy personal space, territories, crowding.* Monterey: Brooks Cole.

Altman, I., & Low, S.M. (Eds.) (1992). *Place attachment.* New York: Plenum Press.

Altman, I., & Rogoff, B. (1987). World views in psychology: trait, interactional, organismic, and transactional perspectives. *In* D. Stokols & I. Altman (Eds.), *Handbook of environmental psychology* (pp. 7–40). New York: Wiley.

Ambiente Italia Research Institute (2003). *European common indicators: Towards a local sustainability profile. Final project report.* Milano (Italy): Ambiente Italia Research Institute.

Amérigo, M. (2009). Concepciones del ser humano y la naturaleza desde el antropocentrismo y el biosferismo (Conceptions of the human being and nature from anthropocentrism and biosphereism). *Medio Ambiente y Comportamiento Humano, 10*, 217–234.

Amérigo, M., Aragonés, J.I., Sevillano, V., & Cortés, B. (2005). La estructura de las creencias sobre la problemática medioambiental (The structure of beliefs about environmental issues). *Psicothema, 17*, 257–262.

Amphoux, P. (2002). Ambiance et conception: De l'analyse des ambiances à la conception architecturale et urbaine. *Conférence internationale Herbert Simon, Sciences de l'ingénierie, sciences de la conception.* Actes du colloque du 15–16 mars 2002. Lyon.

Andersson, E., & McPhearson, T. (2018). Making sense of biodiversity: The affordances of systems ecology. *Frontiers in Psychology, 9*, 594.

Andrade, C., Lima, L., Fornara F., & Bonaiuto, M. (2012). Users' views of hospital environmental quality: Validation of the Perceived Hospital Environment Quality Indicators (PHEQIs). *Journal of Environmental Psychology, 32*, 97–111.

Antilla, L. (2005). Climate of scepticism: US newspaper coverage of the science of climate change. *Global Environmental Change, 15*(4), 338–352.

Appleyard, D. (1970). Styles and methods of structuring a city. *Environment and Behavior, 2*, 100–116.

Apostolidis, T., & Fieulaine, N. (2004). Validation française de l'échelle de temporalité The Zimbardo Time Perspective Inventory. *European Review of Applied Psychology, 54*, 207–217.

Arciszewski, T., & Drozda-Senkowska, E. (2006). Du risque à la menace environnementale: lorsque prévoir rime avec croire. *In* K. Weiss & D. Marchand (Eds.), *Psychologie sociale de l'environnement* (pp. 205–214). Rennes: PUR.

Arisidis, A., Karaletsou, C., & Tsoukala, K. (1992). *Socio-environmental Metamorphoses.* Proceedings 12th International Conference of the IAPS, Chalkidiki, Greece.

Arnocky, S., Stroink, M., & DeCicco, T. (2007). Self-construal predicts environmental concern, cooperation, and conservation. *Journal of Environmental Psychology, 27*, 255–264.

Arruda, A., & de Alba, M. (2007) *Espacios imaginarios y representaciones sociales. Aportes desde Latinoamerica.* Mexico: Anthropos.

Attia, M., Engel, P., & Hildebrandt, G. (1980). Quantification of thermal comfort parameters using a behavioural indicator. *Physiology et Behavior, 24*(5), 901–909.

Augé, M. (1994). *Pour une anthropologie des mondes contemporains.* Paris: Aubier.

Augoyard, J.F. (1979). *Pas à pas. Essai sur le cheminement urbain.* Paris: Éditions du Seuil.

Bachelard, G. (1958). *La poétique de l'espace.* Paris: PUF.

Bailly, E., & Marchand, D. (2019). *Penser la qualité: la ville résiliente résilience et sensible.* Bruxelles: Mardaga.

Bailly, E., & Marchand, D. (2021). *Ville numérique, la qualité urbaine en question.* Bruxelles: Mardaga.

Balundė, A., Jovarauskaitė, L., & Poškus, M.S. (2019). Exploring the relationship between connectedness with nature, environmental identity, and environmental self-identity: A systematic review and meta-analysis. *SAGE Open, 9*(2). https://doi.org/10.1177/2158244019841925

Balundė, A., Perlaviciute, G., & Steg, L. (2019). The relationship between people's environmental considerations and pro-environmental behavior in Lithuania. *Frontiers in Psychology, 10*, 2319.

Bamberg, S. (2013). Applying the stage model of self-regulated behavioral change in a car use reduction intervention. *Journal of Environmental Psychology, 33*, 68–75.

Bamberg, S., & Möser, G. (2007). Twenty years after Hines, Hungerford, and Tomera: A new meta-analysis of psycho-social determinants of pro-environmental behaviour. *Journal of Environmental Psychology, 27*(1), 14–25.

Barker, R.G. (1968). *Ecological psychology. Concepts and methods for studying the environment of human behavior.* Stanford, CA: Stanford University Press.

Barker, R.G. (1969). Wanted: An eco-behavioral science. *In* E.P. Willems & H.L. Raush (Eds.) *Naturalistic viewpoints in psychological research* (pp. 31–43). New York: Holt, Rinehart & Winston.

Barker, R.G. (1978). *Habitats, environments, and human behavior. Studies in ecological and ecobehavioral science from Midwest Psychological Field Station 1947–1972*. San Francisco, CA: Jossey Bass.

Barker, R.G., & Gump, P.V. (1964). *Big school, small school: High school size and student behavior*. Stanford, CA: Stanford University Press.

Barker, R.G., & Schoggen, P. (1973). *Qualities of community life: Methods of measuring environment and behavior applied to an American and an English town*. San Francisco: Jossey-Bass.

Barker, R.G., & Wright, H.F. (1949). Psychological ecology and the problem of psychosocial development. *Child Development, 20,* 131–143.

Barker, R.G., & Wright, H.F. (1955). *Midwest and its children*. New York: Row, Peterson and Company.

Barrera-Hernández, L.F., Sotelo-Castillo, M.A., Echeverría-Castro, S.B., & Tapia-Fonllem, C.O. (2020). Connectedness to nature: Its impact on sustainable behaviors and happiness in children. *Frontiers in Psychology, 11,* 276.

Barthe, Y. (2010). Le syndrome du bâtiment malsain: un problème de santé mentale? *Le concours médical, 132*(9), 9–10.

Barthe, Y., & Jouzel, J.N. (2005). Risque, incertitude et pacification des conflits. *In* C. Lahellec (Ed.), *Risques et crises alimentaires* (pp. 207–216). Paris: Tec & Doc.

Barthes, R. (1967). Sémiologie et Urbanisme. *In* R. Barthes (Ed.), *L'aventure sémiologique* (pp. 261–272). Paris: Seuil.

Bassand, M., & Brulhardt, M.C. (1980). *Mobilité spatiale. Bilan et analyse des recherches en Suisse*. Saint-Saphorin: Georgi.

Bassili, J.N., & Brown, R.D. (2005). Implicit and explicit attitudes: Research, challenges, and theory. *In* D. Albaracín, B.T. Johnson, & M.P. Zanna (Eds.), *The handbook of attitudes* (pp. 543–574). Mahwah, NJ: Erlbaum.

Batel, S. (2020). Research on the social acceptance of renewable energy technologies: Past, present and future. *Energy Research & Social Science, 68,* 101544.

Batel, S., Castro, P., Devine-wright, P., & Howarth, C. (2016). Developing a critical agenda to understand pro-environmental actions: contributions from Social Representations and Social Practices Theories. *Wiley Interdisciplinary Reviews: Climate Change,* 7(5), 727–745.

Batel, S., & Devine-Wright, P. (2020). Using NIMBY rhetoric as a political resource to negotiate responses to local energy infrastructure: A power line case study. *Local Environment: The International Journal of Justice and Sustainability, 25*(5), 338–350.

Batel, S., Devine-Wright, P., Wold, L., Egeland, H., Jacobsen, G., & Aas, O. (2015). The role of (de)essentialisation within siting conflicts: An interdisciplinary approach. *Journal of Environmental Psychology, 44,* 149–159.

Baum, A., Aiello, J.R., & Calesnick, L.E. (1978). Crowding and personal control: Social density and the development of learned helplessness. *Journal of Personality and Social Psychology, 36*(9), 1000–1011.

Becker, E., & Jahn, T. (2006). *Social ecology: Outlines of a science of social relationships with nature*. Frankfurt: Campus.

Bell, S.L., Foley, R., Houghton, F., Maddrell, A., & Williams, A.M. (2018). From therapeutic landscapes to healthy spaces, places and practices: A scoping review. *Social Sciences and Medicine, 196,* 123–130.

Bergquist, M., Nilsson, A., & Schultz, P.W. (2019). A meta-analysis of field-experiments using social norms to promote pro-environmental behaviors. *Global Environmental Change, 59,* 101941.

Bernardi, N., & Kowaltowski, D.C. (2006). Environmental comfort in school buildings: A case study of awareness and participation of users. *Environment and Behavior, 38*(2), 155–172.

Bernstein, J., & Szuster, B.W. (2018). The new environmental paradigm scale: Reassessing the operationalization of contemporary environmentalism. *The Journal of Environmental Education, 50*(2), 73–83. https://doi.org/10.1080/00958964.2018.1512946

Bertalanffy, L.V. (1950). The theory of open systems in physics and biology. *Science, 111,* 23–29.

Berthoz, A. (1991). Reference frames for the perception and control of movement. *In* J. Paillard (Ed.), *Brain and space* (pp. 81–111). Oxford: Oxford University Press.

Bertoldo, R., Mays, C., Böhm, G., Poortinga, W., Poumadère, M., Tvinnereim, E., Arnold, A., Steentjes, K., & Pidgeon, N. (2019). Scientific truth or debate: On the link between perceived scientific consensus and belief in anthropogenic climate change. *Public Understanding of Science, 28*(7), 778–796.

Bertoldo, R., Poumadère, M., & Rodrigues, L.C. (2015). When meters start to talk: The public's encounter with smart meters in France. *Energy Research and Social Science, 9,* 146–156.

Bethelmy, L.C., & Corraliza, J.A. (2019). Transcendence and sublime experience in nature: Awe and inspiring energy. *Frontiers in Psychology, 10,* 509.

Bettencourt, L., & Castro, P. (2015). Diversity in the maps of a Lisbon neighbourhood: Community and 'official' discourses about the renewed Mouraria. *Culture and Local Governance / Culture et gouvernance locale, 5*(1–2), 23–44.

Bilotta, E., Ariccio, S., Leone, L., & Bonaiuto, M. (2019). The cumulative risk model to encompass perceived urban safety and well-being. *Visions for Sustainability, 11,* 68–82.

Bilotta, E., Vaid, U., & Evans, G.W. (2019). Environmental stress. *In* L. Steg & J.I.M. de Groot (Eds.). *Environmental psychology* (pp. 36–44). London: BPS Blackwell.

Binder, A. (1972). A new context for psychology: Social ecology. *American Psychologist, 27,* 903–908.

Birkinshaw, J., Foss, N., & Lindenberg, S. (2014). Combining purpose with profits: How to make your pro-social goals pay. *MIT Sloan Management Review, 55*(3), 48–56.

Blanc, N., Emelianoff, C., & Rochard, H. (2022). *Réparer la Terre par le bas. Manifeste pour un environnementalisme ordinaire.* Paris: Le Bord de l'eau.

Blesius, J.C. (2013). Discours sur la culture du risque, entre approches négative et positive. Vers une éducation aux risques? Etude comparée du Québec et de la France. *Géographie et cultures, 88,* 249–265.

Bogan, W.J. (1973). Environmental education redefined. *The Journal of Environmental Education, 4*(4), 1–3.

Bogner, F.X., & Wiseman, M. (1999). Towards measuring adolescent environmental perception. *European Psychologist, 4,* 139–151.

Böhm, G., & Tanner (2019), Environmental risk perception. *In* L. Steg & J.I.M. de Groot (Eds.), *Environmental psychology: An introduction* (pp. 15–25). Hoboken, NJ: Wiley & Sons Ltd.

Bonaiuto, M., Aiello, A., Perugini, M., Bonnes, M., & Ercolani, A.P. (1999). Multi-dimensional perception of residential environment quality and neighbourhood attachment in the urban environment. *Journal of Environmental Psychology, 19,* 331–352.

Bonaiuto, M., & Alves, S. (2012). Residential places and neighborhoods: Toward healthy life, social integration, and reputable residence. *In* S.D. Clayton (Ed.), *The Oxford handbook of environmental and conservation psychology* (pp. 221–247). New York: Oxford University Press.

Bonaiuto, M., Alves, S., De Dominicis, S., & Petruccelli, I. (2016). Place attachment and natural hazard risk: Research review and agenda. *Journal of Environmental Psychology, 48,* 33–53.

Bonaiuto, M., Ariccio, S., Fornara, F., Piccinin, G., & Lizzani, G. (2019). La valutazione post-occupativa in un intervento di riqualificazione di edilizia residenziale pubblica a Roma: soddisfazione residenziale e relazione con l'ente gestore. *In* P.V. Dell'Aira & P. Guarini (Eds.), *Residenza pubblica. Condivisione identitaria. Esperienze di recupero dell'abitazione sociale* (pp. 72–79). Macerata: Quodlibet.

Bonaiuto, M., Bonnes, M., & Continisio, M. (2004). Neighborhood evaluation within a multi-place perspective on urban activities. *Environment and Behavior, 36,* 41–69.

Bonaiuto, M., Breakwell, G.M., & Cano, I. (1996). Identity processes and environmental threat: the effects of nationalism and local identity upon perception of beach pollution. *Journal of Community & Applied Social Psychology, 6*(3), 157–175.

Bonaiuto, M., & Fornara, F. (2017). Residential satisfaction and perceived urban quality. *In* J. Stein (Ed.), *Reference module in neuroscience and biobehavioral psychology* (pp. 1–5). Oxford: Elsevier.

Bonaiuto, M., Fornara, F., Alves, S., Ferreira, I., Mao, Y., Moffat, E., Piccinin, G., & Rahimi, L. (2015). Urban environment and well-being: cross-cultural studies on Perceived Residential Environment Quality Indicators (PREQIs). *Cognitive Processing, 16,* 165–169.

Bonaiuto, M., Fornara, F., Ariccio, S., Ganucci Cancellieri, U., & Rahimi, L. (2015). Perceived Residential Environment Quality Indicators (PREQIs) relevance for UN-HABITAT City Prosperity Index (CPI). *Habitat International, 45,* 53–63.

Bonaiuto, M., Mao, Y., Roberts, S., Psalti, A., Ariccio, S., Ganucci Cancellieri, U., & Csikszentmihalyi, M. (2016). Optimal experience and personal growth: Flow and the consolidation of place identity. *Frontiers in Psychology, 7,* 1654.

Bonnefoy, B. (2007). Les odeurs de la ville. *Villes en Parallèle, 28*(1), 124–139.

Bonnefoy, B., Demarque, C., le Conte, J., & Feliot-Rippeault, M. (2014). Penser globalement, agir localement. Comment les distances spatiales et temporelles modulent notre relation à l'environnement. *In* K. Weiss, D. Marchand, & S. Depeau (Eds.), *L'individu au risque de l'environnement* (pp. 245–269). Paris: InPress.

Bonnes, M., & Bonaiuto, M. (1995). Expert and layperson evaluation of urban environmental quality: The 'natural' versus the 'built' environment. *In* Y. Guerrier, N. Alexander, J. Chase, & M. O'Brien (Eds.), *Values and the environment: A social science perspective* (pp. 151–163). New York: Wiley.

Bonnes, M., & Bonaiuto, M. (2002). Environmental psychology: From spatial-physical environment to sustainable development. *In* R.B. Bechtel & A. Churchman (Eds.), *Handbook of environmental psychology* (pp. 28–54). New York: Wiley.

Bonnes, M., Bonaiuto, M., Metastasio, R., Aiello, A., & Sensales, G. (1997). Environmental discourse and ecological responsability in media communication in

Italy. *In* R. García-Mira, C. Arce, & J.M. Sabucedo (Eds.), *Responsabilidad ecológica y gestión de los recursos ambientales* (Ecological responsibility and management of environmental resources) (pp. 99–135). A Coruña: Diputación Provincial de A Coruña.

Bonnes, M., & Secchiaroli, G. (1992). *Psicologia ambientale: introduzione alla psicologia sociale dell'ambiente*. Venezia: Nuova Italia Scientifica.

Bonnes, M., & Secchiaroli, G. (1995). *Environmental Psychology, a psycho-social introduction*. London: Sage.

Bookchin, M. (1996). *The philosophy of social ecology: Essays on dialectical naturalism*. Montreal, CA: Black Rose Books.

Borja, S., Courty, G., & Ramadier, T. (2015). Les mobiles sont-ils tous mobiles? Critiques et questions autour de la mobilité et de son capital. *In* V. Kaufman, E. Ravalet, & E. Dupuit (Eds.), *Mobilité et motilité: mode d'emploi* (pp. 197–243). Neûchatel: Éditions Alphil - Presses universitaires suisses.

Borraz, O. (2008). *Les politiques du risque*. Paris: Les presses de Sciences Po.

Bottero, M., Caprioli, C., Cotella, G., & Santangelo, M. (2019). Sustainable cities: A reflection on potentialities and limits based on existing eco-districts in Europe. *Sustainability, 11*(20), 5794.

Bouman, T., van der Werff, E., Perlaviciute, G., & Steg, L. (2021). Environmental values and identities at the personal and group level. *Current Opinion in Behavioral Sciences, 42*, 47–53.

Bourdieu, P. (1979). *La distinction*. Paris: Les Editions de Minuit.

Bourdieu P. (1980). *Le sens pratique*. Paris: Editions de Minuit.

Bourdieu, P. (1993). *La misère du monde*. Paris: Seuil.

Bourg, D., Joly, P.B., & Kaufmann, A. (Eds.) (2013). *Du risque à la menace, penser la catastrophe*. Paris: PUF.

Boykoff, M.T., & Boykoff, J.M. (2007). Climate change and journalistic norms: A case-study of US mass-media coverage. *Geoforum, 38*, 1190–1204.

Brancalion, P.H.S., Broadbent, E.N., De-Miguel, S., Cardil, A., Rosa, M.R., Almeida, C.T., Almeida, D.R.A., Chakravarty, S., Zhou, M., Gamarra, J.G.P., Liang, J., Crouzeilles, R., Hérault, B., Aragão, L.E.O.C., Silva, C.A., & Almeyda-Zambrano, A.M. (2020). Emerging threats linking tropical deforestation and the COVID-19 pandemic. *Perspectives in Ecology and Conservation, 18*(4), 243–246.

Breakwell, G.M. (Ed.) (1992). *Social psychology of identity and self-concept*. Surrey: Surrey University Press.

Brinkman, I. (2009). Landscape and Nostalgia: Angolan refugees in Namibia remembering home and forced removals. *In* M. Bollig & O. Bubenzer (Eds.), *African landscapes: Interdisciplinary approaches* (pp. 275–294). New York: Springer.

Broadbent, G. (1980). *Signs, Symbols and Architecture*. London: John Wiley & Sons.

Bronfenbrenner, U. (1974). The origins of alienation. *Scientific American, 231*(2), 53–61.

Bronfenbrenner, U. (1977a). Lewinian space and ecological substance. *Journal of social sciences, 32*, 513–531.

Bronfenbrenner, U. (1977b). Toward an experimental ecology of human development. *American Psychologist, 32*, 513–531.

Bronfenbrenner, U. (1979). *The ecology of human development: Experiments by nature and design*. Cambridge, MA and London: Harvard University Press.

Bronfenbrenner, U. (1986). Ecology of the family as a context for human development: Research perspectives. *Developmental Psychology, 22*, 723–742.

Bronfenbrenner, U. (1993). The ecology of cognitive development: Research models and fugitive findings. *In* R. Wonziak & K. Fischer (Eds.), *Development in context: Acting and thinking in specific environments* (pp. 3–44). Hillsdale, NJ: Erlbaum.

Bronfenbrenner, U., & Morris, P.A. (1998). The ecology of developmental processes. *In* W. Damon & R.M. Lerner (Eds.), *Handbook of child psychology, Vol. 1: Theoretical models of human development* (5th ed., pp. 993–1023). New York: Wiley.

Bronfenbrenner, U., & Morris, P.A. (2006). The bioecological model of human development. *In* W. Damon & R.M. Lerner (Eds.), *Handbook of child psychology, Vol. 1: Theoretical models of human development* (6th ed., pp. 793–828). New York: Wiley.

Brower, S. (1980). Territory in urban settings. *In* I. Altman, A. Rapoport, & J.F. Wohwill (Eds.), *Culture and environment* (pp. 179–207). New York: Plenum Press.

Brown, B.B., Werner, C.M., Amburgey, J.W., & Szalay, C. (2007). Walkable route perceptions and physical features: Converging evidence for en route walking experiences. *Environment and Behavior, 39*(1), 34–61.

Brown, S.D., & Middelton, D. (2008). La mémoire et l'espace dans les travaux de Maurice Halbwachs. *In* A. Arruda, B. Madiot, & E. Lage (Eds.), *Une approche engagée en psychologie sociale. L'œuvre de Denise Jodelet* (pp. 147–172). Saint Agde: Erès.

Brown, T., Keane, T., & Kaplan, S. (1986). Aesthetics and management: bridging the gap. *Landscape and Urban Planning, 13*, 1–10.

Brundtland, G.H. (1987). *Our common future.* Oxford: Oxford University Press.

Brunswik, E. (1943). Organismic achievement and environmental probability. *Psychological Review, 50*(3), 255–272.

Bullard, R. D. (1990). *Dumping in Dixie: Race, class, and environmental quality.* Boulder, CO: Westview PressBulletin d'épidémiologie hebdomadaire (2007). *Les syndromes psychogènes: connaissances acquises et études de cas, 15–16,* 24 avril 2007.

Burgess, E.W. (1925). The growth of the City: An introduction to a research project. *In* R. Park et al. (Eds.), *The City* (pp. 35–41). Chicago: University of Chicago Press.

Burningham, K. (2000). Using the language of NIMBY: A topic for research not an activity for researchers. *Local Environment, 5,* 55–67.

Büscher, M., Urry, J., & Witchger, K. (2011) *Mobile methods.* London: Routledge.

Callon, M., Lascoumes, P., & Barthe, Y. (2001). *Agir dans un monde incertain. Essai sur la démocratie technique.* Paris: Le seuil.

Campbell-Sills, L., & Stein, M.B. (2007), Psychometric Analysis and Refinement of the Connor-Davidson Resilience Scale (CD-RISC): Validation of a 10-item measure of resilience. *Journal of Traumatic Stress, 20*(6), 1019–1028.

Canter, D. (1970) (Ed.). *Architectural psychology: proceedings of the Dalandhui conference 1969.* London: RIBA Publications.

Canter, D. (1974a) (Ed.). *A short course in architectural psychology.* Sydney: Architectural Psychology Research Unit, University of Sydney.

Canter, D. (1974b). *Psychology for Architects.* London: Applied Science.

Canter, D. (1977). *The Psychology of Place.* London: Architectural Press.

Canter, D., & Lee, T. (1974) (Eds.). *Psychology and the Built Environment.* London: Architectural Press.

do Canto, N.R., Grunert, K.G., & de Barcellos, M.D. (2022). Goal-framing theory in environmental behaviours: review, future research agenda and possible applications in behavioural change. *Journal of Social Marketing.* DOI 10.1108/JSOCM-03-2021-0058

Capaldi, C.A., Dopko, R.L., & Zelenski, J.M. (2014). The relationship between nature connectedness and happiness: A meta-analysis. *Frontiers in Psychology, 5,* 976.

Capstick, S., Whitmarsh, L., Poortinga, W., Pidgeon, N., & Upham, P. (2015). International trends in public perceptions of climate change over the past quarter century. *Climate Change, 6*(1), 35–61.

Carpman, J.R., & Grant, M.A. (2002). Wayfinding: A broad view. *In* R. Bechtel & A. Churchman (Eds.), *Handbook of Environmental Psychology* (pp. 427–442). New York: Wiley.

Carson, R. (1962, réédition 2002). *Silent spring.* Boston, MA: Houghton Mifflin.

Casal, A. (2006). *Usines d'assainissement des eaux et phénomène Nimby: les conditions environnementales, sociales et individuelles de l'acceptabilité.* Thèse de doctorat, Université Paris Descartes.

Casal, A., & Devine-Wright, P. (2014). Du Nimby à l'acceptation des ouvrages favorables à l'environnement. *In* D. Marchand, S. Depeau, & K. Weiss (Eds.), *L'individu au risque de l'Environnement* (pp. 321–345). Paris: InPress.

Castello, L. (2010). *Rethinking the meaning of place. Conceiving place in architecture-urbanism.* London: Routledge.

Castells, M. (1996). *The Rise of the Network Society, The Information Age: Economy, Society and Culture (Vol. 1).* Oxford: Blackwell.

Castrechini, A., Pol, E., & Guàrdia-Olmos, J. (2014). Media representations of environmental issues: From scientific to political discourse. *European Review of Applied Psychology, 64*(5), 213–220.

Castro, P. (2021). A dynamic view of local knowledge and epistemic bonds to place: Implications for senses of place and the governance of biodiversity conservation. *In* C.M. Raymond, L.C. Manzo, D.R. Williams, A. Di Masso & T. von Wirth (Eds.), *Changing sense of places: Navigating global challenges* (pp. 259–270). Cambridge: Cambridge University Press. http://dx.doi.org/10.1017/9781108769471.023

Castro, P., Batel, S., Devine-Wright, H., Kronberger, N., Mouro, C., Weiss, K., & Wagner, W. (2010). Redesigning nature and managing risk: Social representation, change and resistance. *In* A. Abdel-Hadi, M. Tolman, & S. Soliman (Eds.), *Environment, health and sustainable development* (pp. 227–241). Göttingen: Hogrefe & Huber.

Cervinka, R., Röderer, K., & Hefler, E. (2012). Are nature lovers happy? On various indicators of well-being and connectedness with nature. *Jounral of Health Psychology, 17*(3), 379–388.

Chateauraynaud, F., & Torny, D. (1999). *Les sombres précurseurs. Une sociologie pragmatique de l'alerte et du risque.* Paris: Éditions EHESS.

Chelkoff, G., Thibaud, J.P., Bardyn, J.L., Belchun, & B., Leroux, M. (1997). *Ambiances sous la ville: une approche écologique des espaces publics souterrains.* Grenoble: CRESSON, Plan Urbain.

Cheshire, J. (2021). Why eye-catching graphics are vital for getting to grips with climate change. *The conversation,* https://theconversation.com/why-eye-catching-graphics-are-vital-for-getting-to-grips-with-climate-change-165983

Choay, F. (2006) *Pour une anthropologie de l'espace.* Paris: Seuil.

Chombart de Lauwe, P. (1976). Appropriation of space and social change. *In* P. Korosec-Serfaty (Ed.), *Appropriation of space. Proceedings of the Strasbourg International Architectural Psychology Conference (IAPC)* (pp. 23–77). Louvain-La-Neuve: CIACO.

Chwialkowska, A. (2019). How sustainability influencers drive green lifestyle adoption on social media: The process of green lifestyle adoption explained through the lenses of the minority influence model and social learning theory. *Management of Sustainable Development Sibiu, 11*(1), 33–42.

Cialdini, R.B., Reno, R.R., & Kallgren, C.A. (1990). A focus theory of normative conduct: Recycling the concept of norms to reduce littering in public places. *Journal of Personality and Social Psychology, 58*(6), 1015.

Clayton, S. (2020). Climate anxiety: Psychological responses to climate change. *Journal of Anxiety Disorders, 74*, 102263.

Clayton, S., Devine-Wright, P., Stern, P., Whitmarsh, L., Carrico, A.R., Steg, L., Swim, J., & Bonnes, M. (2015). Psychological research and global climate change. *Nature Climate Change 5*, 640–646. https://doi.org/10.1038/nclimate2622

Clayton, S., Devine-Wright, P., Swim, J., Bonnes, M., Steg, L., Whitmarsh, L., & Carrico, A. (2016). Expanding the role for psychology in addressing environmental challenges. *American Psychologist, 71*(3), 199–215.

Clayton, S., & Karazsia, B.T. (2020). Development and validation of a measure of climate change anxiety. *Journal of Environmenal Psychology, 69*, 101434.

Clayton, S., & Myers, G. (2015). *Conservation psychology: Understanding and promoting human care for nature.* (2nd ed.). Oxford: Blackwell.

CoE, (2016). *Council of Europe landscape convention.* Strasbourg: Council of Europe Treaty Office.

Coffey, Y., Bhullar, N., Durkin, J., Islam, M.S., & Usher, K. (2021). Understanding eco-anxiety: A systematic scoping review of current literature and identified knowledge gaps. *The Journal of Climate Change and Health, 3*, 100047.

Cohen, S. (1980). Aftereffects of stress on human performance and social behavior: A review of research and theory. *Psychological Bulletin, 88*, 82–108.

Cohen, S., Evans, G.W., Krantz, D.S., & Stokols, D. (1986). *Behavior, health, and environmental stress.* New York: Plenum.

Cohen, S., Kessler, R.C., & Gordon, L. (Eds.). (1995). *Measuring stress.* New York: Oxford University Press.

Collado, S., Staats, H., & Corraliza, J.A. (2013). Experiencing nature in children's summer camps: Affective, cognitive and behavioural consequences. *Journal of Environmental Psychology, 33*, 37–44.

Collins, C.M., & Chambers, S.M. (2005). Psychological and situational influences on commuter-transport-mode choice. *Environment and Behavior, 37*(5), 640–661.

Comelli, T., Anguelovski, I., & Chu, E. (2018). Socio-spatial legibility, discipline, and gentrification through favela upgrading in Rio de Janeiro. *City, 22*(5–6), 633–656.

Connor, K.M., & Davidson, J.R.T. (2003). Development of a new resilience scale: The Connor–Davidson Resilience Scale (CDRISC). *Depression and Anxiety, 18*, 76–82.

Contrada, R.J., & Baum, A. (Eds.). (2011). *The handbook of stress science.* New York: Springer.

Convention on Biological Diversity (1992). Available at https://www.cbd.int/convention/text/

Coombs, T. (2015). What equivocality teaches us about crisis what equivocality teaches us. *Journal of Contingencies and Crisis Managament, 23*(3), 125–128.

Cordoza, M., Ulrich, R.S., Manulik, B.J., Gardiner, S.K., Fitzpatrick, P.S., Hazen, T., & Perkins, R.S. (2018). Impact of nurses taking daily work breaks in a hospital garden on burnout. *American Journal of Critical Care, 27*(6), 509–512.

Corral-Verdugo, V., Corral-Frías, N., Frías, M., Lucas, M.Y., & Peña, E. (2021). Positive environments and precautionary behaviors during the COVID-19 outbreak. *Frontiers in Psychology, 12*, 624155.

Corral-Verdugo, V., Pato, C., & Torres, N. (2021). Testing a tridimensional model of sustainable behavior: Self-care, caring for others and caring for the planet. *Environment, Development, and Sustainability, 23*, 12867–12882.

Courant, F., Biscay, J.F., Boutillet, D., Rizza, C., Simoné, M., Vinet, F., & Weiss, K. (2021). *Mission sur la transparence, l'information et la participation de tous à la gestion des risques majeurs, technologiques ou naturels.* Paris: Ministère de la Transition Ecologique.

Cowell, R., & Devine-Wright, P. (2018). A 'delivery-democracy dilemma'? Mapping and explaining policy change for public engagement with energy infrastructure. *Journal of Environmental Policy and Planning, 20*(4), 499–517.

Cox, R. (2013). *Environmental communication and the public sphere.* London: Sage.

Cox, R., & Depoe, S. (2015). Emergence and growth of the "field" of environmental communication. *In* A. Hansen, & R. Cox (Eds.), *The Routledge handbook of environment and communication* (pp. 33–45). London: Routledge.

Craik, K., & Feimer, N. (1987). Environmental assessment. *In* D. Stokols & I. Altman (Eds.), *Handbook of Environmental Psychology, vol. 2* (pp. 891–918). New York: Wiley.

Craik, K., & Zube, F. (Eds.) (1976). *Perceiving environmental quality: Research and applications.* New York: Plenum Press.

Crasson, M. (2005). L'hypersensibilité à l'électricité: une approche multidisciplinaire pour un problème multifactoriel. *Revue européenne de psychologie appliquée, 55*, 51–67.

Crocq, L., Huberson, S., & Vraie, B. (2009). *Gérer les grandes crises sanitaires, économiques, politiques et économiques.* Paris: Odile Jacob.

Csíkszentmihályi, M. (1990). The psychology of optimal expérience. *Journal of Leisure Research, 24*(1), 93–94.

d'Arienzo, R., & Younès, C. (Eds.) (2018). *Synergies urbaines: pour un métabolisme collectif des villes.* Genève: MetisPresses.

Daniel, T.C., & Boster, R.S. (1976). *Measuring landscape aesthetics: The scenic beauty estimation method. USDA Forest Service Research Paper RM-167.* Fort Collins, CO: Rocky Mountain and Range Experiment Station.

Darwin, C. (1859). *On the origin of species by means of natural selection.* London: John Murray.

Dautun, C. (2007). *Contribution à l'étude des crises de grande ampleur: Connaissance et aide à la décision pour la Sécurité Civile. Sciences de l'environnement.* Ecole Nationale Supérieure des Mines de Saint-Etienne.

Dawes, R.M. (1973). The commons dilemma game: An *N*-person mixed motive game with a dominating strategy for defection. *ORI Research Bulletin, 13*, 1–12.

Dawes, R.M. (1980). Social dilemmas. *Annual Review of Psychology, 31*, 169–193.

de Alba Gonzales, M. (2010). Representaciones Sociales del Centro historico de la Ciudad de Mexico: una ventana a la memoria urbana. *In* P. Ramirez Kuri (Ed.), *Las Disputas por la Ciudad* (pp. 345–364). Mexico: UNAM-Porrúa.

Dear, M. (1992). Understanding and overcoming the NIMBY syndrome. *Journal of the American Planning Association, 58*, 288–300.

Debarbieux, B. (2004). De l'objet spatial à l'effet géographique, *In* B. Debarbieux & M-C. Fourny (Eds.), *L'effet géographique* (pp. 11–33). Grenoble: Publications de la MSH-Alpes.

Defays, D. (1991). Incertitude. *In* R. Doron & F. Parot (Eds.), *Dictionnaire de psychologie*. Paris: Presses universitaires de France.

De Groot, J.I., & Steg, L. (2008). Value orientations to explain beliefs related and biospheric value orientations. *Environment and Behavior, 40*(3), 330–354.

Demarque, C. (2011). *Perspective temporelle future et communication engageante, une approche psychosociale du rapport au temps dans le domaine de l'environnement*. Thèse de doctorat. Université de Provence.

Denis, M. (1997). *Langage et cognition spatiale*. Paris: Dunod.

Depeau, S. (2003). *L'enfant en ville: autonomie de déplacement et accessibilité environnementale*. Thèse de doctorat en psychologie. Université R. Descartes.

Depeau, S., Chardonnel, S., André-Poyaud, I., Lepetit A., Jambon, F., Quesseveur, E., & Gombaud, J. (2017). What about routines and informal situations in children's daily life and their well-being? *Travel behavior and society, 9*, 70–80.

Depeau, S., & Quesseveur, E. (2014). A la recherche d'espaces invisibles de la mobilité: usages, apports et limites des techniques GPS dans l'étude des déplacements urbains à l'échelle pédestre. *Netcom, 28* (1–2), 35–54.

Depeau, S., Tabaka, K., Dias, P., Duroudier, S., Kerouanton, C., Lepetit, A., Chardonnel, S., Andre-Poyaud, I., Mericskay, B., Moffat, E. (2023). When children move to middle school: a small transition or a major change in their daily travel autonomy? *Journal of Urban Research*.

Devine-Wright, P. (2011) Public engagement with large-scale renewable energy: Breaking the NIMBY cycle. *Wiley Interdisciplinary Reviews: Climate Change, 2*, 19–26.

Devine-Wright, P., & Batel, S. (2017). My neighbourhood, my country or my planet? The influence of multiple place attachments and climate change concern on social acceptance of energy infrastructure. *Global Environmental Change, 47*, 110–120.

Dias, P., & Ramadier, T. (2015). Social trajectory and socio-spatial representation of urban space: The relation between social and cognitive structures. *Journal of environmental psychology*, 41, 135–144. DOI: http://10.1016/j.jenvp.2014.12.002

Dias, P., & Ramadier, T. (2016). Fragmentations et ségrégations de l'espace urbain: Une approche par les cognitions socio-spatiales dans la relation individu/milieu. *Les impromptus du LPED: Autour de la fragmentation, 1*, 12–24.

Díaz-Pont, J., Maeseele, P., Sjölander, A.E., Mishra, M., & Foxwell-Norton, K. (Eds.). (2020). *The local and the digital in environmental communication*. Heidelberg: Springer Nature.

Diebolt, W., Helias, A., Bidou, D., & Crepey, G. (2005). *Les inégalités écologiques en milieu urbain*. Paris: Inspection Générale de l'Environnement.

Diener, E. (1984). Subjective well-being. *Psychological Bulletin, 95*, 524–575.

Dijkstra, J.K., Kretschmer, T., Lindenberg, S., & Veenstra, R. (2015). Hedonic, instrumental, and normative motives: Differentiating patterns for popular, accepted, and rejected adolescents. *The Journal of Early Adolescence, 35*, 308–328.

Di Masso, A., Williams, D.R., Raymond, C.M., Buchecker, M., Degenhardt, B., Devine-Wright, P., Hertzog, A., Lewicka, M., Manzo, L., Shahrad, A., Stedman, R., Verbrugge, L., & von Wirth, T. (2019). Between fixities and flows: Navigating place attachments in an increasingly mobile world. *Journal of Environmental Psychology, 61*, 125–133.

Dixon, J., & Durrheim, K. (2000). Displacing place-identity: A discursive approach to locating self and other. *British Journal of Social Psychology, 39*(1), 27–44.

Doise, W. (1982). *L'explication en psychologie sociale*. Paris: Presses Universitaires de France.

Doise, W. (1992). L'ancrage dans les études sur les représentations sociales. *Bulletin de psychologie, 45,* 189–195.

Douglas, M. (1966). *Purity and danger: An analysis of concepts of pollution and taboo.* London: Routledge & Kegan Paul.

Douglas, M. (1979). *Cultural bias.* London: Royal Anthropological Institute.

Dovidio, J.F., & Gaertner, S.L. (1986). Prejudice, discrimination, and racism: Historical trends and contemporary approaches. *In* J. Dovidio & S.L. Gaertner (Eds.). *Prejudice, discrimination and racism* (pp. 1–34). New York: Academic Press.

Downs, R.M., & Stea, D. (Eds.). (1973). *Image and environment: Cognitive mapping and spatial behavior.* Chicago: AldineTransaction.

Downs, T.J., Ross, L., Goble, R., Subedi, R., Greenberg, S., & Taylor, O. (2011). Vulnerability, risk perception, and health profile of marginalized people exposed to multiple built-environment. Stressors in Worcester, Massachusetts: A pilot project. *Risk Analysis, 31*(4), 609–628.

Drozda-Senkowska, E. (2020). Conclusion—Final contributions to a research agenda on social threats. *In* D. Jodelet, J. Vala, & E. Drozda-Senkowska (Eds.), *Societies Under Threat* (Vol. 3, pp. 213–220). New York: Springer International Publishing.

Duclos, D. (1987). La construction sociale du risque: le cas des ouvriers de la chimie face aux dangers industriels. *Revue française de sociologie, 28*(1), 17–42.

Dumur, E., Bernard, Y., & Boy, G. (2004). Designing for comfort. *In* C.M. Weikert (Ed.), *Human factors in design* (pp. 111–127). Maastricht: Shaker Publishing.

Duncan, M., & Mummery, K. (2005). Psychosocial and environmental factors associated with physical activity among city dwellers in regional Queensland. *Preventive Medicine, 40,* 363–372.

Dunlap, R.E., & McCright, A.M. (2008). A widening gap: Republican and democratic views on climate change. *Environment: Science and Policy for Sustainable Development, 50*(5), 26–35.

Dunlap, R.E., & Van Liere, K.D. (1978). The "New Environmental Paradigm". *The Journal of Environmental Education, 9,* 10–19. http://dx.doi.org/10.1080/00958964.1978.10801875

Dunlap, R.E., van Liere, K.D., Mertig, A.G., & Jones, R.E. (2000). Measuring endorsement of the New Ecological Paradigm: A revised NEP scale. *Journal of Social Issues, 56,* 425–442.

Dweck, C.S., & Goetz, T.E. (1978). Attributions and learned helplessness. *In* J.H. Harvey, W. Ickes & R.F. Kidd, (Eds.). *New directions in attribution research: Volume 1 Chap 6* (pp. 153–176). London: Psychology Press.

Ebbinghaus, H. (1908). *Psychology: An elementary text-book.* New York: Cornall University Library.

Eco, U. (1989). *Lector in fabula.* Paris: Livre de Poche.

Efese (2016). *Rapport intermédiaire.* Thema Analyses, Commissariat général au développement durable, Service de l'économie, de l'évaluation et de l'intégration du développement durable.

Emelianoff, C. (2010). Les inégalités écologiques et environnementales, au point de rupture d'un modèle de développement? *URBIA. Les Cahiers du développement urbain durable, 11,* 181–202.

Emery, F.E., & Trist, E. (1965). The causal texture of organizational environments. *Human Relations, 18*(1), 12–32.

Engels, A., Hüther, O., Schäfer, M., & Held, H. (2013). Public climate-change skepticism, energy preferences and political participation. *Global Environmental Change, 23*(5), 1018–1027.

Engels, F. (1845) *Die Lage der arbeitenden Klasse in England (The Condition of the Working Class in England)*. First Published: Leipzig in 1845; in English in 1887. Available at: https://www.marxists.org/archive/marx/works/1845/condition-working-class/index.htm

Engels, F. (1872) *The housing question*. Reprinted by the Co-operative Publishing Society of Foreign Workers Transcribed: Zodiac, June 1995. Available at: https://www.marxists.org/archive/marx/works/1872/housing-question/

European Environmental Agency. (2004). Environmental quality. *EEA Glossary*. Available at https://www.eea.europa.eu/help/glossary/eea-glossary/environmental-quality

Euzen, A., Eymard, L., & Gail, F. (Eds.) (2013). *Le développement durable à découvert*. Paris: CNRS Editions.

Evans, G.W. (Ed.) (1982). *Environmental stress*. New York: Cambridge University Press.

Evans, G.W. (2003). The built environment and mental health. *Journal of Urban Health, 80*, 536–555.

Evans, G.W. (2021). The physical context of human development. *Current Directions in Psychological Science, 30*, 41–48.

Evans, G.W., & Cohen, S. (1987). Environmental stress. *In* D. Stokols & I. Altman (Eds.), *Handbook of environmental psychology* (pp. 571–610). New York: Wiley.

Federal Facility Council (2001). Learning from our buildings: A state-of-the-practice summary of post–occupancy evaluation. *Federal Facilities Council Technical Report No. 145*. Washington, DC: Federal Facilities Council.

Feldman, R.M. (1990). Settlement-identity: Psychological bonds with home places in a mobile society. *Environment and Behavior, 22*(2), 183–229.

Félonneau, M.L. (2004). Love and loathing of the city: Urbanophilia and urbanophobia, topological identity and perceived incivilities. *Journal of Environmental Psychology, 24*, 43–52.

Ferreira, I.A., Johansson, M., Sternudd, C., & Fornara, F. (2016). Transport walking in urban neighbourhoods. Impact of perceived neighbourhood qualities and emotional relationship. *Landscape and Urban Planning, 150*, 60–69.

Festinger, L. (1957). *A theory of cognitive dissonance*. Stanford: Stanford University Press.

Fischer, C.S. (1976). *The urban experience. Sociology, Urban, cities and towns*. New York: Harcourt Brace Jovanovich.

Flurin, C. (2017). Eco-districts: Development and evaluation. A European case study. *Procedia Environmental Sciences, 37*, 34–45.

Fink, S. (1986). *Crisis management: Planning for the inevitable*. New York: American Management Association.

Firey, W. (1945). Sentiment and symbolism as ecological variables. *American Sociological Review, 10*, 140–148.

Fischer, G.N. (1992). *Psychologie sociale de l'environnement*. Toulouse: Privat.

Fischer, G.N. (1997). *Psychologie de l'Environnement social*. Paris: Dunod.

Fishbein, M., & Ajzen, I. (1975). *Beliefs, attitudes, intention and behaviour: An introduction to theory and research*. Reading, MA: Addison Wesley.

Fleury-Bahi, G. (2008). Environmental risk: Perception and target with local, versus global evaluation. *Psychological Reports, 102*, 185–193.

Fleury-Bahi, G., Navarro, O., & Pol, E. (Eds.) (2017). *Handbook of environmental psychology and QOL research*. New York: Springer.

Fleury-Bahi, G., Préau, M., Annabi-Attia, T., Marcouyeux, A., & Wittenberg, I. (2015). Perceived health and quality of life: The effect of exposure to atmospheric pollution. *Journal of Risk Research, 18*(2), 127–138.

Folke, C. (2006) Resilience: the emergence of a perspective for social-ecological systems analyses. *Global Environmental Change, 16*(3), 253–267.

Fornara, F., Lai, A.E., Bonaiuto, M., & Pazzaglia, F. (2019). Residential place attachment as an adaptive strategy for coping with the reduction of spatial abilities in old age. *Frontiers in Psychology, 10,* 856.

Fornara, F., Ariccio, S., Rioux, L., Moffat, E., Mariette, J., Bonnes, M., & Bonaiuto, M. (2018). Test of PREQIs' factorial structure and reliability in France and of a Neighbourhood Attachment prediction model: A study on a French sample in Paris (Vérification de la structure factorielle et de la fiabilité des preqis en France et test d'un modèle de prédiction de l'attachement au quartier: une étude sur un échantillon parisien). *Pratiques Psychologiques, 24,* 131–156.

Fornara, F., Bonaiuto, M., & Bonnes, M. (2006). Perceived hospital environment quality indicators: A study of orthopaedic units. *Journal of Environmental Psychology, 26,* 321–334.

Fornara, F., Bonaiuto, M., & Bonnes, M. (2010). Cross-validation of abbreviated Perceived Residential Environment Quality (PREQ) and Neighbourhood Attachment (NA) Indicators. *Environment and Behavior, 42,* 171–196.

Fried, M. (1982). Residential attachment: Source of residential and community satisfaction. *Journal of Social Issues, 38,* 109–119.

Fuhrer, U., Kaiser, F.G., & Hartig, T. (1993). Place attachment and mobility during leisure time. *Journal of Environmental Psychology, 13,* 309–321.

Furman, A. (2012). Desire lines: Determining pathways through the city. *In* M. Pacetti, G. Passerini, C.A. Brebbia, & G. Latini (Eds.). *The Sustainable City VII,* Vol. 1 (pp. 23–33). Southampton: Wit Press.

Gallez, C., & Kaufmann, V. (2009). Aux racines de la mobilité en sciences sociales.: Contribution au cadre d'analyse socio-historique de la mobilité urbaine. *In* M. Flonneau & V. Guigueno. (Eds.), *De l'histoire des transports à l'histoire de la mobilité?* (pp. 41–55). Rennes: Presses Universitaires de Rennes.

García-Mira, R. (Coord.) (2014). *Low Carbon at Work. Modeling Agents and Organizations to achieve Transitions to a Low Carbon Europe. LOCAW Final Report.* A Coruña: Instituto Xoan Vicente Viqueira.

García-Mira, R. (Coord.) (2017). *Green Lifestyles, Alternative Models and Upscaling Regional Sustainability. GLAMURS Final Report.* A Coruña: Instituto Xoan Vicente Viqueira.

García-Mira, R., Dumitru, A., Alonso-Betanzos, A., Sánchez-Maroño, N., Fontenla-Romero, O., Polhill, J.G., & Craig, T. (2017). Testing scenarios to achieve workplace sustainability goals using Backcasting and Agent-based Modeling, *Environment & Behavior, 49(9),* 1007–1037.

Gärling, T., Book, A., & Lindberg, E. (1986). Spatial orientation and wayfinding in the designed environment: A conceptual analysis and some suggestions for postoccupancy evaluation. *Journal of Architectural and Planning Research, 3,* 55–64.

Gehl, J. (1987, 2011 revisited ed.). *Life between buildings: Using Public Space.* Washington, Covelo, London: Island Press

Gibson, J.J. (1950). *The perception of the visual word.* Boston: Houghton Mifflin.

Gibson, J.J. (1966). *The senses considered as perceptual systems.* Boston: Houghton Mifflin.

Gibson, J.J. (1979). *The ecological approach to visual perception.* Boston: Houghton Mifflin.

Gibson, J.J., & Crooks, L. (1938). A theoretical field-analysis of automobile-driving. *The American Journal of Psychology, 51,* 453–471.

Gibson, B., & Werner, C. (1994). Airport waiting areas as behavior settings: The role of legibility cues in communicating the setting program. *Journal of Personality and Social Psychology, 66*(6), 1049–1060.

Gieseking, J., & Manglod, W. (2014). *The people, place and space reader.* New York: Routledge.

Gifford, J., & Gifford, R. (2000). FISH 3: A microworld for studying social dilemmas and resource management. *Behavior Research Methods, Instrumentation, and Computers, 32,* 417–422.

Gifford, R. (1995). Natural Psychology: An Introduction. *Journal of Environmental Psychology, 15,* 167–168.

Gifford R. (2002). *Environmental Psychology: Principles and practice.* Boston: Allyn and Bacon.

Gifford, R. (2011). The dragons of inaction: Psychological barriers that limit climate change mitigation and adaptation. *American Psychologist, 66*(4), 290.

Gifford, R. (2014a). Environmental psychology matters. *Annual Review of Psychology, 65,* 541–579.

Gifford, R. (2014b). *Environmental psychology: Principles and practice.* (5th ed.). Colville, WA: Optimal Books.

Gifford, R., Scannell, L., Kormos, C., Smolova, L., Biel, A., Boncu, S., … & Uzzell, D. (2009). Temporal pessimism and spatial optimism in environmental assessments: An 18-nation study. *Journal of Environmental Psychology (29),* 1–12.

Göckeritz, S., Schultz, P.W., & Rendón, T., Cialdini, R.B., Goldstein, N., & Griskevicius, V. (2010). Descriptive normative beliefs and conservation behavior: The moderating role of personal involvement and injunctive normative beliefs. *European Journal of Social Psychology, 40,* 514–523.

Goffman, E. (1973). *La mise en scène de la vie quotidienne. Les relations en public.* Paris: Les éditions de Minuit.

Goldszlagier, J. (2015). The anchoring effect: The role of cognitive psychology in studying judicial decision-making. *Les Cahiers de la Justice, 4 (4),* 507–531.

Golledge, R.G. (1992). Place Recognition and Wayfinding: Making Sense of Space. *Geoforum, 23*(2), 199–214.

Granié, M., Varet, F. & Torres, J. (2018). Les trajets à pied comme temps et objets de socialisation chez les collégiens français. *Le sujet dans la cité, 7,* 73–86.

Graumann, C.F. (1974). Psychology and the world of things. *Journal of Phenomenological Psychology, 4,* 389–404.

Graumann, C.F. (1976). The concept of appropriation (aneignung) and modes of appropriation of space. *In* P. Korosec-Serfaty (Ed.), *Appropriation of space. Proceedings of the Strasbourg International Architectural Psychology Conference (IAPC)* (pp. 113–125). Louvain-La-Neuve: CIACO. https://iaps.architexturez.net/doc/oai-iaps-id-iaps-00-1976-009

Graumann, C. F. (1999). *Ökologische Perspectiven in der Retrospective.* Fachgruppentagung Umweltpsychologie 26.-28.09.1999 Universität Magdeburg. https://www.psychologie.uni-heidelberg.de/cfg/oekologischeperspektiven.pdf

Grimm, J., & Grimm, W. (2021) *Deutsches Wörterbuch von Jacob Grimm und Wilhelm Grimm,* digital version available from the Trier Center for Digital Humanities, Version 01/21, downloaded on 25.06.2021. https://woerterbuchnetz.de/?sigle=DWB&lemid=GU04404&mode=linking#0.

Gray, J., Whyte, I., & Curry, P. (2018). Ecocentrism: What it means and what it implies. *The Ecological Citizen, 1*, 130–1.

Greenberg, S. (2008). Do Americans have green fatigue? *Newsweek*. Accessed 20 February 2023. https://www.newsweek.com/do-americans-have-green-fatigue-91073

Griffiths, I.D., & Langdon, F.J. (1968). Subjective response to road traffic noise. *Journal of Sound and Vibration*, 8 (91), 16–32.

Groat, L., & Wang, D. (2002) *Architectural Research Methods* Chichester: John Wiley & Sons

Guattari, F. (1989). *Les trois écologies*. Paris: Galilée.

Guillard, M., Navarro, O., & Fleury-Bahi, G. (2019). Flooding experience and assessment of climate change: implication of psychological distance, risk perception and place attachment. *Psyecology, 10*(3), 287–312.

Gump, P.V., & Adelberg, B. (1978). Urbanism from the perspective of ecological psychologists. *Environment and Behavior, 10*, 171–191.

Gustafson, P. (2009). Mobility and Territorial Belonging. *Environment and Behavior, 41*(4), 490–508.

Gustafson, P. (2014). Place attachment in an age of mobility. *In* L. Manzo, & P. Devine-Wright (Eds.). *Place attachment: Advances in theory, methods and applications* (pp. 37–48). London: Routledge.

Haas, V. (2004). Les cartes cognitives: Un outil pour étudier la ville sous ses dimensions sociohistoriques et affectives. *Bulletin de psychologie*, 57 (6), 621–633.

Haeckel, E. (1866). *Generelle Morphologie der Organismen*. Berlin: Reimer.

Halbwachs, M. (1925). *Les cadres sociaux de la Mémoire*. Paris: Albin Michel.

Hall, E.T. (1966). *The Hidden dimension*. New York: Doubleday and Co. et 1971 pour la traduction française *La dimension cachée*. Paris: Seuil.

Hall, S. (2017) *Identités et culture. Politiques des cultural studies*. Paris, Amsterdam.

Hansen, P.G. (2016). The definition of nudge and libertarian paternalism: Does the hand fit the glove? *European Journal of Risk Regulation, 7*(1), 155–174.

Hardin, G. (1968). The Tragedy of the Commons. *Science, 162*(3859), 1243–1248.

Hardy, G. (1939). *La géographie psychologique*. Paris: Gallimard.

Harré, R. & Lamb, R. (Eds.). (1983). *The encyclopedic dictionary of psychology*. Cambridge: MIT Press.

Hartig, T., Mitchell, R., de Vries, S., & Frumkin, H. (2014). Nature and health. *Annual Review of Public Health, 35*, 207–228.

Hedblom, M., Hedenås, H., Blicharska, M., Adler, S., Knez, I., Mikusiński, G., Svensson, J., Sandström, S., Sandström, P., & Wardle, D.A. (2020). Landscape perception: linking physical monitoring data to perceived landscape properties. *Landscape Research, 45*(2), 179–192.

Heft, H. (2001). *Ecological psychology in context*. Mahwah, NJ: Lawrence Erlbaum.

Heft, H. (2013). Environment, cognition, and culture: Reconsidering the cognitive map. *Journal of Environmental Psychology, 33*, 14–25.

Hegarty, M., Montello, D.R., Richardson, A.E., Ishikawa, T., & Lovelace, K. (2006). Spatial abilities at different scales: Individual differences in aptitude-test performance and spatial-layout learning. *Intelligence, 34*(2), 151–176.

Hegney, D.G., Buikstra, E., Baker, P., Rogers-Clark, C., Pearce, S., Ross, H., King, C., & Watson-Luke, A. (2007). Individual resilience in rural people: A Queensland study, Australia. *Rural Remote Health*, 7, 1–13.

Heidegger, M. (1958). *Bâtir Habiter Penser. Essais et conférences*. Paris: Gallimard.

Heiderich, D. (2010). *Plan de gestion de crise: organiser, gérer et communiquer en situation de crise*. Paris: Dunod.

Hellpach, W. (1911a). *Die geopsychischen Erscheinungen – Die Menschenseele unter dem Einfluss von Wetter und Klima, Boden und Landschaft*. Leipzig: Engelmann.

Hellpach, W. (1911b). Geopsyche. Leipzig: W. Engelmann.

Hellpach, W. (1924). Psychologie der Umwelt. *In* E. Abderhalden (Ed.), *Handbuch der biologischen Arbeitsmethoden* Abt. VI, Teil C, Heft 3, (pp. 109–218). Wien: Urban & Schwarzenberg.

Hellpach, W. (1939). *Mensch und Volk der Großstadt*. Stuttgart: Enke.

Hellpach, W. (1951). *Sozialpsychologie* (3rd ed.). Stuttgart: Ferdinand Enke.

Henn, L., Otto, S., & Kaiser, F.G. (2020). Positive spillover: The result of attitude change. *Journal of Environmental Psychology, 69,* 101429.

Hidalgo, C., & Hernandez, B. (2001). Place attachment: Conceptual and empirical questions. *Journal of Environmental Psychology, 21*, 273–281.

Hirtle, S.C., & Jonides, J. (1985). Evidence of hierarchies in cognitive maps. *Memory and Cognition*, *13*(3), 208–217.

Hoot, R.E., & Friedman, H. (2011). Connectedness and environmental behavior: Sense of interconnectedness and pro-environmental behavior. *International Journal of Transpersonal Studies*, *30*(1–2), 89–100.

Howell, A.J., Dopko, R.L., Passmore, H.A., & Buro, K. (2011). Nature connectedness: Associations with well-being and mindfulness. *Personality and Individual Differences*, *51*(2), 166–171.

Hume, T., & Barry, J. (2015). Environmental education and education for sustainable development. *In* J.D. Wright (Ed.), *International Encyclopedia of the Social & Behavioral Sciences* (pp. 733–739). Amsterdam: Elsevier.

IRSN (2016). *Baromètre IRSN 2016 sur la perception des risques et de la sécurité par les Français : les principaux constats*. Paris: The IRSN Publishing. https://barometre.irsn.fr/

Ittelson, W.H. (1973). *Environment and cognition*. London: Seminar Press.

Jacobs, J. (1961). *The death and life of Great American cities*. New York: Random House.

James, W. (1890). *The principles of psychology*. New York: Holt.

Jencks, J. (1977). *The language of post-modern architecture*. London: Rizzoli.

Jodelet, D. (1982). Les representations socio-spatiales de la ville. *In* P.H. Derycke (Ed.), *Conceptions de l'espace* (pp. 145–177). Paris: Université de Paris X-Nanterre.

Jodelet, D. (1987). The study of people-environment relations in France. *In* I. Altman & D Stockols (Eds.), *Handbook of environmental psychology* (pp. 1171–1193). New York: Wiley.

Jodelet, D. (1991). Représentation sociale. *In* R. Zazzo (Ed.), *Grand Dictionnaire de la Psychologie* (pp. 668–672). Paris: Larousse.

Jodelet, D. (1996). Las representaciones sociales del medio ambiente. *In* L. Iniguez, & E. Pol (Eds.), *Cognicion, representacion y apropriacion del espacio. Monografias Psico-socio-ambientales* (pp. 29–44). Barcelone: Publicaciones de la Universitat de Barcelona.

Jodelet, D. (2015a). Les représentations sociales de l'environnement. *In* D. Jodelet (Ed.), *Représentations sociales et mondes de vie* (pp. 149–158). Paris: Archives Contemporaines.

Jodelet, D. (2015b). Production de mise en sens de l'espace et pratiques sociales. *In* D. Germanos & M. Liapi (Eds.), *Digital proceedings of the symposium with international participation: Places for Learning expériences. Think, make, change* (pp. 66–77). Athènes: Greek National Documentation.

Jodelet, D. (2017). Les menaces: passer du mot au concept. *In* S. Caillaud, V. Bonnot, & E. Drozda-Senkowska (Eds.), *Menaces sociales et environnementales: repenser la société des risques* (pp. 17–30). Rennes: PUR.

Jodelet, D., & Milgram, S. (1976). Psychological maps of Paris. *In* H. Proshansky, W.H. Ittelson, & L.G. Rivlin (Eds.), *Environmental psychology: people and their physical settings* (pp. 104–124). New York: Holt, Rinehart and Winston.

Joffe, H. (2003). Risk: From perception to social representation. *British Journal of Social Psychology, 42,* 55–73.

Joffe, H., & Orfali, B. (2005). De la perception à la représentation du risque: Le rôle des médias. *Hermes, La Revue, 41*(1), 121–129.

Jorgensen, B.S., & Stedman, R.C. (2006). A comparative analysis of prediction of sense of place dimensions: Attachment to, dependence on and identification with lakeshore proprieties. *Journal of Environmental Management, 79,* 316–327.

Joule, R.V., & Beauvois, J.L. (1998). *La soumission librement consentie.* Paris: PUF.

Joule, R.V., & Beauvois, J.L. (2017). *Petit traité de manipulation à l'usage des honnêtes gens.* Grenoble: PUG.

Kahn, P.H. (1999). *The human relationship with nature: Development and culture.* Cambridge: MIT Press.

Kahneman, D., Diener, E., & Schwarz, N. (Eds.). (1999). *Well-being: The foundation of hedonic psychology.* New York: Russell Sage Foundation.

Kaiser, F.G. (2021). Climate change mitigation within the Campbell paradigm: Doing the right thing for a reason and against all odds. *Current Opinion in Behavioral Sciences, 42,* 70–75.

Kaiser, F.G., Brügger, A., Hartig, T., Bogner, F.X., & Gutscher, H. (2014). Appreciation of nature and appreciation of environmental protection: How stable are these attitudes and which comes first? *European Review of Applied Psychology/Revue Européenne de Psychologie Appliquée, 64,* 269–277.

Kaiser, F.G., Byrka, K., & Hartig, T. (2010). Reviving Campbell's paradigm for attitude research. *Personality and Social Psychology Review, 14,* 351–367.

Kaiser, F.G., Hartig, T., Brügger, A., & Duvier, C. (2013). Environmental protection and nature as distinct attitudinal objects: An application of the Campbell paradigm. *Environment and Behavior, 45,* 369–398.

Kaiser, F.G., & Wilson, M. (2019). The Campbell paradigm as a behavior-predictive reinterpretation of the classical tripartite model of attitudes. *European Psychologist, 24,* 359–374.

Kals, E., & Ittner, H. (2003). Children's environmental identity: indicators and behavioural impacts. *In* S. Clayton & S. Opotow (Eds.), *Identity and the natural environment* (*pp.*135–157). Cambridge: MIT Press.

Kals, E., Schumacher, D., & Montada, L. (1999). Emotional affinity toward nature as a motivational basis to protect nature. *Environment and Behavior, 31,* 178–202.

Kaminski, G. (1976). *Umweltpsychologie: Perspektiven, Probleme, Praxis.* Stuttgart: Klett.

Kaplan, R., & Kaplan, S. (1989). *The experience of nature: A psychological perspective.* New York: Cambridge University Press.

Kaplan, S. (1995). The restorative benefits of nature: Toward an integrative framework. *Journal of Environmental Psychology, 15*(3), 169–182.

Karnas, G. (2000). *Contrôle et incertitude en psychologie du travail et en ergonomie.* Leçon inaugurale donnée dans le cadre de la chaire Francqui au titre belge à l'Université catholique de Louvain, Louvain-le-Nauve, 2000.

Katsuki, F., & Constantinidis, C. (2014). Bottom-up and top-down attention: Different processes and overlapping neural systems. *The Neuroscientists, 20*(5), 509–521.

Katz, D., & Kahn, R.L. (1966). *The social psychology of organizations.* New York: John Wiley & Sons.

Kermarec, F., Dor, F. (2010). Appréhender les questions locales en santé environnement en partenariat avec les sciences humaines et sociales, *Environnement, risques et santé, 9*(1), 61–69.

Kitchin, R.M. (1994). Cognitive maps: what are they and why study them?, *Journal of Environmental Psychology, 14*, 1–19.

Klein, D.C., Fencil-Morse, E., & Seligman, M.E. (1976). Learned helplessness, depression, and the attribution of failure. *Journal of Personality and Social Psychology, 33*(5), 508–516.

Knopf, R.C. (1987). Human behavior, cognition and affect in the natural environment. *In* D. Stokols & I. Altman (Eds.), *Handbook of environmental psychology, Vol.1* (pp. 783–825). New York: Wiley.

Koffka, K. (1935). Le comportement molaire et son environnement. *In* M. Flückiger & K. Klaue (Eds.). *La perception de l'environnement* (pp. 143–160). *Textes de base en psychologie.* Lausanne: Delachaux et Niestle.

Koole, S.L., & Van den Berg, A.E. (2005). Lost in the wilderness: Terror management, action orientation, and nature evaluation. *Journal of Personality and Social Psychology, 88*, 1014–1028.

Korosec-Serfaty, P. (Ed.) (1978). *Appropriation of space.* Proceedings of the Strasbourg Conference -3 IAPC, Estrasburg, 1976. Louvain-la-Neuve: Ciaco. http://perlaserfaty.net/appropriation-de-l-espace/

Kosslyn, S.M., Pomerantz, J.P. (1977). Imagery, propositions, and the form of internal representations. *Cognitive Psychology, 9*, 52–76.

Kouabenan, D.R. (2007). *Psychologie des risques.* Paris: De Boeck.

Kouabenan, D.R., & Cadet, B. (2005). Risk evaluation and accident analysis. *In* A. Columbus (Ed.), *Advances in Psychology Research* (pp. 61–80). Hauppauge: Nova Science Publishers.

Kozhevnikov, M., & Hegarty, M. (2001). A dissociation between object manipulation spatial ability and spatial orientation ability. *Memory & Cognition, 29*(5), 745–756. https://doi.org/10.3758/BF03200477

Kruse, L. (1974). *Räumliche Umwelt. Die Phänomenologie des räumlichen Verhaltens als Beitrag zu einer psychologischen Umwelttheorie.* Berlin: de Gruyter.

Kruse, L. (1986). Drehbücher für Verhaltensschauplätze oder Scripts für Settings. *In* G. Kaminski (Ed.), *Ordnung und Variabilität im Alltagsgeschehen* (pp. 135–153). Göttingen: Hogrefe.

Kruse, L. (1995). Globale Umweltveränderungen. Eine Herausforderung für die Psychologie. *Psychologische Rundschau, 46, 81*–92.

Kruse, L., & Funke, J. (2022). Umweltpsychologie. *In* T.Meier, F.Keppler, U. Mager, U. Platt & F. Reents (Eds.) *Umwelt interdisziplinär.* Grundlagen - Konzepte - Handlungsfelder. Open access by Heidelberg University Publishing (https://archiv.ub.uni-heidelberg.de/)

Kruse, L., & Graumann, C.F. (1987). Environmental psychology in Germany. *In* D. Stokols & I. Altman (Eds.), *Handbook of environmental psychology* (pp. 1195–1225). New York: Wiley.

Kruse, L., Graumann, C.F. & Lantermann, E.D. (Eds.) (1990). *Ökologische Psychologie. Ein Handbuch in Schlüsselbegriffen.* München: Psychologie Verlags Union.

Kuipers, B. (1978). Modeling spatial knowledge. *Cognitive Science, 2*, 129–153.

Kuo, M., Barnes, M., & Jordan, C. (2019). Do experiences with nature promote learning? Converging evidence of a cause-and-effect relationship. *Frontiers in Psychology, 10*(305). https://doi.org/10.3389/fpsyg.2019.00305

Kusenbach, M. (2003). Street phenomenology: The Go-Along as ethnographic research tool. *Ethnography, 4*(3), 455–485.

Kyttä, M. (2004). The role and significance of children s autonomous mobility for environmental child-friendliness in the light of the Bullerby-model. *In* L. Horelli, & M. Prezza (Eds.), *Child-friendly environments: Approaches and lessons* (pp. 142–156). Helsinki: Helsinki University of Technology, Centre for Urban Regional Studies.

Kyttä, M., Oliver, M., Ikeda, E., Ahmadi, E., Omiya, I. & Laatikainen, T. (2018). Children as urbanites: Mapping the affordances and behavior settings of urban environments for Finnish and Japanese children. *Children's Geographies, 16*(3), 319–332.

Lachaux, J.P. (2013). *Le Cerveau Attentif. Contrôle, Maîtrise et Lâcher-Prise.* Paris: Odile Jacob.

Ladouceur, R., Gosselin, P., & Dugas, M. (2000). Experimental manipulation of intolerance of uncertainty: A study of a theoretical model of worry. *Behaviour Research and Therapy, 38*(9), 933–941.

Lagadec, P. (1991). La gestion des crises: outils de réflexion à l'usage des décideurs. *Science, XIII*, 326.

Lalli, M. (1992). Urban-related identity: Theory, measurement, and empirical findings. *Journal of Environmental Psychology, 12*, 285–303.

Lannoy, P., & Ramadier, T. (2007). *La mobilité généralisée: formes et valeurs de la mobilité quotidienne.* Louvain-la-Neuve: Académia-Bruylant.

Lavadinho, S. (2011). *Le renouveau de la marche urbaine: Terrains, acteurs et politiques.* Thèse de doctorat. ENS LYON.

Lazard, A., & Atkinson, L. (2015). Putting environmental infographics center stage: The role of visuals at the elaboration likelihood model's critical point of persuasion. *Science Communication, 37*(1), 6–33.

Ledrut, R. (1973). *Les images de la ville.* Paris: Anthropos.

Lefebvre, H. (1968). *Le droit à la ville.* Paris: Anthropos.

Lee, T. (1976). *Psychology and the environment.* Methuen: Methuen Young Books.

Leiserowitz, A.A. (2005). American risk perceptions: Is climate change dangerous? *Risk Analysis, 25*(6), 1433–1442.

Levine, M. (1982) You-are-here maps: Psychological considerations. *Environment and Behavior, 14*, 221–237.

Levy, E. (2001). Saisir l'accessibilité. Les trajets-voyageurs à la gare du Nord. *In* M. Grosjean & J.P. Thibaud (Eds.), *L'espace urbain en méthodes* (pp. 47–62). Marseille: Parenthèses.

Lévy, J., & Lussault, J. (Eds.) (2013). *Dictionnaire de la géographie et de l'espace des sociétés.* Paris: Belin.

Levy-Leboyer, C. (1980). *Psychologie et environnement.* Paris: PUF.

Lewandowsky, S., Gignac, G.E., & Vaughan, S. (2012). Supplementary information: The pivotal role of perceived scientific consensus in acceptance of science. *Nature Climate Change, 3*(4), 399–404.

Lewicka, M. (2010). What makes neighborhood different from home and city? Effects of place scale on place attachment. *Journal of Environmental Psychology, 30*, 35–51.

Lewicka, M. (2011). Place attachment: How far have we come in the last 40 years? *Journal of Environmental Psychology, 31*(3), 207–230.

Lewin, K. (1936). *Principles of topological psychology* (F. Heider & G.M. Heider, Trans.). New York: McGraw-Hill.

Lewin, K. (1943) Psychologische Ökologie. In: Feldtheorie in den Sozialwissenschaften. (pp. 206-222). Bern: Huber and 1982 in Kurt Lewin. Feldtheorie (C.F.Graumann (Ed.) Bd. 4 der Kurt-Lewin Werkausgabe (pp. 291.312). Bern/Stuttgart: Huber/Klett-Cotta. (Engl.: 1951 Psychological ecology. *In* Field theory in social science. (pp.170-187). New York: Harper.

Lewin, K. (1951). Fieldtheory in social science. New York: Harper, (1st ed. 1943). Feldtheorie in den Sozialwissenschaften. Bern Huber.

Liberman, N., & Trope, Y. (2008). The psychology of transcending the here and now. *Science, 322*, 1201–1205.

Lima, M.L., Moreira, S., & Marques, S. (2012). Participatory community involvement in planning processes of building project - A social psychological approach. *Umweltpsychologie, 16*(1), 68–87.

Linask, L., Magnus, R., & Kull, K. (2015). Applying Jakob von Uexküll's concept of *Umwelt* to human experience and development. *In* G. Mey & H. Günther (Eds,), *The life space of the urban child. Perspectives on Martha Muchow's classic study* (pp. 175–192). New Brunswick-London: Transaction Publishers.

Lindenberg, S., Six, F., & Keizer, K. (2020). Social contagion and goal framing: The sustainability of rule compliance. *In* D. Daniel Sokol & B. van Rooij (Eds.), *Cambridge handbook of compliance* (pp. 422-437). Cambridge: Cambridge University Press.

Lindenberg, S., & Steg, L. (2013a). Goal-framing theory and norm-guided environmental behavior. *In* H. van Trijp (Ed.), *Encouraging Sustainable Behavior* (pp. 37–54). New York: Psychology Press.

Lindenberg, S., & Steg, L. (2013b). What makes organizations in market democracies adopt environmentally-friendly policies? *In* A.H. Huffman & S.R. Klein (Eds.), *Green organizations. Driving change with I-O psychology* (pp. 93–114). New York: Routledge/Psychology Press.

Lloyd, W.F. (1837/1968). *Lectures on population, value, poor laws and rent*. New York: August M. Kelley.

Loomis, J.M., Blascovich, J.J., & Beall, A.C. (1999). Immersive virtual environment technology as a basic research tool in psychology. *Behavior Research Methods, Instruments, & Computers, 31*, 557–564. https://doi.org/10.3758/BF03200735

Lord, S., & Piché, D. (2018). *Vieillissement et aménagement: Perspectives plurielles*. Montréal: Presses de l'Université de Montréal.

Lorenzoni, I., Leiserowitz, A., Doria, M.D.F., Poortinga, W., & Pidgeon, N.F. (2006). Cross-national comparisons of image associations with "global warming" and "climate change" among laypeople in the United States of America and Great Britain. *Journal of Risk Research, 9*(3), 265–281.

Lubis, M.I., & Langston, J.D. (2015). Understanding landscape change using participatory mapping and geographic information systems: Case study in North Sulawesi, Indonesia. *Procedia Environmental Sciences, 24*, 206–214.

Lupton, D. (2013). *Risk* (2e éd.). London: Routledge.

Luthar, S.S., Cicchetti, D., & Becker, B. (2000). The construct of resilience: A critical evaluation and guidelines for future work. *Child Development, 71*, 543–562.

Lynch, K. (1960) *The image of the city*. Cambridge: MIT Press.

Maffesoli, M., Freund, J., Bozonnet, J.P., & Bellotto, B. (1979). *Espaces et imaginaire*. Grenoble: Presses Universitaires de Grenoble.

Maloney, M.P., & Ward, M.P. (1973). Ecology: Let's hear from the people. An objective scale for the measurement of ecological attitudes and knowledge. *American Psychologist, 28*, 583–586.

Malpas, J. (1999). *Place and experience: A philosophical topography.* Cambridge: Cambridge University Press.

Manning, P. (1965) *Office design: A study of environment.* Liverpool: Department of Building Science, University of Liverpool.

Manzo, L., & Devine-Wright, P. (2021). *Place attachment* (2nd ed.). New York: Routledge.

Mao, Y., Fornara, F., Manca, S., Bonnes, M., & Bonaiuto, M. (2015). Perceived Residential Environment Quality Indicators (PREQIs) and Neighborhood Attachment: A confirmation study on a Chinese sample in Chongqing. *PsyCh Journal, 4*, 123–137.

Marazziti, D., Cianconi, P., Mucci, F., Foresi, L., Chiarantini, I., & Della Vecchia, A. (2021). Climate change, environment pollution, COVID-19 pandemic and mental health. *Science of the Total Environment, 773*, 145182.

Marchand, D. (2007). *Analyse psychologique des freins et des motivations des propriétaires de maisons individuelles dans leur projet de rénovation thermique.* Rapport final sur le panel de propriétaires de maisons individuelles. CSTB. MITECH. 76 p.

Marchand, D., Brisson, G., & Plante, S. (2014). L'apport des sciences sociales à la gestion du risque sanitaire environnemental. *In* D. Marchand, S. Depeau, & K. Weiss (Eds.), *L'individu au risque de l'environnement* (pp. 199–230). Paris: InPress.

Marchand, D., & Pol, E. (2021). *La perception. In* J. Monnet & K. Demailly (Eds.), *Dictionnaire pluriel de la marche en ville.* Paris: L'œil d'Or.

Marchand, D., Ramalho, O., Laffitte, J.D., Chaventré, F., Collignan, B., & Weiss, K. (2012). *PSYCOBAT - Du syndrome des bâtiments malsains au syndrome psychogène collectif : quelle est la part de l'environnement et de la subjectivité dans l'expression des syndromes sanitaires collectifs survenant dans les bâtiments et pour quelles modalités de gestion ?* Rapport final, Programme de recherche PRIMEQUAL/PREDIT, MEDDTL, Paris.

Marchand, D., & Weiss, K. (2009). Représentations sociales du confort dans le train : vers une conceptualisation de la notion de confort social. *Les Cahiers Internationaux de Psychologie Sociale, 4*(84), 107–124.

Marchand, D., Weiss, K., & Laffitte, J.D. (2010). Syndrome des bâtiments malsains ou syndrome psychogène collectif ? La raison face aux croyances. *Environnement, risques et santé, 9*(5), 401–407.

Marchand, D., Weiss, K., Ramalho, O., Chaventré, F., & Collignan, B. (2017). L'incertitude, un facteur explicatif de l'évolution des crises environnementales. Le rôle de l'incertitude dans la construction sociale des problématiques environnementales. *Bulletin de psychologie, 70*(2), 548.

Marchand, D., Weiss, K., & Zouhri, B. (2017). Emerging risks and quality of life: towards new dimensions of well-being?. *In* G. Fleury-Bahi, O. Navarro & E. Pol (Eds.), *Handbook of environmental psychology and QOL* (pp. 531–542). London: Springer.

Marczak, M., & Sorokowski, P. (2018). Emotional connectedness to nature is meaningfully related to modernization. Evidence from the Meru of Kenya. *Frontiers in Psychology, 9*, 1789.

Marié, M. (1985). De l'aménagement au ménagement du territoire en Provence. *Le Genre Humain, 1*(12), 71–92.

Marié, M. (1996). Aménager ou ménager le territoire ? *Annales des Ponts et Chaussées, 77*, 67–76.

Markus, T.A., Whyman, P., Morgan, J., Whitton, D., Maver, T., Canter, D., & Fleming, J. (1972). *Building performance, building performance research unit*. London: Applied Science Publishers.

Marry S., Baulac M., Marchand D., Defrance J., & Ramalho, O. (2010). Evaluation multicritères des nuisances et de la perception en milieu urbain. *10ème congrès français d'acoustique*, Apr 2010, Lyon, France.

Martinez-Alier, J. (2002). *The environmentalism of the poor. A study of ecological conflicts and valuation*. Cheltenham, Northampton: Edward Elgar.

Maruyama, M. (1963). The second cybernetics: Deviation-amplifying mutual causal processes. *American Scientist, 51*, 164–179.

Maslow, A.H. (1968). *Toward a psychology of being*, (2nd ed.). Princeton, NJ: Van Nostrand.

Massey, D. (2005). *For space*. London: Sage.

Mayer, F.S., & Frantz, C.M. (2004). The connectedness to nature scale: a measure of individuals' feeling in community with nature. *Journal of Environmental Psychology, 24*, 503–515.

Mayer, F.S., Frantz, C.M., Bruehlman-Senecal, E., & Dolliver, K. (2009). Why is nature beneficial? The role of connectedness to nature. *Environment and Behavior, 41*, 607–643.

Mccright, A.M., Dunlap, R.E., & Marquart-Pyatt, S.T. (2016). Political ideology and views about climate change in the European Union. *Environmental Politics, 25*(2), 338–358.

McEwen, B.S. (2012). Brain on stress: How the social environment gets under the skin. *Proceedings of the National Academy of Sciences, 109*, 17180–17185.

McIntyre, D. (1973). A guide to thermal comfort. *Applied Ergonomics, 4*(2), 66–72.

Meadows, D., Meadows, D., Randers, J., & Behrens, W.W. (1972). *The limits to growth*. Washington, DC: Potomac Associates Books.

Melcion, N., & Bidaud, C. (2018). La psychologie sociale au service de la biodiversité. *Sciences Eaux & Territoires, 25*, 34–37.

Meilinger, T., Knauff, M., & et Bülthoff, H. H. (2008). Working memory in wayfinding—A dual task experiment in a Virtual city, *Cognitive Science, 32*(4), 755–770.

Mena, A., Olivos, P., Loureiro, A., & Navarro, O. (2020). Effects of contact with nature on connectedness, environmental identity and evoked contents. *Psyecology, 11*(1), 21–36.

Menatti, L., & Casado da Rocha, A. (2016). Landscape and health: Connecting psychology, aesthetics, and philosophy through the concept of affordance. *Frontiers in Psychology, 7*, 571.

Mercer, C. (1975). *Living in cities: Psychology and the urban environment*. London: Penguin.

Michel-Guillou, E., Lalanne, P.A., & Krien, N. (2015). Hommes et aléas: appréhension des risques côtiers par des usagers et des gestionnaires de communes littorales. *Pratiques Psychologiques, 21*(1), 35–53.

Michelson, W.H. (1970/1976). *Man and his urban environment: A sociological approach* (2nd ed., 1976; first published in 1970 ed.). Reading, MA: Addison-Wesley.

Mikellides, B. (1980). *Architecture for people. Explorations in a new humane environment*. London: Studio Vista.

Milburn, T., & Watman, K. (1981*). On the nature of threat: A social psychological analysis.* New York: Praeger.

Milfont, T. (2010). Global warming, climate change and human psychology. *In* V. Corral-Verdugo, C.H. Garcia Cadena, & M. Frias-Armenta (Eds.), *Psychological approaches to sustainability* (pp. 19–42). New York: Nova Science Publishers.

Milfont, T., Abrahamse, W., & McCarthy, N. (2011). Spatial and temporal biases in assessments of environmental conditions in New Zealand. *New Zealand Journal of Psychology, 40*(2), 56–67.

Milfont, T.L., & Demarque, C. (2015). Understanding environmental issues with temporal lenses: issues of temporality and individual differences. *In* M. Stolarski, W. van Beek, & N. Fieulaine (Eds.), *Time perspective theory: Review, research and application - Essays in Honor of Philip Zimbardo* (pp. 371–384). Switzerland: Springer.

Milfont, T.L., & Duckitt, J. (2004). The structure of environmental attitudes: A first and second-order confirmatory factor analysis. *Journal of Environmental Psychology, 24,* 289–303.

Miller, J. G. (1978). *Living systems.* New York: McGraw-HillMishel, M.H. (1988). Uncertainty in illness. *Journal of Nursing Scholarship, 20,* 225–232.

Mitscherlich, A. (1965). *Die Unwirtlichkeit unserer Städte. Anstiftung zum Unfrieden.* Frankfurt: Suhrkamp.

Moffat, É. (2016). *La satisfaction environnementale au travail des employés de bureaux.* Thèse de doctorat. Université Paris Ouest Nanterre.

Moffat, É., Mogenet, J.L., & Rioux, L. (2016). Développement et validation d'une Échelle de Satisfaction Environnementale au Travail (ÉSET). *Psychologie française, 61,* 196–206.

Moles, A., & Rohmer, E. (1978). *Psychosociologie de l'espace.* Paris: l'Harmattan.

Moliner, P. (1996). *Images et représentations sociales. De la théorie des représentations sociales à l'étude des images sociales.* Grenoble: Presses Universitaires de Grenoble.

Moore, G. (1988). Effects of the spatial definition of behavior settings on children's behavior: a quasi-experimental field study. *Journal of Environmental Psychology, 6,* 205–231.

Moore, J. (2000). Placing Home in context. *Journal of Environmental Psychology, 20,* 207–217.

Moos, R.H. (1979). Social ecological perspectives on health. *In* G.C. Stone, F. Cohen, & N.E. Adler (Eds.), *Health psychology: A handbook* (pp. 523–547). San Francisco, CA: Jossey Bass.

Morais, J. (1987). Stimuli, processus, représentations. *In* D. Siguan (Ed.), *Comportement, cognition, conscience; la psychologie à la recherche de son objet.* Symposium de l'association de psychologie scientifique de langue française. Paris: PUF.

Morin, E. (2004). *La Méthode, Ethique.* Paris: Seuil.

Morris, P. (1961) 'Homes for Today and Tomorrow' report by Sir Parker Morris for the Ministry of Housing and Local Government, 1961. BADDA2543. *Museum of Domestic Design & Architecture,* Middlesex University. Accessed November 03, 2020. https://moda.mdx.ac.uk/object/badda2543/

Morval, J., & Corbière, M. (2000). L'appropriation de l'espace. Un concept à la recherche d'une définition. *European Review of Applied Psychology / Revue Européenne de Psychologie Appliquée, 50*(1), 127–133.

Moscardo, G., & Pearce, J. (2019). Eco-fatigue and its potential impact on sustainable touristexperiences. *In* J. Pearce (Ed.) *BEST EN Think Tank XIX Conference Proceedings: Creating Sustainable Tourist Experiences* (pp. 140–164). Townsville: James Cook University.

Moscovici, S. (1961, 1976). *La psychanalyse, son image, son public.* Paris: PUF.

Moscovici, S. (1986). L'ère des représentations sociales. *In* W. Doise & A. Palmonari (Eds.), *L'étude des représentations sociales* (pp. 34–80). Neuchâtel: Delachaux et Niestlé.

Moscovici, S. (1994). Social representations and pragmatic communication. *Social Science Information, 33*(2), 163–177.

Moser, G. (1992). *Les stress urbains.* Paris: Armand Colin.

Moser, G. (1998). Attribution causale et sentiment d'insécurité de victimes de différents types de vols. *Les Cahiers Internationaux de Psychologie Sociale, 39,* 43–52.

Moser, G. (2009). *Psychologie environnementale.* Bruxelles: de Boeck.

Moser, G., Legendre, A., & Ratiu, E. (2003). City dwellers' relationship networks: patterns of adjustment to environemental constraints. *In* R. Garcia-Mira, J.M. Sabucedo Cameselle & J. Romay Martinez (Eds.), *Culture, Environmental action and sustainability* (pp. 161–170). Göttingen: Hogrefe & Huber.

Moser, G., & Weiss, K. (Eds.) (2003). *Espaces de vie. Aspects de la relation homme-environnement.* Paris: Armand Colin.

Muchow, M., & Muchow, H.H. (1935): *Der Lebensraum des Großstadtkindes* (Reprint 1978). Bensheim: Päd extra. Translated as The life space of the urban child and published as part of G. Mey & H. Günther, (2015), (Eds.). *The life space of the urban child: Perspectives on Martha Muchows's classic study* (pp. 63–146). New Brunswick: Transaction Publishers.

Naus, J., Spaargaren, G., Van Vliet, B.J.M., & Van der Horst, H.M. (2014). Smart grids, information flows and emerging domestic energy practices. *Energy Policy, 68,* 436–446.

Navarro, O. (2016). Les représentations sociales dans le champ de l'environnement. *In* G. Lo Monaco, S. Delouvée & P. Rateau (Eds.). *Les représentations sociales. Théories, méthodes et applications* (pp. 263–273). Louvain-la-Neuve: De Boeck.

Navarro, O., & Michel-Guillou, E. (2014). Analyse des risques et menaces environnementales: Un regard psycho-socio-environnementale. *In* D. Marchand, S. Depeau, & K. Weiss (Dir.), *L'individu au risque de l'environnement. Regards croisés de la psychologie environnementale* (pp. 271–298). Paris: Editions InPress.

Navarro, O., Tapia-Fonllem, C., Fraijo-Sing, B., Roussiau, N., Ortiz-Valdez, A., Guillard, M., Wittenberg, I., & Fleury-Bahi, G. (2020). Connectedness to nature and its relationship with spirituality, wellbeing and sustainable

Nipperteng, C.E. (1996). *Home and work.* Chicago & London: University of Chicago Press.

Nisbet, E.K., Zelenski, J.M., & Murphy, S.A. (2011). Happiness is in our nature: Exploring nature relatedness as a contributor to subjective well-being. *Journal of Happiness Studies, 13,* 303–322.

Nisbet, M.C., & Myers, T. (2007). The polls—trends: Twenty years of public opinion about global warming. *Public Opinion Quarterly, 71*(3), 444–470.

Nogué, J., & Vicente, J. (2004). Landscape and national identity in Catalonia. *Political Geography, 23*(2), 113–132.

Nolan, J., Schultz, P.W., Cialdini, R.B., Goldstein, N., & Griskivicius, V. (2008). Normative social influence is underdetected. *Pers Soc Psychol Bull. 2008 Jul; 34*(7):913-23.

Nora, P. (1997). *Les lieux de mémoire.* Paris: Quarto, Gallimard.

Norton, T., & Grecu, N. (2015). Publics, communication campaigns, and persuasive communication. *In* A. Hansen & R. Cox (Eds.), *The Routledge handbook of environment and communication* (pp. 374–387). London: Routledge.

Ntanos, S., Kyriakopoulos, G., Skordoulis, M., Chalikias, M., & Arabatzis, G. (2019). An Application of the New Environmental Paradigm (NEP) Scale in a Greek Context. *Energies, 12*(2), 239. https://doi.org/10.3390/en12020239

Nussbaum, M. (2012). *Capabilités. Comment créer les conditions d'un monde plus juste?* Paris: Flammarion.

Oborne, D.J., & Gruneberg, M.M. (1983). *The physical environment at work.* Chichester: John Wiley & Sons.

OECD. (2003). *Les risques émergents au XXIème siècle. Vers un programme d'action.* Paris: OECD Publishing.

O'Keefe, J. & Nadel, L. (1978). *The Hippocampus as a Cognitive Map.* Oxford: Oxford University Press.Olivos, P., & Aragonés, J.I. (2014). Medio ambiente, self y conectividad con la naturaleza. *Revista Mexicana de Psicología, 3*, 71–77.

Olivos, P., Aragonés, J.I., & Navarro, O. (2013). Educación ambiental: itinerario en la naturaleza y su relación con conectividad. preocupaciones ambientales y conducta. *Revista Latinoamericana de Psicología, 45*(3), 501–511.

Olivos, P., & Clayton, S. (2017). Self, nature and wellbeing: sense of connectedness and environmental identity for quality of life. *In* G. Fleury-Bahi, E. Pol, & O. Navarro. (Eds.), *Handbook of environmental psychology and QOL research* (pp. 107–126). New York: Springer.

Olivos-Jara, P., Segura-Fernández, R., Rubio-Pérez, C., & Felipe-García, B. (2020). Biophilia and Biophobia as emotional attribution to nature in children of 5 years old. *Frontiers in Psychology, 11*, 511.

Osmond, H. (1957). Function as the Basis of Psychiatric Ward Design. *Psychiatric Services, 8*(4), 23-27. https://doi.org/10.1176/ps.8.4.23

Oullier, O., & Sauneron, S. (2011). « Nudges verts »: de nouvelles incitations pour des comportements écologiques. *Note d'analyse du Centre d'Analyse Stratégique, 216*, 1–12.

Paciuk, M. (1990). The role of personal control of the environment in thermal comfort and satisfaction at the workplace. *In* R.I. Selby, K.H. Anthony, J. Choi, & B. Orland (Eds.) *Coming of age* (pp. 303–312). Edmond: Environmental Design Research Association.

Paivio, A. (1971). *Imagery and verbal processes*, New York, Holt, Rinehart & Winston.

Paluck, R.J., & Esser, A.H. (1971). Territorial behavior as an indicator of changes in clinical behavioral condition of severely retarded boys. *American Journal of Mental Deficiency, 76*(3), 284–290.

Paquot, T. (1990). *Homo urbanus, essai sur l'urbanisation du monde et des mœurs.* Paris: Le Félin.

Park, R., Burgess, E.W., & McKenzie, R.D. (1925). *The city.* Chicago, IL: University of Chicago Press.

Pasca, L., & Aragonés, J.I. (2021). Contacto con la naturaleza: Favoreciendo la conectividad con la naturaleza y el bienestar. *Revista CES Psicologia, 14*(1), 100–111.

Passafaro, P., Rimano, A., Piccini, M.P., Metastasio, R., Gambardella, V., Gullace, G., & Lettieri, C. (2014). The bicycle and the city: Desires and emotions versus attitudes, habits and norms. *Journal of Environmental Psychology, 38*, 76–83.

Patterson, M.E., & Williams, D.R. (2005). Maintaining research traditions on place: Diversity of thought and scientific progress. *Journal of Environmental Psychology, 25*(4), 361–380.

Payre, W., Cestac, J., & Delhomme, P. (2015). Fully automated driving: Impact of trust and practice on manual control recovery. *The Journal of the Human Factors and Ergonomics Society, 58*(2), 229–241.

Pelenc, J., Ballect, J., & Dedeurwaerdere, T. (2015). *Weak versus strong sustainability.* Brief for GSDR 2015.

Pellow, D.N. (2000). Environmental inequality formation: Toward a theory of environmental justice. *American Behavioral Scientist, 43*(4), 581–601.

Peng, J., Strijker, D., & Wu, Q. (2020). Place identity: how far have we come in exploring its meanings?. *Frontiers in psychology, 11,* 294.

Perkins, D.V., Burns, T.F., Perry, J.C., Nielsen, K.P. (1988). Behavior setting theory and community psychology: An analysis and critique. *Journal of Community Psychology, 16,* October, 355–372.

Peretti-Watel, P. (2003). *Sociologie du risque.* Paris: Armand Colin.

Peterson, C., Maier, S.F., & Seligman, M.E. (1995). *Learned helplessness: A theory for the age of personal control.* New York: Oxford University Press.

Peterson, C., & Seligman, M.E. (1983). Learned helplessness and victimization. *Journal of Social Issues, 39*(2), 103–116.

Petiteau, J.Y., Renoux, B. Tallagrand, D., Tixier, N., & Toussaint, M. (2018) (Eds.). *Dockers à Nantes – L'expérience des itinéraires.* Annecy: Les presses du réel.

Piaget, J., & Inhelder, B. (1948). *La représentation de l'espace chez l'enfant.* Paris: PUF.

Piaget, J., & Inhelder, B. (1959). *La Genèse des Structures Logiques Elémentaires.* Neuchâtel: Delachaux & Niestlé.

Pihkala, P. (2020). Anxiety and the ecological crisis: An analysis of eco-anxiety and climate anxiety. *Sustainability, 12,* 7836.

Piaget, J., Inherler, B. (1963). Les images mentales. *In* P. Fraisse & J. Piajet, *Traité de psychologie expérimentale,* vol VII. Paris: PUF.

Pineau, C. (1980). *Psychologie différentielle du confort; Etude des besoins individuels en matière de confort dans les logements.* Unpublished Doctoral dissertation, Université Paris Descartes.

Pirages, D. C., & Ehrlich, P. R. (1974). *Ark II; social response to environmental imperatives.* San Francisco: Freeman.

Pol, E. (1993a). Procesos psicológicos en el uso y organización del espacio. *In* M. Amerigo, J.I. Aragonés, & J.A. Corraliza (Eds.), *El comportamiento en el Medio Construido y Natural (Behavior in the natural and built environment)* (pp. 121–134). Badajoz, Spain: Agencia del Medio Ambiente. Junta de Extremadura.

Pol, E. (1993b). *Environmental psychology in Europe: From architectural psychology to green psychology.* Aldershot: Avebury.

Pol, E. (1996). La apropiación del espacio (The appropriation of space). *In* L. Íñiguez & E. Pol (Eds.), *Cognición, representación y apropiación del espacio. Monografies Psico/Socio/Ambientals.* Barcelona: PUB. (Original, 1994, en Familia y Sociedad, 12, 233-249).

Pol, E. (2002a). Environmental, management: A perspective from environmental psychology. *In* R.B. Bechtel & A. Churchman (Eds.), *Handbook of environmental psychology* (pp. 55–84). New York: Wiley & Sons.

Pol, E. (2002b). El modelo dual de la apropiación del espacio. *In* R. Garcia-Mira, J. Sabucedo-Cameselle, & J. Romay-Martinez (Eds.), *Psicología medio ambiente. Aspectos psicosociales, educativos ymetodológicos* (pp. 123–132). A Coruña: Dialnet.

Pol, E. (2006). Blueprints for a history of environmental psychology (I): From first born to American transition. *Medio Ambiente y Comportamiento Humano, 7*(2), 95–113.

Pol, E. (2007). Blueprints for a history of environmental psychology (II): From architectural psychology to challenge of sustainability. *Medio Ambiente y Comportamiento Humano, 8* (1/2), 1–28.

Pol, E. (2020). Superar la ecofatiga, abandonar la ecoansiedad (Overcome eco-fatigue, abandon eco-anxiety). *Circle, 9,* 36–37.

Pol, E., Castrechini A., Carmona M., Ramírez A., & Manolov R. (2017). Communication, crise et « durabilité ». Instabilité et incertitude des messages. *Bulletin de Psychologie, 70*(2), 87–104.

Pol, E., Castrechini A., & Carrus, G. (2017). Quality of Life and Sustainability: The End of Quality at Any Price. *In* G. Fleury-Bahi, E. Pol & O. Navarro (Eds). *Handbook of Environmental Psychology and Quality of Life Research* (pp. 11–39). New York: Springer.

Pol, E., Di Masso, A., Castrechini, A., Bonet, M., & Vidal, T. (2006). Psychological parameters to understand and manage the NIMBY effect. *European Review of Applied Psychology, 56*(1), 43–51.

Pol, E., Moreno, E., & Castrechini, A. (2010). Gestión Ambiental como gestión de comportamientos. (Environmental Managemet as behavior management). *In* J.I. Aragonés & M. Amérigo (Eds.), *Psicología ambiental* (pp. 379–398). Madrid: Piramide.

Pol, E., Vidal, T., & Romeo, M. (2001). Supuestos de cambio de actitud y conducta usados en las campañas de publicidad y los programas de promoción ambiental. El modelo de las 4 esferas. *Estudios de psicología, 22*(1), 111–126.

Polat, S., & Dostoglu, N. (2017). Measuring place identity in public open spaces. *Proceedings of the Institution of Civil Engineers-Urban Design and Planning, 170*(5), 217–230.

Poortinga, W., Spence, A., Whitmarsh, L., Capstick, S., & Pidgeon, N.F. (2011). Uncertain climate: An investigation into public scepticism about anthropogenic climate change. *Global Environmental Change, 21*(3), 1015–1024.

Pörtner, H.O., Scholes, R.J., Agard, J., et al. (2021). *Scientific outcome of the IPBES-IPCC co-sponsored workshop on biodiversity and climate change.* Bonn: IPBES secretariat.

Proshansky, H. (1976). Appropriation and misappropriation of space. *In* P. Korosec-Serfaty (Ed.), *Proceedings of the Strasbourg International Architectural Psychology Conference* (pp. 31–45). Louvain-La Neuve: CIACO. https://iaps.architexturez. net/doc/oai-iaps-id-iaps-00-1976-002

Proshansky, H. (1978). The city and self-identity. *Environment and Behavior, 10*(2), 147–169.

Proshansky, H., Fabian, A.K., & Kaminoff, R. (1983). Place-identity: Physical world socialization of the self. *Journal of Environmental Psychology, 3,* 57–83.

Proshansky, H., Ittelson, W.H., & Rivlin, L.G. (Eds.) (1970). *Environmental psychology: People and their physical settings.* New York: Holt, Rinehart & Winston.

Proudfoot, J. (2019). Traumatic landscapes: Two geographies of addiction. *Social Sciences and Medicine, 228,* 194–201.

Pylyshyn, Z. (1973). What the mind's eye tells the mind's brain: A critical of mental imagery. *Psychological Bulletin, 80,* 1–24.

Ramadier, T. (2010). *La géométrie socio-cognitive de la mobilité quotidienne : distinction et continuité spatiale en milieu urbain.* Manuscrit de l'Habilitation à diriger des recherches. Université de Nîmes.

Ramadier, T. (2020). Articuler cognition spatiale et cognition environnementale pour saisir les représentations socio-cognitives de l'espace, Revue internationale de géomatique, 30 (1-2), 13-35.

Ramadier, T., & Depeau, S. (2011). Introduction. *In* S. Depeau & T. Ramadier (Eds.), *Se déplacer pour se situer* (pp. 9–24). Rennes: Presses Universitaires de Rennes.

Ramadier, T., & Moser, G. (1998). Social legibility, the cognitive map and urban behaviour. *Journal of Environmental Psychology, 18*, 307–319.

Ramos, I.L., Bernardo, F., Ribeiro, S.C., & Van Eetvelde, V. (2016). Landscape identity: Implications for policy making. *Land Use Policy, 53*, 36–43.

Rapoport, A. (1969). *House form and culture.* East Lansing (Michigan State University): Prentice-Hall.

Rapoport, A. (1982). *The Meaning if the Built Environment: a nonverbal communication approach.* Beverley Hills, CA: Sage.

Rasch, G. (1980). *Probabilistic models for some intelligence and attainment tests.* Chicago: University of Chicago Press (Original work published 1960).

Rateau, P., Moliner, P., Guimelli, C., & Abric, J.-C. (2011). Social representation theory. *In* P.A.M. Van Lange, A. Kruglanski, & J. Higgins (Eds.), *Handbook of the theories of social psychology* (pp. 478–498). Thousand Oaks, CA: Sage.

Raymond, C.M., Brown, G., & Weber, D. (2010). The measurement of place attachment: Personal, community, and environmental connections. *Journal of Environmental Psychology, 30,* 422–434.

Raymond, C.M., Fazey, I., Reed, M.S., Stringer, L.C., Robinson, G.M., & Evely, A.C. (2010). Integrating local and scientific knowledge for environmental management. *Journal of Environmental Management, 91*(8), 1766–1777.

Real-Deus, E. (2010). Les dangers du développement durable. *In* K. Weiss & F. Girandola (Eds.), *Psychologie et développement durable* (pp. 37–50). Paris: InPress.

Renn, O. (2008). *Risk governance: Coping with uncertainty in a complex world.* London: Earthscan.

Renn, O., & Rohrmann, B. (2000). Cross–cultural risk perception: State and challenges. *In* O. Renn & B. Rohrmann (Eds.), *Cross-cultural risk perception* (pp. 211233). New York: Springer.

Riechmann, J. (2015). *Autoconstrucción. La transformación cultural que necesitamos.* Madrid: Catarata.

Roberts, T., & Parks, B. (2007). *A climate of injustice.* Cambridge, London: MIT Press.

Rogers, C.R. (1961, 2005). *Le développement de la personne.* Paris: Dunod.

Roig, B., & Brocal, F. (2018). Introduction: Needs on emerging risk and management. *In* B. Roig, K. Weiss, & V. Thireau, V. (Eds.) *Management of emerging public health issues and risks* (pp. xvii–xxi). London: Elsevier (Academic Press).

Rosenberg, M.J., & Hovland, C.I. (1960). Cognitive, affective, and behavioral components of attitudes. *In* C.I. Hovland & M.J. Rosenberg (Eds.), *Attitude organization and change: An analysis of consistency among attitude components* (pp. 1–14). New Haven, CT: Yale University Press.

Rossignol, N., Delvenne, P., & Turcanu, C. (2015). Rethinking vulnerability analysis and governance with emphasis on a participatory approach. *Risk Analysis, 35*(1), 129–141.

Roussel, J. (2016). *Le confort de la marche dans l'espace public parisien. Représentations, pratiques, enjeux.* Thèse de doctorat. Université de Paris.

Roux-Dufort, C. (2007). A passion for imperfections. *In* C. Pearson, C. Roux-Dufort & J.A. Clair (Eds.), *International handook of organizational crisis management* (pp. 221–252). London: Sage.

Ryff, C.D. (1989). Happiness is everything, or is it? Explorations of the meaning of psychological well-being. *Journal of Personality and Social Psychology, 57,* 1069–1081.

Ryff, C.D. (2013). Psychological well-being revisited: Advances in the science and practice of Eudaimonia. *Psychotherapy and Psychosomatics, 83*, 10–28.

Sadalla, E. K, Burroughs, W. J., & Staplin, L. J. (1980). Reference points in spatial cognition. *Journal of Experimental Psychology: Human Learning and Memory, 6*(5), 516-528.

Scannel, L., & Gifford, R. (2010). Defining place attachment: A tripartite organizing framework. *Journal of Environmental Psychology, 30*, 1–10.

Scannel, L., & Gifford, R. (2014). The psychology of place attachment. *In* R. Gifford (Ed.), *Environmental psychology: Principles and practice* (5th ed., pp. 272–300). Victoria: Optimal Books.

Schama, S. (1995). *Landscape and memory.* New York: Knopf.

Schlosberg, D. (2007). *Defining environmental justice. Theories, movements, and nature.* Oxford: Oxford University Press.

Schmitt, M.T., & Branscombe, N.R. (2002). The meaning and consequences of perceived discrimination in disadvantaged and privileged social groups. *In* W. Stroebe & M. Hewstone (Eds.), *European Review of Social Psychology* (Vol. 12, pp. 167–199). Chichester: Wiley.

Schmuck, P., & Schultz, P.W. (Eds.) (2002). *Psychology of sustainable development.* Norwell, MA: Kluwer.

Schroeder, H.W. (2007). Place experience, gestalt and the human-nature relationship. *Journal of Environmental Psychology, 27*(4), 293–309.

Schultz, W. (1998). Changing behavior with normative feedback interventions: A field experiment on curbside recycling. *Basic and Applied Social Psychology, 21*(1), 25–36.

Schultz, W. (2002). Inclusion with nature: The psychology of human-nature relations. *In* P. Schmuck & W.P. Schultz (Eds.), *Psychology of sustainable development* (pp. 61–78). Boston, MA: Kluwer Academic Publishers.

Schultz, W., & Kaiser, F.G. (2012). Promoting pro-environmental behavior. *In* S. Clayton (Ed.), *The Oxford handbook of environmental and conservation psychology* (pp. 556–580). New York: Oxford University Press.

Schultz, W., Khazian, A., & Zaleski, A. (2008). Using normative social influence to promote conservation among hotel guests. *Social Influence, 3*, 4–23.

Schultz, W., Shriver, C., Tabanico, J., & Khazian, A. (2004). Implicit connections with nature. *Journal of Environmental Psychology, 24*(1), 31–42.

Schulz, A., Williams, D., Israel, B., Becker, A., Parker, E., James, S.A., & Jackson, J. (2000). Unfair treatment, neighborhood effects, and mental health in the detroit metropolitan area. *Journal of Health and Social Behavior, 41*(3), 314–332.

Schwartz, S.H. (1992). Universals in the content and structure of values: Theoretical advances and empirical tests in 20 countries. *Advances in Experimental Social Psychology, 25*, 1–65.

Schwartz, S.H., Cieciuch, J., Vecchione, M., Davidov, E., Fischer, R., Beierlein, C., ... & Konty, M. (2012). Refining the theory of basic individual values. *Journal of Personality and Social Psychology, 103*(4), 663.

Schwartz, S.H., & Howard, J. (1981). A normative decision-making model of altruism. *In* J.P. Rushton & R.M. Sorrentino (Eds.), *Altruism and helping behavior* (pp. 189–211). Hillsdale, NJ: Lawrence Erlbaum.

Seamon, D. (2018). *Life takes place: Phenomenology, lifeworlds and place making.* New York: Routledge.

Seeger, M.W. (2006). Best Practices in Crisis Communication: An Expert Panel Process. *Journal of Applied Communication Research, 34*(3), 232–244. https://doi.org/10.1080/00909880600769944

Seeger, M.W., Sellnow, T., & Ulmer, R. (1998). Communication, organization, and crisis. *Annals of the International Communication Association, 21*(1), 231–276.

Seligman, M. (2002). *Authentic happiness: Using the new positive psychology to realize your potential for lasting fulfillment.* New York: Free Press.

Seligman, M.E. (1975). *Helplessness: On depression, development, and death.* New York: Freeman.

Seligman, M.E. (1990/2006). *Learned Optimism: How to Change Your Mind and Your Life.* New York: Vintage.

Seligman, M.E., & Csikszentmihalyi, M. (2000). Positive psychology: An introduction. *American Psychologist, 55,* 5–14.

Selye, H. (1956). *The stress of life.* New York: McGraw Hill.

Serfaty-Garzon, P. (1985). Expériences et pratiques de la maison. *In* I. Altman et C. Werner (Dir.), *Home Environment. Man, Behavior and Environment. Advances in Theory and Research* (Vol. 8, pp. 65–86). New York: Plenum Press. http://perlaserfaty.net/wp-content/uploads/2017/01/Experience-and-use-of-the-dwelling-an-article-by-Perla-Ser-1.pdf

Serfaty-Garzon, P. (2002). L'appropriation de l'espace. *In* M. Segaud, J. Brun & J.C. Driant (Ed.), *Dictionnaire critique du logement et de l'habitat, sous le regard des sciences sociales* (pp. 27–30). Paris: Armand Colin.

Serfaty-Garzon, P. (2003). *Chez soi. Les territoires de l'intimité.* Paris : Armand Colin.

Serfaty-Garzon, P. (2016). *Quand votre maison vous est contée.* Montréal: Bayard Canada.

Serido, J., Tang, C., Ahn, S., & Shim, S. (2020). Financial behavior change and progress toward self-sufficiency: A goal-framing theory application. *Emerging Adulthood, 8*(6), 521–529.

Sèze, C. (1994). Confort moderne. Une nouvelle culture du bien-être. *Autrement, 20,* 110–124.

Shoggen, P. (1983). Behavior settings and the quality of life. *Journal of Community Psychology, 2,* 144–157.

Simmel, G. (1903). *Die Grosstädte und das Geistesleben.* Dresden: Petermann [*The Metropolis and Mental Life.* The Sociology of Georg Simmel' New York: Free Press, 1976].

Simmel, G. (1908a). *Soziologie.* Leipzig: Duncker & Humblot.

Simmel, G. (1908b). Über das Wesen der Sozialpsychologie. *Archiv für Sozialwissenschaft und Sozialpolitik, 26*(2), 285–291.

Simmel, G. (1984). Métropoles et mentalité. *In* Y. Grafmeyer & I. Joseph (Eds.). *L'Ecole de chicago. Naissance de l'écologie urbaine* (Vol 41, num 3, 2017, pp. 87–105). Paris: Aubier.

Slovic, P. (1987). Perception of risk. *Science, 236*(4799), 280–285.

Slovic, P. (1999). Trust, emotion, sex, politics, and science: Surveying the risk-assessment battlefield. *Risk Analysis, 19*(4), 689–701.

Smith, N., & Leiserowitz, A. (2012). The rise of global warming skepticism: exploring affective image associations in the United States over time. *Risk Analysis: An Official Publication of the Society for Risk Analysis, 32*(6), 1021–1032.

Sommer, R. (1969) *Personal space: The behavioral basis of design.* Englewood Cliffs, NJ: Prentice Hall.

Sorokin, P.A. (1927/1998). *Social mobility*. London: Routledge.

Sorokin, P.A. (1947). *Society, culture and personality: Their structures and dynamics: A system of general sociology*. New York: Harper.

Sparkman, G., Weitz, E., Robinson, T., Malhotra, N., & Walton, G. (2020). Developing a scalable dynamic norm menu-based intervention to reduce mean consumption. *Sustainability, 12*, 2453.

Sparks, P.J. (2000). Idiopathic environmental intolerances: Overview. *Occupational Medicine, 15*(3), 497–510.

Spence, A., Poortinga, W., Butler, C., & Pidgeon, N. (2011). Perceptions of climate change and willingness to save energy related to flood experience. *Nature Climate Change, 1*, 46–49.

Spence, A., Poortinga, W., & Pidgeon, N. (2011). The psychological distance of climate change. *Risk Analysis, 32*(6), 0272–4332.

Staats, H. (2012). Restorative environments. *In* S.D. Clayton (Ed.), *The Oxford handbook of environmental and conservation psychology* (pp. 445–458). New York: Oxford University Press.

Stanley, S.K., Hogg, T.H., Levistona, Z., & Walker, I. (2021). From anger to action: Differential impacts of eco-anxiety, eco-depression, and eco-anger on climate action and wellbeing. *The Journal of Climate Change and Health, 1*, 100003.

Steffen, W., Richardson, K., Rockström, J., Cornell, S.E., Fetzer, I., Bennett, E.M., Biggs, R., Carpenter, S.R., de Vries, W., de Wit, C.A., Folke, C., Gerten, D., Heinke, J., Mace, G.M., Persson, L.M., Ramanathan, V., Reyers, B., & Sörlin, S. (2015). Planetary boundaries: Guiding human development on a changing planet. *Science, 347*(6223), 736–745.

Steg, L., & De Groot, J. (2019). *Environmental psychology: An introduction*. New York: Wiley.

Steg, L., Lindenberg, S., & Keizer, K. (2016). Intrinsic motivation, norms and environmental behaviour: The dynamics of overarching goals. *International Review of Environmental and Resource Economics, 9*(1–2), 179–207.

Steg, L., Perlaviciute, G., Van der Werff, E., & Lurvink, J. (2014). The significance of hedonic values for environmentally relevant attitudes, preferences, and actions. *Environment and Behavior, 46*(2), 163–192.

Stengers, I. (2019). *Résister au désastre*. Vernon: Wildproject.

Stern, P.C. (2000). Toward a coherent theory of environmentally significant behavior. *Journal of Social Issues, 56*, 407–424.

Stern, P.C., Dietz, T., & Guagnano, G.A. (1995). Values, Beliefs, and Proenvironmental Action: Attitude Formation Toward Emergent Attitude Objects. *Journal of Applied Social Psychology, 25*(18), 1611-1636. https://doi.org/10.1111/j.1559-1816.1995.tb02636.x

Stern, P.C., Dietz, T., Abel, T., Guagnano, G.A., & Kalof, L. (1999). A Value-Belief-Norm theory of support for social movements: The case of environmentalism. *Human Ecology Review, 6*(2), 81–97.

Stern, W. (1938). General psychology from the personalistic standpoint. New York: MacMillan.

Stokols, D. (1972). On the distinction between density and crowding: Some implications for future research. *Psychological Review, 79*, 275–277.

Stokols, D. (1978). Environmental psychology. *Annual Review of Psychology, 29*, 253–295.

Stokols, D. (2006). Toward a science of transdisciplinary action research. *American Journal of Community Psychology, 38*(1), 63–77.

Stokols, D. (2018). *Social ecology in the Digital Age - Solving complex problems in a globalized world.* London: Academic Press.

Stokols, D., & Altman, I. (Eds.). (1987). *Handbook of environmental psychology* (Vol. 1 & 2). New York: Wiley.

Stokols, D., & Shumaker, S. (1981). People in place: A transactional view of settings. In J. Harvey (Ed.), *Cognition, social behaviour and the environment* (pp. 441–88). Hillsdale, NJ: Lawrence Erlbaum.

Strother, J.B., & Fazal, Z. (2011). Can green fatigue hamper sustainability communication efforts? *2011 IEEE International Professional Communication Conference* (pp. 1–6). Cincinnati: IEEE. doi: 10.1109/IPCC.2011.6087206.

Sullivan, D., & Young, I. (2020). Place attachment style as a predictor of responses to the environmental threat of water contamination. *Environment and Behavior, 52*(1), 3–32.

Sullivan, W.C., & Kaplan, R. (2016). Nature! Small steps that can make a big difference. *HERD: Health Environments Research & Design Journal, 9*(2), 6–10.

Swim, J., Clayton, S., Doherty, T., Gifford, R., Howard, G., Reser, J., Stern, P., & Weber, E. (2009). *Psychology and global climate change: Addressing a multi-faceted phenomenon and set of challenges. A report by the American psychological association's task force on the interface between psychology and global climate change.* New York: APA.

Swim, J., & Whitmarsh, L. (2019). Climate change as a unique environmental problem. In L. Steg & J.I.M. de Groot (Eds.), *Environmental psychology: An introduction* (pp. 26–35). Hoboken, NJ: Wiley & Sons.

Swofford, J., & Slattery, M. (2010). Public attitudes of wind energy in Texas: Local communities in close proximity to wind farms and their effect on decision-making. *Energy Policy, 38*, 2508–2519.

Szasz, A. (1994). *Ecopopulism. Toxic waste and the movement for environmental justice.* Minneapolis, London: University of Minnesota Press.

Tajfel, H. (1981). *Human groups and social categories.* Cambridge: Cambridge University Press.

Taylor, N. (2009). Legibility and aesthetics in urban design. *Journal of Urban Design, 14*(2), 189–202.

Taylor, B., Chapron, G., Kopnina, H., Orlikowska, E., Gray, J., & Piccolo, J.J. (2020). The need for ecocentrism in biodiversity conservation. *Conservation Biology, 34*, 1089–1096.

Thaler, R.H., & Sunstein, C.R. (2008). *Nudge.* New Haven, CT: Yale University Press.

Thibaud, J.P. (2001). La méthode des parcours commentés. In M. Grosjean & J.P. Thibaud (Eds.) *L'espace urbain en méthodes* (pp. 79–99). Paris: Parenthèses.

Thibaud, J.P. (2008). Je, Tu, Il. La marche aux trois personnes. *Revue Urbanisme, 359*, 63–65.

Thomas, R. (2010). *Marcher en ville. Faire corps, prendre corps, donner corps aux ambiances urbaines.* Paris: Éditions des Archives Contemporaines.

Thomashow, M. (1995). *Ecological identity. Becoming a reflective environmentalist.* Cambridge: MIT Press.

Thompson, S.C., & Barton, M.A. (1994). Ecocentric and anthropocentric attitudes toward the environment. *Journal of Environmental Psychology, 14*, 149–157.

Tolman, E.C. (1948). Cognitive maps in rats and men. *Psychological Review, 55*(4), 189–208. https://doi.org/10.1037/h0061626

Tönnies, F. (1887). *Gemeinschaft und Gesellschaft* (Community and Society). Leipzig: Fues's Verlag.

Tripier, P. (2007). Entre art de la guerre et activités civiles, des grammaires d'action à trouver, *Inflexions, 6*, 217–235.

Trope, Y., & Liberman, N. (2003). Temporal construal. *Psychological Review, 110*(3), 403–421.

Trope, Y., & Liberman, N. (2010). Construal-level theory of psychological distance. *Psychological Review, 117*(2), 440–463.

Trowbridge, C.C. (1913). On Fundamental Methods of Orientation and "Imaginary Maps". *Science, 38*(990), 888–897. DOI: 10.1126/science.38.990.888

Tuleya, L.G. (Ed.). (2007). *Thesaurus of psychological index terms* (11th ed.). Washington: American Psychological Association.

Tuan, Y. (1974). *Topophilia: A study on environmental perception, attitudes and values.* Englewood Cliffs, NJ: Prentice-Hall.

Tuan, Y. (1979). *Landscapes of fear.* New York: Pantheon Books.

Tuan, Y. (1980). Rootedness versus sense of place. *Landscape, 24*, 3–8.

Tuan, Y. (1991). Language and the making of place: A narrative-descriptive approach. *Annals of the Association of American Geographers, 81*, 684–696.

Tudge, J.R.H., Mokrova, I., Hatfield, B.E., & Karnik, R.B. (2009). Uses and misuses of Bronfenbrenner's bioecological theory of human development. *Journal of Family Theory & Review, 1*, 198–210.

Turner, B.A. (1976). The organizational interorganizational development of disasters. *Administrative Science Quarterly, 21*(3), 378–397.

Turtle, E. (2008). "Green Fatigue" and "Eco Anxiety". *Columbia Journalism Review.* Accessed 20 February 2023. https://archives.cjr.org/the_observatory/green_fatigue_and_eco_anxiety.php

Twigger-Ross, C., & Uzzell, D. (1996). Place and identity processes. *Journal of Environmental Psychology, 16*(3), 205–220.

Uexküll, J. (1909). *Umwelt und Innenwelt der Tiere* (Environment and inner world of animals.). Berlin: Springer.

Uexküll, J. (1921). *Umwelt und Innenwelt der Tiere* (2nd ed.). Berlin: Springer.

Uexküll, J. (1934). *Streifzüge durch die Umwelten von Tieren und Menschen. Ein Bilderbuch unsichtbarer Welten.* (Forays into the environment of animals and people. A picture book of invisible worlds) Bd. 21 Berlin: Springer. (Engl.: A stroll through the worlds of animal and man. *In* C.H. Schiller (Ed.) (1957). *Instinctive behavior* (pp. 5–80). New York: International University Press.

Uexküll, J. (1936). *Niegeschaute Welten.* Berlin: S. Fischer.

Uexküll, J., & Kriszat, G. (1956). *Streifzüge durch die Umwelten von Tieren und Menschen: Ein Bilderbuch unsichtbarer Welten.* Hamburg: Rowohlt. (1st ed., 1934)

Ulrich, R.S. (1979). Visual landscapes and psychological well-being. *Landscape Research, 4*(1), 17–23.

Ulrich, R.S. (1983). Aesthetic and affective response to natural environment. *In* I. Altman & J. Wohlwill (Eds.), *Human behavior and environment, Vol. 6: Behavior and natural environment* (pp. 85–125). New York: Plenum.

Ulrich, R.S. (1984). View through a window may influence recovery from surgery. *Science, 224*, 42–421.

Ulrich, R.S. (1993). Biophilia, biophobia, and natural landscapes. *In* S. Kellert & E.O. Wilson (Eds.), *The Biophilia hypothesis* (pp. 74–137). Washington, DC: Shearwater/Island Press.

Ulrich, R.S., Simons, R.F., Losito, B.D., Fiorito, E., Miles, M.A., & Zelson, M. (1991). Stress recovery during exposure to natural and urban environments. *Journal of Environmental Psychology, 11*, 201–230.

UN-Habitat. (2020). *The new urban agenda illustrated.* Kenya : UN Habitat.

Urry, J. (2000). Mobile sociology. *British Journal of Sociology, 51*(1), 185–203.

Uzzell, D.L. (1991). Environmental psychological perspectives on landscape. *Landscape Research, 16*(1), 3–10.

Uzzell, D.L. (2000). The psycho-spatial dimension of global environmental problems. *Journal of Environmental Psychology, 20*(4), 307–318.

Uzzell, D.L., & Lewand, K. (1990). The psychology of landscape. *Landscape Design, 189*, 34–35.

Valencia, S.C., Simon, D., Croese, S., Nordqvist, J., Oloko, M., Sharma, T., Taylor Buch, N., & Versace, I. (2019). Adapting the sustainable development goals and the new urban agenda to the city level: Initial reflections from a comparative research project. *International Journal of Urban Sustainable Development, 11*(1), 4–23.

Valera, S., & Pol, E. (1994). El concepto de identidad social urbana: una aproximación entre la Psicología Social y la Psicología Ambiental (The concept of urban social identity: an approach between Social Psychology and Environmental Psychology). *Anuario de Psicología, 62*, 5–24.

Valera, S., Pol, E., & Vidal, T. (2018). Percepción objetual y percepción ambiental (Objects perception and environmental perception). *Elementos básicos de Psicología Ambiental (Basic elements of Environmental Psychology).* Centre de recursos per a l'aprenentage i la Investigació-CRAI- Universitat de Barcelona.

Van Acker, V., Goodwin, P., & Witlox, F. (2016). Key research themes on travel behavior, lifestyle, and sustainable urban mobility. *International Journal of Sustainable Transportation, 10*(1), 25–32.

Van der Klis, M., & Karsten, L. (2009). Commuting partners, dual residences and the meaning of home. *Journal of Environmental Psychology, 29*, 235–245.

Van der Linden, S.L., Leiserowitz, A.A., Feinberg, G.D., & Maibach, E.W. (2015). The scientific consensus on climate change as a gateway belief: Experimental evidence. *PLoS ONE, 10*(2), 2–9.

Van der Werff, E., & Steg, L. (2018). Spillover benefits: Emphasizing different benefits of environmental behavior and its effects on spillover. *Frontiers in Psychology, 9*, 2347.

Van der Werff, E., Steg, L., & Keizer, K. (2014). I am what I am, by looking past the present: The influence of biospheric values and past behavior on environmental self-identity. *Environment and Behavior, 46*(5), 626–657.

VanKamp, R., Leidelmeijer, K., Marsman, G., & DeHollander, A. (2003). Urban environmental quality and human well-being: Toward a conceptual framework and demarcation of concepts; a literature study. *Landscape and Urban Planning, 65*, 5–18.

Van Valkengoed, A., & Steg, L. (2019). *The psychology of climate change adaptation.* Cambridge: Cambridge University Press.

Velarde, D., Fry, G., & Tveit, M. (2007). Health effects of viewing landscapes – Landscape types in environmental psychology. *Urban Forestry & Urban Greening, 6*, 199–212.

Verplanken, B., Aarts, H., Knippenberg, A., & Knippenberg, C. (1994). Attitude versus general habit: Antecedents of travel mode choice. *Journal of Applied Social Psychology, 24*(4), 285–300.

Vidal, T., & Pol, E. (2005). La apropiación del espacio: una propuesta teórica para comprender la vinculación entre las personas y los lugares (The appropriation of space: a theoretical proposal to understand the link between people and places). *Anuario de Psicología, 36,* 281–297.

Vischer, J.C., & Fischer, G.N. (2005). Une approche de l'évaluation des environnements de travail: La méthode diagnostique. *Le Travail Humain, 68*(1), 73–95.

Vita, G., Ivanova, D., Dumitru, A., García-Mira, R., Carrus, G., Stadler, K., Krause, K., Wood, R., & Hertwich, E. (2020). Happier with less? Members of environmental grassroots initiatives reconcile lower carbon emissions with higher life satisfaction and income increases. *Energy Research & Social Science, 60,* 101329.

Von Lindern, E. (2017). Perceived interdependencies between settings as constraints for self-reported restoration. *Journal of Environmental Psychology, 49,* 8–17.

Ward Thompson, C. (2011). Linking landscape and health: The recurring theme. *Landscape and Urban Planning, 99,* 187–195.

Waterman, A.S., Schwartz, S.J., & Conti, R. (2008). The implications of two conceptions of happiness (hedonic enjoyment and eudaimonia) for the understanding of intrinsic motivation. *Journal of Happiness Studies, 9,* 41–79.

Watson, D., & Clark, L.E. (1999). *The PANAS-X: Manual for the positive and negative affect schedule expanded form.* Ames: University of Iowa.

Weber, L., Foss, N., & Lindenberg, S. (2023). The role of cognition and motivation in understanding internal governance and hierarchical failure: A discriminating alignment analysis. Academy of Management Review. doi/10.5465/amr.2019.0035

Weick, K.E. (1995). *Sensemaking in organizations.* California: Sage.

Weisman, J. (1981). Evaluating architectural legibility. Wayfindings in a built environment, *Environment and Behavior, 13*(2), 189–204.

Weiss, K. (2003). Les sites comportementaux. *In* G. Moser & K. Weiss (Eds.), *Espaces de vie : Aspects de la relation homme-environnement* (pp. 247–265). Paris: Armand Colin.

Weiss, K., & Girandola, F. (2010). *Psychologie et développement durable.* Paris: InPress.

Weiss, K., & Rateau, P. (2018). *Psychologie sociale et environnementale.* Paris: InPress.

Wells, N.M., & Phalen, K.B. (2018). Everyday and nearby natural environments. *In* A.S. Devlin (Ed.), *Environmental psychology and human well-being. Effects of built and natural settings* (pp. 221–252). Cambridge, MA: Academic Press.

Whipple, S.S., & Evans, G.W. (2022). The physical environment and social development. *In* P. Smith & C. Hart (Eds.), *The handbook of childhood social development* (3rd ed., pp. 171-188). London: Wiley-Blackwell.

Whitburn, J., Linklater, W., & Abrahamse, W. (2019). Meta-analysis of human connection to nature and proenvironmental behavior. *Conservation Biology, 34*(1), 180–193.

White, M.P., Bratman, G., Pah, S., Young, G., Cracknell, D., & Elliott, L.R. (2020). Affective reactions to losses and gains in biodiversity: Testing a prospect theory approach. *Journal of Environmental Psychology, 72*(14), 101502.

White, M.P., Elliott, L.R., Grellier, J., Economou, T., Bell, S., Bratman, G.N., Gascon, M., Lima, M.L., Lõhmus, M., Nieuwenhuijsen, M., Wemaere, A., Ojala, A., Roiko, A., Schultz, P., van der Bosch, M., & Fleming, L.E. (2021). Associations between green/blue spaces and mental health across 18 countries. *Scientific Reports – Nature, 11,* 8903.

Whitmarsh, L., & O'Neill, S. (2010). Green identity, green living? The role of pro-environmental self-identity in determining consistency across diverse pro-environmental behaviours. *Journal of Environmental Psychology, 30*(3), 305–314.

WHO (1983). *Indoor air pollutants: Exposure and health effects.* Copenhagen: WHO Regional Office for Europe (EURO Reports and Studies, No. 78).

Wicker, A. W. (1979). *An introduction to ecological psychology.* Monterey: Brooks/Cole.

Wicker, A. W. (1992). Making sense of environments. *In* W. B. Walsh, K. H. Craik & R. H. Price (Eds.), *Person–environment Psychology: Models and Perspective.* Hillsdale, NJ: Erlbaum.

Widegren, Ö. (1998). The new environmental paradigm and personal norms. Environment and Behavior, 30(1), 75–100. https://doi.org/10.1177/0013916598301004

Williams, H.T., McMurray, J.R., Kurz, T., & Lambert, F.H. (2015). Network analysis reveals open forums and echo chambers in social media discussions of climate change. *Global environmental change, 32,* 126–138.

Wilson, E.O. (1984). *Biophilia.* Harvard Cambridge, Massachuttets, and London, England: Harvard University Press.

Winkin, Y. & Lavadinko, S. (2010). Comment produire de l'hospitalité pour la marche? Boite à outils pour augmenter le plaisir de marcher en ville, novembre 2010, CERTU.

Witkin, H. A. (1959). The perception of the upright. *Scientific American, 200,* 50–70.

Wohlwill, J.F. (1983). The concept of nature. A psychologist's view. *In* I. Altman & J.F. Wohlwill (Eds.), *Human behavior and environment. Advances in theory and research: Vol.6 Behavior and the natural environment* (pp. 5–37). New York: Plenum Press.

Wolsink, M. (2005). Invalid theory impedes our understanding: A critique on the persistence of the language of NIMBY. *Transations of the Institute of British Geographers, 31,* 85–91.

Wolsko, C., & Lindberg, K. (2013). Experiencing connection with nature: The matrix of psychological well-being, mindfulness, and outdoor recreation. *Ecopsychology, 5*(2), 80–91.

Woods, J. (2010). Are you suffering from eco-fatigue? Psychologies. Accessed 20 February 2019 https://www.psychologies.co.uk/self/are-you-suffering-from-eco-fatigue.html

Yale Program on Climate Change Communication (2019). *Americans are increasingly 'alarmed' about global warming.* Available at: https://climatecommunication.yale.edu/publications/americans-areincreasingly-alarmed-about-global-warming/

Zeiske, N., Venhoeven, L., Steg, L., & van der Werff, E. (2020). The normative route to a sustainable future: examining children's environmental values, identity and personal norms to conserve energy. *Environment and Behavior, Vol 53(10), 1118-1139.*

Zhang, J.W., Howell, R.T., & Iyerc, R. (2014). Engagement with natural beauty moderates the positive relation between connectedness with nature and psychological well-being. *Journal of Environmental Psychology, 38,* 55–63.

Zimring, C.M., & Reizenstein, J.E. (1980). Post-occupancy evaluation: An overview. *Environment and Behavior, 12,* 429–450.

Zimmermann, M., & Toussaint J.-Y. (1998). *Projet urbain, Ménager les gens, aménager la ville.* Mardaga: Architecture, Recherches.

Zwarts, A., & Coolen, H. (2003). The meaning of residential environment features: A case study comparing urban and suburban apartment dwellers. *In* T. Craig (Ed.), *Crossing boundaries. The value of interdisciplinary research - Proceedings of the 3rd conference of the EPUK network* (pp. 80–95). Aberdeen: Robert Gordon University.

For Product Safety Concerns and Information please contact our EU
representative GPSR@taylorandfrancis.com
Taylor & Francis Verlag GmbH, Kaufingerstraße 24, 80331 München, Germany